Date Due

OCT 22 1988	FEB 21 '98	
DEC 6 1989	SEP 8 '98	
DEC 28 1989	OCT 09 2001	
AUG 14 1990	MAR 2 6 2002	
FEB 13 '92		
MAY 03 '95		
APR 22 '97		
FEB 5 '98		
FEB 13 '98		
OCT 14 '98		

The Greek Islands

An imposing Venetian castle presides over Chora, the chief settlement of Astypalaea

The Greek Islands

Brian Dicks

Robert Hale · London

British Library Cataloguing in Publication Data

Dicks, Brian
The Greek Islands.
1. Aegean Islands (Greece and Turkey)—
Description and travel—Guide-books
2. Ionian Islands (Greece)—Description
and travel—Guide-books
I. Title
914.95′0476   DF895

ISBN 0–7090–2590–4

Robert Hale Limited
Clerkenwell House
Clerkenwell Green
London EC1R 0HT

Set in Photina and printed
in Great Britain by BAS Printers Limited,
Over Wallop, Hampshire
Bound by WBC Bookbinders Ltd.

Contents

Appendices

List of Illustrations

Colour plates

Black and white plates

Line drawings

Maps and plans

Foreword

I do not know the age of Brian Dicks. Nor would it be seemly to make enquiries; but I envy him. Patently *his* exploration of Greece began in his student days six years before I first planted my middle-aged feet on the Cycladic island of Andros and began a love affair with the country where I hope to end my days. Consequently, given the advantages of youth and vigour he has had the benefit of visiting a far greater number of the scattered chips which decorate the blue Aegean than I have been allowed to do. However, one common factor links us – a passion for the islands and their people, and an urge to share our treasures with others albeit at the risk of guiding them to places which selfishly we might prefer to keep private. With that in mind, I am grateful to him for not mentioning certain hill villages in Crete and Rhodes where time is still an idea in the mind of God, where villagers are innocent of our mother tongue, and where I find peace.

Brian Dicks states that his prime object is to 'whet readers' appetites for the Greek islands'. I am sure that he will succeed, for within the pages of this splendidly researched book with its attractive little vignettes, sound advice and potted history of the country they intend to visit, they will find the ethos of Greece.

John Ebdon

Preface

The gestation period for this book dates back to the summer of 1962 when my first visit to Greece introduced me to the Argo-Saronic islands that lie close to Athens and Piraeus. To be more exact, it was only the island of Poros that I first got to know well and this was largely on the insistence of my Athenian hosts who, not content in showing me the Greek capital, were anxious that this financially-embarrassed student should at least see something of the Greece that lay beyond the metropolitan boundary. In the early 'sixties foreign tourists had not discovered Poros, though it was well patronized by the Athenians who descended on the island at weekends from an armada of crowded boats that shuttled backwards and forwards from Piraeus. My first trip to Poros, in the company of a large and hospitable Greek party, remains one of the most memorable episodes in my life and on all subsequent returns to Greece, I have revisited the island as much to sentimentally renew an old acquaintance as to enjoy its singular, though now much changed, atmosphere.

Smitten by the charms of Poros, it was inevitable that other islands beckoned. On the Argo-Saronic run the ships from Piraeus had briefly (and tantalizingly) berthed to disembark passengers at Aegina, and on from Poros were the equally enticing and, for me, still unknown, destinations of Hydra and Spetses. On reflection – though I was unaware of it at the time – there was method and elements of planning in the choice of those subsequent island itineraries that formed part of what had quickly become my new-found passion for 'island-hopping'.

From my discovery of the Argo-Saronic group I next moved on to those islands of the Western Cyclades that were easily accessible from the east coast of Attica, and then to my first – albeit fleeting – visit to Euboea, with more extended stays on the northern Sporades to the north and east. But the first real Aegean sea voyage came with my journey from Piraeus to Syros which, on account of its Cycladic centrality, was frequently to form a convenient base for my exploration of this, the traditional heart of the Aegean world. The magic of these 'sea-traced' isles (a term Oscar Wilde applied to Corfu) became the magnet for a succession of summer visits yet, of all Greek island groupings, I am conscious that the more I have visited the Cyclades the more intractable and challenging it becomes to characterize them effectively. Despite their current tourist popularity these often barren islands of flaming sunsets and romantic moonlight share much with the visitor, but they also continue to guard jealously an individual distinctiveness that is deep-rooted and, to all but the indigene, sacrosanct.

13

Such an argument may be used for other Greek island terrains, not least Crete. In fact, many years of Aegean experience were to pass before I accepted what I knew would be the intellectual challenge of that island. Crete has demanded many visits and I am personally aware that I have not even begun to penetrate what can only be described as a complex elusiveness. For those intent on understanding this island, Crete will be found adept in casting long and obstructive shadows, the product of its independent and exclusive spirit. My experience has shown that this Cretan characteristic is to some extent echoed in a number of the eastern and northern Aegean islands that have also fashioned a protective shield that hides all from view but the obvious and, hence, the superficial.

My introduction to the Dodecanese began on a more formal note, being essentially the commencement of an investigative programme for a commissioned book on Rhodes which also entailed extensive travel throughout the island group. Though, by this time, I had written more general books on Greece and the Greeks, this was my first attempt at tackling a Greek island in detail. Rhodes was followed by a similarly structured volume on Corfu whose research also took me to the other Ionian islands. Both books had made it abundantly clear that the Greek islands were the products of an extremely complicated history, facets of which were shared by all, though each island having the capability of moulding the general into something that was particular and peculiar to itself. When the idea was put to me to write about all the major islands of the Aegean and the Ionian, the prospect of portraying them in a single volume was a task I considered with apprehension. On reflection however, such a project seems to have been part of my subconscious plans as far back as my first visit to Poros, yet practical considerations cautioned me of the difficulties in depicting such a multitude of diverse entities. The pages that follow are at least proof that I finally accepted the challenge, and the thoughts and views they contain have largely been conditioned by the impressions I have gained and the experiences I have encountered over the years. But, in view of the time taken in its compilation, this book would have quickly become out of date had it been based on my personal research alone. Hence I am indebted to a large number of historical, topographical and archaeological works, as well as to more official sources of information. A selective list of references is quoted at the back of this book.

The chapters that follow, however, are primarily about island places and island people. The quoted statistics have been kept to a bare minimum and no attempt has been made to cover such items as the prices and qualities of hotels and restaurants, or the times and admission charges to museums and other venues open to the public. These are liable to change and all current information is readily available from the network of Greek National Tourist Organization offices. But a whole section *is* devoted to more general and practical advice for those intending to visit the islands.

As for the main body of the book, an introductory section is followed by a broad summary of Greek history, the remaining chapters dealing with detailed descriptions of the islands which have been grouped according to what is now accepted as the standard regional-geographical classification. Few readers, I feel, will dispute this arrangement, though some might be critical of the compression of material relating to certain islands and the unavoidable selection of material relating to others. The problem of space has dictated this procedure, yet for each individual island and island-grouping an attempt has been made to depict essential characteristics and to convey to the reader local and regional flavours. The larger islands have obviously required lengthier portrayals and more detail has been given to those that currently attract the greatest number of tourists.

The island groupings are accompanied by reference maps, though it has not been possible to include in these every single place-name. Their scales are given in kilometres and miles, but the text refers to distances in kilometres only, for such measurements will confront the visitor on Greek road signs. The problem of the rendering of Greek place names is dicussed elsewhere, my system is that I have used such spellings that seemed to me to be the most familiar to English speaking readers. There will certainly be some who will disagree.

There are many people and organizations that have helped and guided me in the research and writing of this book. To list them all would be a formidable task. I would, however, wish to thank the personnel of the Greek National Tourist Organization, London, for their great assistance and kind permission to use the photographs acknowledged in the subsequent pages. My thanks also go to Mr L. Wuttke for providing the line-drawings at the beginning of each chapter. To my publishers I am indebted for the opportunity to fulfil my long-felt desire to write of the Greek islands.

My prime objectives are to whet readers' appetites for the Greek Islands and to provide the information necessary to plan an Aegean or Ionian visit. Above all, I have tried to provide pointers to those many atmospheric places that visitors would be sorry to miss.

Brian Dicks, September 1986

A Note on Greek Place-names

There is no standard, generally recognized system of transliterating Greek place- and other proper names into the English language. Consequently there are many variant spellings which often cause the visitor considerable confusion, particularly the inconsistency in such important travellers' aids as maps, guidebooks, road signs and tourist publications. In part, the problem results from the number of Greek sounds that have no direct phonetic equivalent in English, and such pronunciation and spelling difficulties are compounded by the contemporary intricacies of the Greek language, which is a legacy of its long and complex development and of the existence of what are, basically, two forms of modern written Greek. In the preparation of this book I have used certain spellings that will not gain universal approval. However, where alternatives exist, I have selected those forms which I consider the more generally acceptable to the English reader.

A section of Chapter 12 reviews the Greek language difficulty in more detail and provides both the Greek and the transliterated Greek versions of the country's main islands, regions, towns and cities. For this I am indebted to the system devised in *Baedeker's-AA guide to Greece*. I trust that readers will not be too bothered by certain renderings that conflict with versions they might consider sacrosanct. The truth of the matter is that visitors to Greece should be prepared for a confrontation with widely differing appellations, for what other country has, for example, the names Hydra, Hydrea, Idhra, Idra, Ithra, Ydra and Ythra for the same Island?

B.D.

THE GREEK ISLANDS

1

The Castaway Stones

Sweetest of sights, the Greek horizon appears.
Sapphire and gold the rise and set of stars.
The Aegean Sea, studded with snowy sails,
Seems like a snake, where swans rendezvous.
The moon, still brighter than the northern sun,
Runs through the cloudless air, and looking down
On the water, smiles to see
The nymphs in every valley of the sea.

Panagiotis Soutsos, trans. Richard Stoneman

The name Greece forcefully inspires many romantic images, chief among which are those that relate to its islands and the seas in which they lie scattered. Down through the centuries writers and poets have celebrated the beauty, mystery and variety of these unique insular worlds, and some of the earliest of Greek literature, not least the epic verses of Homer, carry island descriptions that might well dub for those in contemporary travel and tourism literature. Whereas prosaic portrayals are apt to cloud many less than romantic realities, the very mention of the Greek islands conjures up visions of idyllic retreats and magical paradises of secluded beaches, chocolate-box villages, lethargic harbours and hospitable inhabitants.

For most people the image of a typical Greek island scene is one of dazzling white houses clustered in small villages that perch on sun-baked rocky slopes rising from an indigo, ultramarine or turquoise sea. Further indulgence adds to this mental picture a few whitewashed churches, some ornate dovecots and a collection of windmills with canvas sails furled to tiny triangles. On an eminence the ruins of an ancient temple, or the stones of a crumbling castle, preside over a small, picturesque harbour where boats bob the water and fishermen mend nets in readiness for another night at sea. The vision is completed by a steep, circuitous track leading up to the village along which laden mules and donkeys methodically pick their way in a manner that has remained unchanged for centuries.

It is no exaggeration to state that many Greek islands of the Aegean and Ionian archipelagos conform to this picture-postcard impression. Yet to wallow in generalizations would be tantamount to misrepresentation, for the predominant characteristic of the Greek insular world is its remarkable physical and human variety expressed in the individuality of each island. Seen from the air, they appear very similar (except for shape and in pattern) but in reality the distinctions are marked, for each island has its own landscape and history – consequently its own character, colour and atmosphere. Startling differences are to be found even between islands belonging to the same geographical group and, as Trevor Webster (*Webster's Guide to Greece*) writes, 'If you do find an island that reminds you in some way of another, they are sure to be at opposite ends of the Aegean. The next one in the chain nearly always offers a complete contrast and makes generalizations difficult'.

Official sources recognize some 2000 Greek islands, and collectively they comprise over one-fifth of the nation's land territory – that is, 25,166 square kilometres out of a total of 131,900. Significantly, however, the area of sea that Greece controls is something like 400,000 square kilometres, over three times that of its land area. Of the country's total coastline of 15,021 kilometres, some 11,000 are contributed by its islands. The vast majority of these, it should be noted, are small, barren domains, either uninhabited or, at best, seasonally occupied by goats, sheep and their tenders. These innumerable reefs and islets add romantic weight to the oft-told tale of 'God's castaway stones', for when the creator had finished his work on the world (and for Greece as a whole he had chosen a mountainous and rocky model), he discarded most of his surplus pieces into the Aegean basin, where they patterned themselves into what became a veritable Hellenic polynesia. Some of the Almighty's surplus was, however, windborne in a westerly direction, to form a string of islands along the Ionian approaches to Greece.

To translate fantasy into science, most of the Aegean 'stones' are the peaks of submerged mountain chains geologically explicable in terms of land- and sea-level changes associated with a complicated pattern of fracture zones and great tectonic instability. The islands are, therefore, the structural prolongations of the main mountain massifs responsible for the rugged topographical character of both mainland Greece and the western coast of Asia Minor.

The large island of Euboea and the Sporades group to its north continue into the Aegean the general alignments of the Thessalian ranges and of Othrys and Pelion, respectively, whereas the majority of the Cyclades, the most thickly clustered of the Greek islands, are the south-easterly extensions of Euboea (Andros, Tinos, Mykonos etc) and the promontory of Attica (e.g. Kea, Serifos and Sifnos). From

The church of the Panayi Evangelistra and an ornamental dovecot, Tinos

Mykonos the northern Cycladic chain is continued through Icaria and Samos to form a structural link with the mountainous configuration of western Asia Minor.

By far the most geologically significant chain is the one that can be traced from the rugged Arcadian heart of the Peloponnesus southwards to the island of Cythera, eastwards through the great mountainous bastion of Crete (which effectively closes the Aegean in the south) and north-eastwards through Kassos, Karpathos and Rhodes into south-western Asia Minor. Physically, therefore, the islands of the eastern Aegean – the Dodecanese group, together with Samos, Chios and Lesbos etc – are dislodged portions of the rugged and irregular coast of western Turkey, a geographical fact that has always had considerable political implication, not least today. In similar manner, though currently undisputed, the seven main Ionian islands of Corfu, Paxos, Lefkas, Ithaka, Cephalonia and Zakinthos, together with many smaller territories, are detached segments of the western Greek coasts of

Part of the remains of the Sanctuary of the Great Gods, Samothrace

Epirus, Sterea Hellas and the Peloponnesus. Their insularity is again related to major fracture zones which are also responsible for the Gulfs of Patras and Corinth that separate the Peloponnesus (itself technically an island since the opening of the Corinth Canal in 1893) from mainland Greece proper.

In the formation of the Greek islands, crustal instability has long been accompanied by volcanic activity, earth tremors and associated tidal flooding, and legend, as well as the writings of such early geographers as Strabo and Pliny, speaks of the natural disasters that affected the Greek sea basins. The presence of numerous hot thermal springs and a line of volcanic cones, craters and eruption debris stretching from Methana on the Saronic coast, through to Milos and Santorini (Thera), to Nisyros and Kos, provides tangible evidence of crustal weakness. Nisyros, almost circular in shape, with sulphur springs and an immense crater four kilometres in diameter, illustrates the powerful forces of past volcanic activity, whereas the spectacular Santorini, whose islands encircle a massive drowned caldera (collapsed crater), is a manifestation of still active forces. At the heart of its arrangement of islands are the Kaemenes – the 'Burnt Ones' – partly the product of an eruption in 1956 whose accompanying earth tremors caused considerable local damage.

Earthquakes are still common in the Aegean and Ionian seas, and they have been well documented from ancient times onwards. An ancient stele (commemorative column) discovered at the excavated ruins of Cameiros on the north-west coast of Rhodes bears the inscription 'to the memory of the victims of the earthquake', and similar monuments have been found elsewhere in the islands. Rhodes, together with its neighbouring islands, has suffered numerous tremors. In 227 BC the famous Hellenistic Colossus, one of the ancient world's seven wonders, was tumbled by an earthquake, and in medieval times the ramparts and towers of the great fortifications of the Knights of St John were repeatedly destroyed or weakened. Among the earthquakes that have caused serious damage to the islands in more recent times are those of Crete in 1856, Rhodes in 1926, Kos in 1933 and the Ionian Islands in 1953, when Zakinthos, in particular, suffered greatly.

The tidal waves that accompanied the volcanic eruptions and seismic activity of earliest times were probably reponsible for the tradition of a great flood that affected many parts of the Aegean. Such an event (or series of events) now has the support of scientific and archaeological scholarship, particularly that associated with the destruction of the Bronze Age cities of Minoan Crete. It is significant that the sea god, Poseidon, is constantly referred to by Homer as the 'earth-shaker', and one of the most intriguing theories of Sir Arthur Evans – the 'discoverer' of ancient Crete – related to his ideas on the meaning of the Minoan bull cult and its ritualistic demands, which in all probability were the bases of the Minotaur legend. One warm

June night, when resting in the Villa Ariadne close to his excavations at Knossos, he experienced one of Crete's frequent earthquakes (on average about two severe ones occur each century, with minor tremors every year). He graphically described the incident in his journal: 'Small objects were thrown about, and a pail, full of water, was splashed nearly empty. The movement, which recalled a ship in a storm, though of only a minute and a quarter's duration, already produced the same physical effect on me as a rough sea. A dull noise rose from the ground like the muffled roar of an angry bull.' Imagination and intuition linked this experience and others with a line Evans recalled from the *Iliad*: 'In bulls does the Earth-shaker delight.' There are numerous Homeric references to the activities of Poseidon: 'Up on high the Father of men and gods thundered ominously, and down below Poseidon caused the wide-world and the lofty mountain-tops to quake. Every spur and crest of Ida of the many springs was shaken.' The incidence of seismic destruction at Knossos, and elsewhere, was readily apparent from Evans' excavations, from which it might well be construed that Cretan bull-baiting (as depicted on one of the most famous of the Knossos frescos) and the worship and the legends this fostered, was an attempt by the Minoans to appease the destructive forces of their environment.

As archaeologists and other researchers continue to prove, the step between fable and fact in the Greek island world is often a short and a quick one. When early

24

lat-roofed houses,
hurches and windmills
ompose the scene at Ios

settlers began to concentrate their attention on the Aegean and Ionian seas, the islands were to act as convenient natural stepping-stones, the aids not only to migration and colonization but also to experimentation and progress in seafaring and navigation. As with all long-settled areas, the archipelagos came to inspire beloved myths of the gods and of redoubtable heroes. The mighty Zeus presided over the earth kingdoms from his mountain-tops, and Hades governed the under-world, but the seas were the undisputed domains of Poseidon. Their attractions, mysteries and dangers are encapsulated in the tales of sea monsters and nymphs, of the wily Calypso, the sorceress Circe and the Sirens whose hypnotic wailing lured sailors to their island shores or grounded their ships on rocky reefs.

Jason was one of the first legendary heroes to brave such supernatural challenges, and his exploits in the·*Argo*, one of the first references to a longship, belong to the oldest body of Greek myths. Odysseus was another intrepid sea-adventurer whose wanderings in Greek seas after the fall of Troy lasted some twenty years. Ultimately he returned to his Ionian island of Ithaca, though his destiny was to set sail again as a prophet to people ignorant of boats and the traditions of the sea. The Athenian national hero, Theseus, also knew the Greek seas, and legend has it that the Aegean takes its name from that of his father, Aegeus. With the help of Ariadne, Theseus had slain the Minotaur of the Knossos labyrinth, but on returning home he forgot to raise white sails, the agreed signal that he had successfully accomplished his venture. He obviously had other things on his mind, not least, perhaps, pangs of remorse for having ungratefully abandoned the accommodating Ariadne on the island of Naxos. Seeing his son's ship approaching under black sails, the grief-stricken Aegeus threw himself from the walls of the Athenian Acropolis and drowned in the sea that took his name. Another version of the story places the suicide at Troezen on the Peloponnesian coast opposite the island of Poros – yet both locations would have demanded great strength on Aegeus' part to accomplish such a leap!

Despite their larger-than-life personalities and fantasy scenarios, these and other adventure-voyage traditions are now accepted as being romanticized versions of the movements of early peoples – migrants, explorers and colonists – some, perhaps, intent on exploiting the obsidian of Milos, the marble of Paros, Naxos and Tinos, or the iron of Serifos, Andros and Kythnos. The quest undertaken by Jason and his Argonauts might well have been a search for precious metals greatly in demand by early Aegean civilizations for decorative ornaments, jewellery and ceremonial weapons. Many inventive stories undoubtedly preserve memories of the seafaring and trading prowess of the Cycladic and Minoan cultures (see page 33ff.) whose island colonies acted as bridging points in a sea that linked three continents.

Boat-filled harbours are ubiquitous scenes throughout the islands

In the infancy of shipbuilding and navigation, the close proximity of the Aegean islands meant that, without compass, chart and sextant, early mariners could sail in waters where, except in inclement weather, land was rarely out of sight. Yet the Ionian also claims to be one of the earliest cradles of seamanship, its islands acting as stepping-off points for voyages into the central and western parts of the Mediterranean. It was in the Ionian that European sailors must first have navigated out of sight of land, gradually gaining knowledge of shores where Greek colonies would eventually be founded – for example, in Sicily, southern Italy and as far west as the south of France and the coasts of eastern Iberia. These early voyages might well have been made in vessels similar to the fifty-oared galley that the Phaeceans of Corfu, according to Homer, used to transport Odysseus back to Ithaca.

Whereas the geographical pattern of islands greatly aided early seafaring, a factor of equal importance was that of weather conditions, particularly the direction, strength and, above all, the regularity of seasonal winds on which maritime calendars were ultimately based. In fact, it could be argued that, were it not for

The 'Naval Expedition': a fresco from the Akrotiri excavations on Santorini

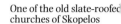
predictable winds, Greek civilization and culture would never have spread so widely. Despite commonly accepted images of placid, lagoon-like waters, the Aegean is a contrary, often treacherous sea, which lends support to the theory that, rather than deriving its name from the unfortunate King Aegeus, it is a corruption of the word *aegis*, meaning 'squall'. Winter storms and high waters often affect the entire basin, confining even the largest ships to the protection of stout harbour walls, and in antiquity it was common for vessels to be hauled ashore in late autumn and to lie beached until the return of more settled, dependable conditions. Even in summer, winds can whip up very heavy seas, sufficient on occasion to disrupt shipping services and ground all smaller craft, especially the caiques, the traditional fishing and inter-island cargo boats, many of which now also specialize in tourism.

From March to November the predominant winds over the Aegean are from the north and, on occasion, blow with considerable force. Known as the *etesians*, by July and August, particularly in the central Aegean, they are supplemented by land and sea winds to produce the *meltemi* which rises to considerable strength in early afternoon, only to fall again as evening approaches. The *meltemi* frequently creates difficulty for shipping, as those who have made the short crossing from Mykonos to Delos will certainly have experienced. Yet for islanders and visitors alike, the summer winds of the Aegean are of considerable personal value since they prevent what otherwise would be excessively high temperatures. They are also responsible for the remarkable clarity of the atmosphere, a crisp brightness and a blue, cloudless sky.

The Ionian Sea is less troubled by disagreeable summer winds; in fact in this season it has lengthy periods of calm. The soft haze that envelops its islands has a wonderfully seductive quality, one that contrasts with the burnished skies of the Aegean. Ernle Bradford (*The Companian Guide to the Greek Islands*) wrote of its being a feminine sea whereas, for him, the Aegean exhibited all the traits of masculinity. Perhaps the ancients also recognized this quality when they named it after Io, the beautiful nymph who attended Hera, the consort of Zeus. Unbridled passion frequently governed the activities of the Father of the Gods, and Aeschylus relates his torrid love-affair with Io. Though above reproach, Zeus was anxious to allay the suspicions of Hera and changed the willing maiden into a heifer. But Hera was wise to the relationship and in a fit of jealous rage ordered a gadfly to sting the animal. Maddened with pain, Io plunged into the sea that came to bear her name and after a marathon swim reached Egypt, where she was restored to human form to become the first in a long line of beauties particularly pleasing to the gods.

Yet, like many beauties, the Ionian can also be a sultry sea, especially in spring and autumn, when for short periods hot, moisture-bearing winds originating over North Africa bring oppressive conditions leaving the islanders short-tempered and restless. These humid *sirokos* were the bane of the British during their occupation of the Ionian Islands. Writing in 1823 from Corfu, Private Wheeler described them as 'the most disagreable evils with which to contend'. It is said that Ionian sailors, touching the decks of their boats at night, can detect the onset of a *siroko* by the heavy dewfall. When it blows, the humidity drawn from the sea is intensive and for its duration indolence reigns.

Few feminine attributes mark the *gregale* or *Grego* (the Greek Wind), the fierce northerly or north-easterly wind which blows mainly in winter. Fortunately its most wild effects are felt not over the islands but off Sicily and Malta. With a full sweep of sea behind it, the *gregale* gives rise to high and dangerous waters. Called

'Euroclydon' in the Acts of the Apostles, it was this wind that was responsible for St Paul's perilous adventures during his voyage to Rome when, from Crete, his boat was driven helplessly across the Ionian to the bay in Malta that bears his name. The King James version of the Bible provides a particularly dramatic account: 'And when the south wind blew softly . . . [we] sailed close to Crete. . . . But not long after there arose against it a tempestuous wind called Euroclydon. . . . And we were exceedingly tossed with a tempest. . . . And when neither sun nor stars in many days appeared . . . all hope that we should be saved was taken away.' Even today the Ionian schooners and coastal traders hesitate to put to sea during the *gregale* months, and most of the open fishing boats are laid up during winter awaiting the light winds of spring and the land breezes of summer.

The physical qualities of the Greek seas, their dependable seasonal rhythms but also their daily moods and frequently unpredictable whims, have played major roles in determining the individual atmospheres and distinctive characters of the islands. The latter are as much seascape as landscape, these terms denoting facets not of a dualism but of a unified whole, for as in all insular worlds land and sea are indivisible: the one cannot be conceived or take form without the other. From the dawn of history the Greek archipelagos have captured the imagination, fed the spirit, converted the soul and instructed the intellect, all to a collective degree that the images the islands project are as much those of the mind as concrete realities. The islands induce a wealth of emotional responses, for the barrenness of many shocks, the lushness of others surprises, the general quality of their light continues to fascinate, while the often fierce forces of their natural elements are capable of evoking feelings of wary respect.

Yet, at the same time, their human lifestyles prompt an embracing sense of timeless control, a comforting traditionalism that has led to a balance between islander and island, between man and nature. This is not to suggest that Greek island life is anachronistic, for changes, some for the better, others questionable, have long affected their towns and cities and are gradually spreading to even the most isolated parts of their countrysides. It is in the latter, however, that man's relationship with his environment is most readily apparent, and there still remain many communities where life offers unrelieved toil and, for some, crushing poverty, the only means of retaliation being migration to island capitals, Athens or abroad.

History has brought the Greek islands periods of prosperity, but its pages are also a catalogue of natural disasters, for man has pillaged, conquered, oppressed and depopulated, conditioning the islanders' acceptance (though this is a generalization) of conflict and hardship, and nurturing, in parts of the Aegean in particular, an innate sense of fatalism. The all-pervading closeness of the past lies at the very forefront of the present, and though some would argue that the islands and their people can be appreciated for their contemporary worth and without recourse to history, those who wish to penetrate beyond the superficialities will benefit from some, albeit generalized, chronological frame of reference. As almost every island has a colourful place in mythology and history, the past is essentially the story of each individual sea-washed territory, or, at least, the combined stories of islands that form a geographical grouping. As Richard Stoneman writes: 'Islands, like men, have their exits and their entrances. Some maintain a reputation, a fascination, through the centuries: others surface briefly . . . and are lost to thought. They catch the imagination at different historical moments.' The Greek islands support this view, for many have, in fact, been fortunate in retaining a sense of importance from earliest times to the present; others, having fallen from grace, have now found a new economic life-blood in tourism; but there are some that remain, in the words of Alexander the Great's general, Antipater 'deserted islands, broken sherds of land held in by the Aegean's belt of noise'.

2

Isles Full of Noises

Among the first settlers of the Aegean were neolithic farmers and fishers whose presence can be traced back to at least 4,000 BC. These peoples had drifted to the islands from the eastern Mediterranean lands and fashioned their implements and weapons from local stone, clay and obsidian. The island of Milos, volcanic in origin, owed its importance to the latter raw material, a glass-like rock formed by the rapid solidification of lava which can be fashioned, like flint, to produce sharp-edged knives, arrowheads and spears. Obsidian was exported as far afield as Egypt and formed the basis of the island's prosperity from the neolithic period to classical times.

Excavations at the prehistoric site of Phylakopi in the north-eastern part of the island have revealed a series of superimposed settlements that provide an important key to the early chronology of the islands. Belonging to what archaeologists call the Cycladic culture, Phylakopi was established in the third millennium BC and subsequently came under the influence of the Bronze Age civilization of Minoan Crete. Its excavated layers have brought to light a wealth of artistic artefacts, particularly stylized marble figurines, generally of fertility goddesses and sometimes representing harp-players. Similar objects found in graves and sanctuaries throughout the southern Aegean and along its Greek and Asia Minor shores indicate the importance of early trading undertaken, perhaps, by those intrepid sailors whom the Greeks later personalized with heroic names, embroidering their maritime adventures with tales of fantasy. A fine collection of figurines can be seen in the local museum on Naxos as well as in the National Archaeological Museum in Athens, which also houses the famous flying-fish fresco recovered from Phylakopi.

The Cycladic culture developed at the same time as that of the Minoan on Crete, and the evidence from Phylakopi speaks of increasing Cretan influence as Minoan colonies were established on several islands including Thera and Cythera. The name 'Minoan', after the legendary King Minos and the story of the Minotaur, was given by Sir Arthur Evans whose excavations at Knossos first revealed evidence of an advanced Cretan Bronze Age civilization. From large palace complexes – Knossos, Mallia and Phaestos – with their refined courtly lifestyles, the Minoans developed a centrally directed economy and, in the period *c.*2000-1450 BC, dominated the Aegean with a powerful trading network. The palaces were exceptionally large and of great complexity, having advanced engineering works, such as intricate water-supply systems, and refined construction methods incorporating multi-storey occupancy. Rooms were richly decorated with frescos, fine examples of which can be seen in the Iraklion Archaeological Museum together with intricately engraved jewellery, votive sculptures and other objects relating to the Minoans' distinctive religious beliefs. Inscribed tablets found at Knossos and elsewhere belong to what are known as Linear A and Linear B. The former is a syllabic script of the Minoan language, whereas the latter, deciphered by Michael Ventris in 1952, is a hieroglyphic form of Greek (indicating later mainland influence) which provides information on economic organization and the goods held in the vast palace storerooms.

The most dramatic evidence of Minoan influence in other islands comes from the excavations at Akrotiri on the island of Thera. The excavators found no palace there but a number of large houses, suggesting that the island was run by a plutocracy of rich merchants and ship-owners with close trading links with North Africa. The frescos of Akrotiri, now in Athens, are of a remarkably high artistic quality. Ironically this wealthy island, nurtured by the Minoan culture, was instrumental in its decline, for in the mid-fifteenth century BC Thera suffered an eruption whose force is said to have produced the greatest explosion in global history – many times more violent than that of Krakatoa in 1883. Much of the southern Aegean suffered from the accompanying earthquakes, tidal floods and volcanic dust, and the devastation of Crete paved the way for invaders (some maintain a local revolt) to topple the Minoan hierarchy. Thereafter only Knossos was heavily populated and ruled by the Mycenaeans from the Greek mainland.

Taking their name from the powerful fortress-city of Mycenae in the Argolid, the Mycenaeans were the first speakers of the Greek tongue, their script being Linear B. Initially dominated by the Minoans but later the conquerors of Crete, by 1300 BC these Greeks, whom Homer refers to as Achaeans, were operating from powerfully defended strongholds and appear to have recognized the overlordship of a chieftain-king known to early Greek literature as Agamemnon. It was his forces, in combination with the armies of other Achaean leaders, who successfully laid siege to Troy. Mycenaean power was based on naval strength and important commercial outlets throughout the Aegean and eastern Mediterranean generally, the islands of Rhodes and Cyprus being vitally important colonies. Homer's *Iliad* and *Odyssey*, though written later, refer to the Mycenaean period and contain much information on the general way of life.

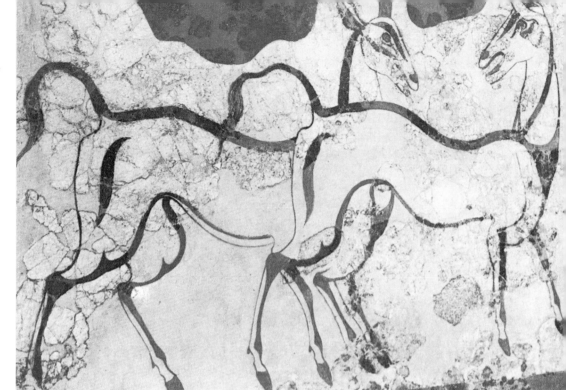

The 'Oryx Fresco' from the Minoan excavations at Akrotiri, Santorini

Floor mosaic from the 'House of Dolphins', Delos

One of the many luxuriou
villas in the 'Theatre
Quarter', Delos

Mycenaean culture declined suddenly in the thirteenth or twelfth century, probably from the combined assaults of the Dorians and those whom Egyptian sources refer to as 'the Sea Peoples' – the Phoenicians.

The Dorians, the first iron-users in Greece, entered the country from the north. Unlike the Mycenaeans, who had originally functioned as a conquering aristocracy, they came as land-hungry migrants whose pillaging and destruction gradually gave way to permanent settlement. History has labelled them illiterate, ruthless warriors, but such stigmas were also attached to the Vikings before detailed research and excavation put the record straight. The Dorian period certainly ushered in a centuries-long 'Dark Age' when aesthetic skills apparently declined, but within this seemingly cultural void a vital spark ignited a fire that was ultimately to blaze as the proud beacon of classical Greek civilization. The Dorians, together with Ionian

36

colonists from the coasts of Asia Minor, first settled around the edge of the Aegean before moving on to the islands themselves, where they took over old Minoan-Mycenaean sites. On Rhodes, for example, they occupied the cities of Cameiros, Ialysos and Lindos, combining these with Astypalaea on Kos and Halicarnassus and Knidos on the Asia Minor coast, to form the Dorian Hexapolis, a religious, economic and political confederation. This acted as a balance of power against the Ionian states which had amalgamated and established their chief centre at Ephesus. Throughout the Aegean, however, many of the old Minoan-Mycenaean trading routes were controlled by the Phoenecians, the Greek name given to the Canaanites whose homeland was the narrow coastal plain of the Levant. The islands have many place-names derived from Phoenician influence.

From this fusion of assorted peoples, but largely as the result of Phoenician influence, a universal Greek alphabet and language developed. This was to play a major role in the cultural unification of the Greeks, though political accord was not endemic and arose only when imposed from outside. In fact, when the curtain rises at the end of the Dark Age, Greece is fragmented into numerous independent states, the majority going their own way and jealously guarding their sovereignty. These, the city states or *poleis* (singular *polis*) exhibited the processes of world political history in microcosm, for treaties were made, boundaries negotiated, alliances and leagues founded, ambassadors exchanged and war and peace declared. They were immensely creative in evolving new forms of government which might best be summarized as the transition from autocratic monarchy to democracy, though the path to the latter was frequently interrupted by periods of oligarchy, tyranny and dictatorship. Their contribution to literature, architecture, pictorial art, philosophy and science is inestimable and best revealed in classical Athens' so-called 'Golden Age', though other city states reached similar peaks of cultural achievement and prestige.

Coveted by the mainland states and often subjected to their government, the islands also played their own individual parts in the rise of classical civilization: Aegina in the sixth century was a prosperous trading centre and introduced the first European coinage; Naxos long dominated the southern Aegean both politically and economically; Samos flourished under Polycrates and claimed the age's largest temple; Lesbos was the home of outstanding lyric poets; Kos had a medical school famous throughout the ancient world; and Delos took its place along with Olympia and Delphi as one of the three great pan-hellenic sanctuaries. In the fine arts many of the islands also excelled and have provided the museums of the world with some of the most renowned pieces of sculpture, not least the 'Victory of Samothrace' which, in the Louvre, vies in popularity with the equally famous Aphrodite (Venus) of Milos, though the latter is a Hellenistic work.

Like their counterparts on the Greek mainland, the island states took part in the unprecedented wave of colonial expansion which placed Greek cities along the shores of the Mediterranean and the Black Sea – in the words of Plato 'like frogs round a pond'. Although many of the Ionian Islands contain evidence of Mycenaean settlement and feature strongly in Homer's *Odyssey* as the lands of King Alcinous and the Phaeceans (the scene of the shipwrecked Odysseus' romantic episode with Nausicaa), they are brought fully into the light of history and the orbit of classical civilization with the founding of Corfu (Corcyra) as a colony of Corinth, its site being the Palaeopolis on the Kanoni peninsula to the south of the modern town. Once founded, its favoured trading position at the western approaches to Greece guaranteed its commercial success, and soon Corfu was exploring the Ionian and Adriatic waters in search of its own colonial outposts. Building up a powerful navy, Corfu reacted against Corinthian control and, though it would be misleading to suggest that it was in any way the prime cause of the Peloponnesian War, this policy of independence was certainly one of the apples of discord that ultimately led to the great conflict between the classical city states. The opening pages of Thucydides' *The Peloponnesian War* details the succession of events that led to the political turmoil.

However, the war postdates another period of bloodshed which initially affected the Greek islands. Largely on account of the piecemeal opportunities they offered for conquest, they were the first parts of Greece to feel the brunt of the Persian menace. In 499 BC a bold attack was launched on Naxos and though, on this occasion, the Persians were driven off, they returned nine years later with massive forces that pillaged the island and conquered the remainder of the Cyclades. This gave Darius the confidence to meet the Greeks at Marathon, but here the Athenians and Plataeans staged a brilliant victory which was repeated ten years later when the Persian fleet, commanded by Xerxes, was largely destroyed at the Battle of Salamis.

Hardly had many of the city states rebuilt their economies following Persian destruction than they were plunged into the conflict between Athens and Sparta, the Peloponnesian War, from 431 to 404 BC. Most of the Aegean islands nominally supported Athens, though not Milos, which was savagely attacked for its pro-Spartan sympathies. The Ionian islands also sided with Athens and were the scene of many battles and massacres. When it became more than apparent that Athens would lose the war, there was a major swing in allegiance in favour of Sparta. Such was the determination of Athens that within decades of its defeat it was actively rebuilding its empire in the Aegean. But many islands, including Rhodes, Kos and Chios, rejected the idea of co-operation at a time when a new political danger was poised to destroy the independent integrity of the city states and bring the classical era to a swift, though not ignoble end.

Whilst warfare, intrigue and rivalry flourished amongst the Greeks, a Macedonian king, Philip II, had been raising and strengthening an army that was quickly to subjugate the Greek peninsula and islands. This he accomplished in two decisive battles in 338 BC at Chaeronia near the Boeotian town of Livadia. The Greeks were forced to accept his leadership and, as a result, reluctantly to support a new offensive against the Persian Empire. But Philip was assassinated in 336 BC, and the Persian campaign, which had all the traits of a Hellenic crusade, fell to the leadership of his power-thirsty son, Alexander, whose brilliant victories forged him a vast empire spreading Hellenism as far east as the River Indus. The Greek cities were now demoted to subordinate roles as other centres such as Antioch, the time-honoured Babylon and the newly founded Alexandria flourished as international emporiums. Yet some of the islands were to gain a new lease of economic and cultural life under the protection of Alexander's Hellenistic empire, especially Rhodes, which had been quick to recognize the advantages of siding with Macedonia. Their combined forces had succeeded in destroying the rival trading city of Tyre, and further Macedonian conquests gave Rhodes unrestricted access to Cyprus, Cicilia, Syria and Egypt. Alexander, it appears, had a great admiration for Rhodes and helped to promote it commercially. When the city of Alexandria was founded in 331 BC, the young ruler proved his admiration by adopting a system of government based on that of Rhodes, which was further honoured by naming the island opposite the harbour Antirodos.

A medieval castle and ancient acropolis occupy the rugged limestone rock above the village of Lindos

Alexander's untimely death from fever at Babylon was followed by a merciless struggle for the control of the great cosmopolitan empire. The result was its partition into what quickly became warring states ruled by self-styled kings, Greece and its islands coming under the rule of Cassander's Macedonian empire. Only Antigonus of Syria and Asia Minor had the will to restore the empire's unity, and the strategic position of his lands, together with his firm command of the sea, enabled him to seduce the allegiance of much of southern Greece and the islands. Initially only Rhodes was strong enough to resist incorporation into a new Aegean League but soon other Greek cities and islands campaigned for independence. Many of them appealed to Rome for protection against the territorial ambitions of Macedonia and Asia Minor and, following something like 150 years of political chaos, in 168 BC the Roman legions defeated the Macedonian phalanx of Philip V's son, Perseus, at Pydna. Acquisition of the old city states and islands followed, and the plundering of Corinth in 146 BC completed Rome's appropriation of Greece. Of all the islands, Rome particularly favoured Delos by declaring it a free port, an act that greatly promoted its development as a trading centre, gaining for itself infamy as a major slave market. Its prosperity was, however, shortlived, for it fell to many plunderers, and when Pausanius visited the island in the second century AD, its population had been reduced to a mere handful of custodians dutifully maintaining the otherwise deserted sanctuaries.

As with all ancient religious centres, the site of Delos attracted the early Christian Church, anxious to establish itself in places that had been centres of paganism. But the settlement failed to last long in a sea that came to be ravaged by pirates. It was the island of Patmos in the Dodecanese that was to gain a revered reputation in Christian history. Here, tradition has it, the Apostle John was sent into exile during the reign of the Roman Emperor Domitian (AD 81–96), and Patmos became the place where he wrote his Revelations before moving on as a teacher to Ephesus, where he died at a ripe age.

Christianity was assured prominence in Greek life when Constantine, converted to the faith, established it as the religion of the Roman Empire. The old colonial city of Byzantium on the Bosporus was renamed Constantinople and became the capital of the Empire's eastern half. Some forty-four years later the Bishop of Constantinople was granted jurisdiction over the Church in Asia Minor and the Balkans, thus establishing the legitimacy of the future Greek Orthodox faith. As throughout Greece, the islands were to receive a number of large basilican churches, episcopal and monastic, while smaller, provincial architectural varieties became the focuses of all local communities.

The Christian Byzantine Empire outlasted the Roman Empire in the west by many centuries, though it was continually subjected to external threats in the form of barbarian (Goth, Hun, Vandal, Slav and Bulgar) and Arab attacks. Great effort was expended by Byzantium in the protection of its Greek islands, though the majority became the pawns in a ruthless game of medieval power politics. Many fell victim to barbarian pillage and Arab attack, Crete, for example, being dominated by Saracen Arabs between 823 and 961. They founded the town of Rabd-el-Kandak, later known as Candia and today as Iraklion.

But Byzantium's greatest threat was to come from within the realms of Christendom itself. The Empire's control of the Ionian islands was precarious, and by the twelfth century they had fallen to the Normans of southern Italy and Sicily who honoured the trading rights which had earlier been conferred on the Venetians by the Byzantine emperors. Corfu, in particular, was an important refurbishing point on the crusaders' route to and from the East. It was here in 1203 that the forces of the infamous Fourth Crusade assembled. Geoffrey de Villehardouin, the appointed chronicler to the campaign, describes the mighty fleet as it left the island: 'It was a more wonderful sight than has ever been seen before. As far as the eye can reach, the sea is covered with sails of ships and galleys. Our hearts were filled with joy and we felt that our armament could undertake the conquest of the world.'

What the Fourth Crusade did conquer in 1204 was not the Moslem 'infidel' but Constantinople. The treachery was masterminded by Venice, which had little to lose, for a year earlier the Republic and the crusaders had been excommunicated for their pillage of the Adriatic city of Zara, where 'They turned the swords they had consecrated to the service of Christianity against Christians.' Dethroning the Emperor, they partitioned the Byzantine Empire into Latin states, but it was Venice, from both strategic and commercial points of view, that secured the choicest of the Greek lands.

The islands, however, presented something of a problem. Realizing the difficulties of administering discontinuous territories, the Venetians awarded land grants and dependencies in return for trading privileges in the newly created fiefdoms. The occupation of the Aegean was left to notable Catholic lords – Ghizi, Dandoli, Giustianini, Barozzi, Michieti and, most important of all, Marco Sanudi, a bucaneering nephew of the Doge. After taking Naxos, the reduction of the other islands followed and all paid homage – some twenty small vassal states – to Sanudi as Duke of Naxos. What became collectively known as the Duchy of the Archipelago stretched from the Sporades in the north to Santorini in the south. Based on a prosperous agriculture and sea trade, the Duchy, under a number of dynasties, was the most durable of the Greek Latin states, lasting from 1207 until the Turkish Ottoman raids of 1566, though the island of Tinos resisted until 1718. Many traces of Venetian-Italian rule can be found in the islands, including Church and military architecture, Italian family names and Italian words and phrases mingled with Greek speech. Often segregation resulted, as in Syros where there remain distinct divisions in the town: one with its houses built around the peak on which the Roman Catholic cathedral stands, the other clustered under the shadow of the Greek Orthodox cathedral.

Ever eager to break Venetian trading monopoly in the eastern Mediterranean, the Genoese, by the time of the Fourth Crusade, had installed themselves on Crete. Here, with the help of the islanders, they resisted Venetian intervention, but in 1210 they were driven out, and the appointment of Jacopo Tiepolo as first governor began Crete's long period of rule by the Republic. Venetian government was oppressive, and attempts to impose Latin lifestyles on the fiercely independent Cretan character was met with many revolts. Only towards the end of the Republic's rule, when Ottoman pressure necessitated local support, was the regime relaxed and the heavy and unjust taxation reduced. Significantly, Crete was one of the last Greek-speaking territories to fall to the Turks, the resistance of Candia being legendary, the siege lasting twenty-three years and ending in favour of the Turks in 1669.

The other major Venetian possessions in Greece were the Ionian islands. The Republic held them in unbroken possession for 410 years (1387–1797), and the islands, Corfu in particular, grew rich as centres of East-West trade, further enabling

Icons in the Monastery of the Holy Mother, Samos

the Venetians to control the entire Adriatic. As strongly defended Christian territories, the Ionian islands resisted Ottoman conquest, and their lengthy period under Venetian rule, followed by shorter periods of French and British control, has given them special characteristics (see page 235ff.), although they have always been, and remain, undeniably Greek in spirit.

What the Ionian islands stood for in the west – in terms of the challenge they presented the Turks – was matched in the east by the Order of St John of Jerusalem, whose knights, following the loss to the Arabs of their Palestinian possessions, established themselves with papal support on Rhodes and the other Dodecanese islands, their occupation lasting from 1309 to 1522. Originating as a hospice whose purpose was the lodging and succouring of Christian pilgrims on their way to the Holy Land, the Order soon transformed itself into a military body whose prime objectives became the defence of the Church against the encroaches of Islam. Rhodes and the other islands were strongly fortified and resisted the two great sieges of the Sultan of Egypt and Mohammed the Conqueror in 1444 and 1480 respectively.

Constantinople had fallen to Mohammed in 1453, finally ending the Byzantine Empire, which had been retaken from the Latin rulers by the Palaeologos family. Thereafter the city remained in Ottoman hands and formed a major military base for their progressive control of the Aegean. Rhodes was now menaced as never before and for the next seventy years remained the sole eastern bulwark of

Christianity in the Mediterranean. The Knights were finally defeated by the massive
forces of Sultan Suleiman II (the Magnificent), but capitulation was on honourable
terms, the Order being allowed twelve days to leave the islands, and all Rhodians
wishing to follow them into exile were free to do so. Led by Grand Master Villiers
de l'Isle Adam, some 180 knights and 4,000 islanders left Rhodes on 1 January
1523, thus placing almost the entire Aegean under Turkish sovereignty. 'Nothing
in the world was ever so well lost as was Rhodes,' remarked Emperor Charles V
on hearing the story of the knights' gallant defence against forces that vastly
outnumbered them. Initially the knights withdrew to Candia, then to Viterbo and
Civitavecchia in Italy, before reforming the Order in Malta in 1530 under a grant
of Charles V.

It would be unfair to perpetuate the view of the Turkish occupation of Greece
as one of unmitigated disaster. Despite corruption, heavy taxation and periods of
savage repression, the Greeks – the islanders in particular – were allowed considerable latitude, and many were adept at manipulating the Turkish power to their
own political and economic advantages. The genius of the Turks was for conquest
rather than administration, and as far as possible they employed their conquered
subjects to run the machinery of the empire. Many islanders were actively engaged
in shipping and commerce, and a lively black market also developed, flouting the

Ottoman ban on trade with the West. As in earlier centuries, piracy was also endemic in the Aegean, and the ships of corsairs preyed on trading vessels as well as on harbour towns and island villages. One of the most infamous corsairs was Khair-ed-Din (know to the West as Barbarossa), who plundered the Greek seas and carried off into slavery the inhabitants of many a local community. Part in retaliation, part as a means of economic survival, some islanders took to piracy themselves, their leaders growing rich and, by the nineteenth century, gaining respectability as merchant skippers – though still with an eye for the main chance.

There were other plunderers of Greek waters – those in search of precious antiquities for wealthy European patrons. The temples and sanctuaries of islands such as Aegina, Delos, Kos and Rhodes were robbed of many of their artistic treasures, the Turkish authorities, provided they were recompensed, turning a blind eye to such often savage forays. Towards the end of the Turkish period the wanton pilfering of archaeological and historical sites became common practice, though ultimately it became a battle for acquisition between Britain and France, which explains why so much of Greece's artistic heritage gravitated to the British Museum and the Louvre.

Already by the middle of the eighteenth century the Ottoman Empire was stricken with symptoms – corruption, intrigue and insurrection – that earned it the title 'the sick man of Europe'. Russia, under Catherine the Great, saw the chance of forging from Ottoman territories a client Greek state extending across the Bosporus, thereby ensuring access from the Black Sea to the Mediterranean. In 1770 a Russian fleet was discharged into the Aegean and captured over a dozen islands, a move met by strong protests and threats from the Great Powers of Europe. In 1774 the Russians were forced to withdraw, but not before they had established the right for their ships to pass freely through what had previously been an enclosed Turkish waterway. Ironically, Russia at this time had few ships but increasingly Greek vessels flew the Russian flag, their captains developing a virtual monopoly in Aegean-Black Sea trade.

Greece's sea captains were to play major roles in the country's bitter struggle for liberation from the four centuries of Turkish rule. The standard of revolt was raised in 1821, and the War of Independence was to last for nine bloodthirsty years as a succession of brutal sieges, horrific slaughters and sadistic acts of reprisal by both sides. Either independently or by combining their fleets, the merchant-corsairs of Hydra, Spetses and Psara (known as the Naval Islands) successfully harried Turkish shipping, and each island had admirals whose heroic deeds (slightly embroidered with time) are now part of modern Greek folklore. The memories of Miaoulis, Bouboulino, Canaris and others are represented in the names of streets, squares and quaysides in many a Greek port. Patriots, brigands and outlaws, plotting against the Turks or escaping from their reprisals, also gravitated to the islands, not least to Skiathos which on a number of occasions was the meeting-place for such *klepht* (guerrilla) leaders as Kolokotronis, Botsaris, Nikotsaras and Karaiskakis, all also considered heroes of the War of Independence. Some islands were the scene of great slaughter: in June 1822 the Turks massacred or enslaved almost all of the 75,000 inhabitants of Chios, and similar acts of carnage were committed on nearby Psara.

Not having been subject to Turkish rule, the Ionian islands escaped the human and physical devastation of the War of Indpendence. Between 1815 and 1864 the islands were a British protectorate governed by High Commissioners whose policies, as directed from Britain, were those of enforcing a somewhat precarious neutrality to the events in other parts of Greece. Yet Corfu and the other islands were to play significant roles in the revolution. Based largely on their Venetian traditions, the Ionians enjoyed a higher standard of living and education than their mainland and Aegean compatriots, and the ideas of the French Revolution, enthusiastically received in Greece, were transmitted through both literary and political channels. Byron and other notable campaigning philhellenes spent many weeks in the islands as guests of the government, which also accepted, though not officially, many Greeks fleeing from Turkish reprisals.

A leading figure in the history of modern Greece, and Corfu's greatest son, is Count John Capo d'Istria (Capodistrias). His house is preserved in Corfu town, and his remains are buried in a simple tomb in the seventeenth-century Platytera monastery. As a vigorous defender of the Greek revolutionary cause, his considerable political skill and diplomatic experience (gained in the service of the Russian Tsar Alexander) made him the obvious choice as the country's first national leader. Ultimately the Great Powers had been forced to intervene in what had become a protracted period of carnage, and the decisive battle in Greece's favour took place at Navarino in the south-west Peloponnesus where a combined British, French and Russian fleet annihilated the Turkish navy. The appointment of Capodistrias had reflected the need to secure foreign confidence in Greece, yet his major problem was curbing petty factionalism, and a violent clash with the militant clans of the Mani in the southern Peloponnesus culminated in his assassination at Nauplia on 9 October 1831.

The Great Powers again intervened to stem the turmoil that followed Capodistrias' death, and the Treaty of London, attended by diplomats of Britain, France, Russia and Bavaria, magnanimously accepted Greece's full independence provided it was under the heriditary sovereignship of Otho, son of King Ludwig of Bavaria. His original kingdom was small both in territorial size and in population. Its continental frontier extended from the Gulf of Arta in the west to the Gulf of Volos in the east, and the only island groupings were those of the Cyclades and the northern Sporades. The inclusion of the Cyclades was the outcome of considerable debate on the part of the Great Powers, but France was eager to protect the Catholic communities on islands such as Naxos, Tinos, Syros and Santorini. Syros had also been a refuge for those Greeks that had managed to escape from the massacre in Chios.

The nationalist and territorial ambitions of Greece were far from satisfied by these boundaries awarded in 1832. To them the political division of the Aegean, excluding many islands, including Crete, was totally unacceptable, and such a partition further hindered the highly important maritime traffic on which the new state was to depend. Essentially there were two Greek communities – the territorial and the extra-territorial – and throughout the nineteenth century and until the Lausanne Treaty of 1923, Greek politics were preoccupied with the liberation of the Greek-inhabited regions still under Turkish control. This irredentism, gaining the title 'The Great Idea', was championed by Eleutherios Venizelos, the Cretan-born statesman who worked both for the union of his native island with Greece and for the greater aim of consolidating the Greek people as they had been territorially and culturally united under the Byzantine Empire.

The first territorial gains came in 1864, when Britain ceded the Ionian islands to Greece. Their acquisition was an immense gain not only in wealth and population but particularly in prestige, for Ionian society (as noted) was highly stratified and its aristocratic culture, rooted in the centuries of Venetian rule and moulded in the principles of British statehood, proved of great benefit to Athenian politics. By the 1860s Ionian agitation for union with Greece had developed into a powerful move-ment, and Britain's decision to cede the islands was a reluctant concession to Greek feelings disguised as an unprecedented gesture of goodwill to the new King George I (formerly Prince William of Denmark) who had replaced the unpopular Otho. Fur-ther territory was acquired by the Congress of Berlin in 1878, which gave Greece the mainland province of Thessaly and part of Epirus, but it was not until the 1912 Balkan War that Greece gained further islands in the Aegean. The alliance of Greece, Bulgaria, Serbia and Montenegro against the Turks resulted in the annexation by Greece of further Epirot territory, the region known today as Greek Macedonia, the islands of the northern and eastern Aegean – Thasos, Samothrace, Lemnos, Chios, Samos and Icaria etc – and Crete.

The struggle for the union of Crete with Greece had taken on its own special characteristics. Numerous insurrections against Turkish rule and periods of blood-shed had punctuated island life throughout the nineteenth century, and the Cretan rallying cry, now immortalized as the title of one of Kazantzakis' regional novels, was 'Freedom and Death'. In 1898, following a period of compromise, inactivity and rivalries, the Great Powers forced the Turks to leave and granted Crete autonomous status under a High Commissioner, Prince George, younger son of George I. Though the Prince was warmly welcomed, many Cretans refused to settle for half measure, and unrest again broke out, culminating with Venizelos leading an abortive revolution in 1905. As a staunch republican, Venizelos' career took him to Athens in 1910 when he was elected deputy and then prime minister. It was he who brought the Balkan Wars to a victorious climax, thus achieving one of his burning ambitions, the official unification of his native island with Greece.

Prior to the First World War, therefore, Greece had acquired the majority of the Aegean Islands, the exceptions being Imbros and Tenedos, and the Dodecanese. The latter would have been included but for the fact that they had been occupied by Italy as a result of the Italian-Turkish War (the Libyan War) of 1911–12. The Greeks made many bold bids for them, and Italy's reluctance to cede them must be viewed in the light of the country's long desire for expansion in the eastern Mediterranean. It was not until Italy's defeat in the Second World War that the Dodecanese were granted union with Greece, the date being May 1947. The Italian occupation survives as a bitter memory to the Dodecanese islanders, especially to the Rhodians.

Fascism reigned throughout much of Italy's rule, the pretensions of which are obvious from the inscription Mussolini placed at the entrance to the restored Palace

The tranquil bays around Poros are sheltered by the mountains of the Argolid

The reconstructed Palace of the Grand Masters, Rhodes

Aegina's Temple of Aphaea stands in a commanding position above the island's east coast

Pashalimani harbour (the classical Zea), Piraeus, is centre of both commerce and recreation

of the Grand Masters. In large gold letters it reads: 'During the reign of his majesty Victor Emmanuel 3rd, King of Italy and Albania and Emperor of Ethiopia, with Benito Mussolini, the Duke of Fascism, at the head of government and Cesare Maria de Vecchi, Count of Val Cismon, the governor of the Italian islands of the Aegean, this ancient fortress, built by the Knights of St John on the unprofaned Roman defence was reconstructed and restored, giving back strength and splendour to its new role as the seat of government of the city of fortitude, defender of western civilization under the rule and religion of Rome. (The year of our Lord, 1940, eighteenth year of the Fascist era.)' It is interesting to note that the Rhodians have not troubled to remove Mussolini's magniloquent inscription. Instead, adjacent to the Italian notice is a Greek statement accompanied by a clumsy English translation. It reads: 'Reigning Paul on the twenty-ninth of June, nineteen hundred and forty-seven, by decision of the Military Governor of the Dodecanese, Vice-Admiral Pericles Ionnides, this rebuilt palace of the Great Magister of the Knights has been declared an historical monument to be preserved, thus rendered to the history of the unconquered Dodecanese people, who have maintained undiminished, during all foreign occupations, the idea of freedom, inexhaustible fountain of the eternal Greek civilization.'

For the Greeks the Dodecanese islands proved to be as great a psychological prize as a territorial one, for during World War II Mussolini had bullied and threatened Greece from occupied Albania where some 125,000 Italian troops were concentrated. On 28 October 1940 the Italian minister in Athens presented an ultimatum to the Greek General Metaxas demanding the cession of parts of Epirus to Albania, which technically meant to Italy. Through Metaxas' defiant 'no' ('*ochi*') to Mussolini's pressures, Britain, facing the Axis powers alone, gained her only fighting ally outside the empire. Mussolini's troops had expected little resistance, but all Italian counter-offensives were beaten back in what was virtually a spontaneous uprising by the Greeks. '*Ochi* Day' is still celebrated as a Greek national holiday, second only to Independence Day.

By 1941 the German timetable had caught up with Greece, and many of the 58,000 British and Imperial forces then in the country were forced to take refuge in the islands, especially in Crete, where, with local support, they made a bold stand. But on 20 May the island witnessed a spectacular invasion by German paratroopers, forcing thousands of British, Australian and New Zealand troops to escape across the mountains to the south coast from whence they were conveyed to Egypt. An imposing eagle, off the main road five kilometres west of Canea, is the German memorial to their assault. The Cretans have chosen to leave the eagle as a memorial to their own valour in the operations!

The majority of the Greek islands were involved in the period of civil strife that followed World War II, a period of grave internal struggles, involving Communist, royalist and other factions. As throughout the Greek mainland, the economic and social life of the islands was greatly impaired, compounding the long-existing problems stemming from their meagre resource bases. It was natural that tourism was seen as a general answer and, as a result of concerted effort, many of the islands have witnessed an unprecedented economic boom, though one that has been periodically interrupted by Greece's largely unstable internal politics in which the Cyprus issue has played a significant role.

In the 1960s inclusive tours to Greece were exceptions rather than the rule, if one discounts the educational (and decidedly up-market) varieties. Today the majority of the country's visitors use the services of the 'package tour' operators, the most important source areas being the UK, USA, West Germany, France, Italy, Switzerland and the Scandinavian countries, with many of these nationals 'adopting' a particular island or insular group. Corfu, Rhodes, Crete and Mykonos have reaped great financial rewards from tourism – an industry that has, however, been selective, certainly initially, in terms of its island development. Currently the Greek islands can be divided into a number of categories – those experiencing a high level of tourism, those earmarked for development, and those (now sought-after by the 'purists') where the slow rhythm of traditional life continues.

Yet commercialization tends to be contagious, the popularity of one island having an important overspill effect on its neighbours. The tourist saturation of Mykonos, for example, has led to the increasing development of nearby Paros and, to a lesser extent, Naxos, whereas the current appeal of Kos is related not only to its own individual attractions but to the long-established tourism character of Rhodes. In the case of Mykonos its overspill effect is largely the product of dissatisfaction on the part of both visitors and Greeks with the island's inflated prices, claustrophobic summer crowds and cosmopolitan *avant-garde* atmosphere that has swamped its Cycladic lifestyle. The search for authentic insular retreats is, however, a process that ultimately rebounds on itself, especially as more and more escapees follow the pattern set by others. Ever conscious of the state of the market and the changing level of popularity of island destinations, developers are quick to move in with their often over-sized hotels and bungalow villages. As commercialization moves apace, and provided island conditions are conducive, airports appear or existing runways are altered to accommodate the larger charter aircraft. Within the last twenty years islands such as Skiathos, Kos and Santorini have followed the precedents set by others to become profit-conscious holiday destinations.

Here, of course, lies the dilemma, for some of the Greek islands suffer from the worse socio-economic problems in Greece, a fact reflected in the high rate of out-

The Oriental influence is quick to surface throughout the Greek islands

migration of their native inhabitants. Any developments seen to reverse this long-established trend have to be greeted with some element of enthusiasm. Without doubt tourism is now the life-blood of many a Greek island, and there is little evidence to suggest that this general trend will not continue. In some islands the massive annual, though largely seasonal influx of visitors has led to a certain unpleasantness on the part of islanders not in for the 'kill', the latter adopting an attitude of indifference and, at times, resentment to the holiday crowds. For those gleaning the profits – many of them opportunists from Athens and other parts of Greece – excessive price-gouging is common; Mykonos, for example, rates as one of Greece's most expensive areas outside the *haute couture* districts of Athens. Yet, equally, there are islands that have managed to take such changes of economic circumstances in their strides, reaping the benefits of tourism without financially abusing the visitor, and maintaining that warm and hospitable attitude that is so often held as being one of the main tenets of the Greek character. Peace, quiet and friendly relaxation can still be found on many of the lesser-visited islands where, however, the 'get-away-from-it-all' atmosphere usually goes hand-in-hand with a more primitive style of accommodation. As in all vacation regions it is a matter of individual taste and choice, though many who once knew those now over-commercialized parts of the Aegean and Ionian will appreciate and sympathize with Byron's sentiment in 'The Isles of Greece' that,

Eternal summer gilds them yet,
But all, except their sun, is set.

51

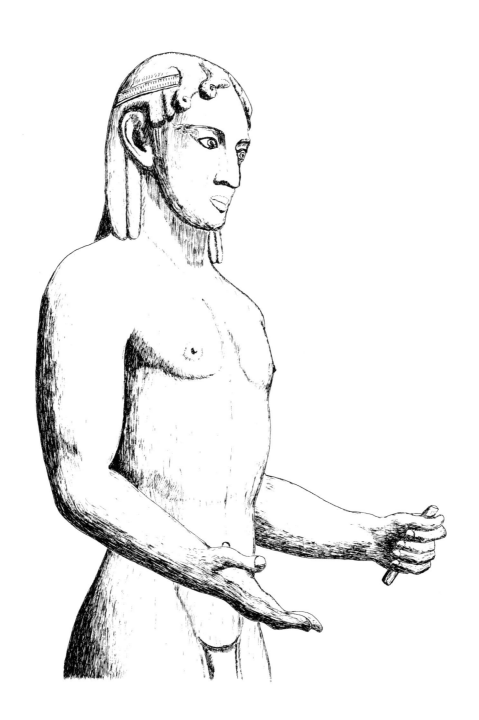

3

Piraeus – Point of Departure

Despite the ever-increasing numbers of annual visitors now reaching the more popular Greek islands by air – either direct from foreign airports or, principally via Athens, on *Olympic Airways* domestic services – the main centre for island communications is the large, bustling port-city of Piraeus which has scheduled sea connections with most of the officially listed island ports. Geography dictates that its shipping lanes favour Aegean destinations, but much of the atmosphere of Piraeus also stems from its international shipping services to European ports and those of the eastern Mediterranean and Middle East. Though Greece has other important mainland ports, such as Patras, Volos, Kavala, Igoumenitsa and Alexandroupolis (and each have their island connections), Piraeus is the undisputed centre of the country's sea-borne commerce and passenger traffic.

For this reason Piraeus is the terminus of the main railway line from northern and central Greece, of the Peloponnesian Railway and also of the frequent electric trains from central Athens and the conurbation's northern suburbs. All three stations are located close to the inner harbour of Kantharos (also known as Megas Limin – 'Grand Harbour') where, overlooking its vessel-congested waters, are the large offices of the national and international shipping companies – Chandris, Epirotiki, Nomikos, Ēfthymiadis, Hellenic Mediterranean, P & O Orient, Adriatica and Oceanic – together with their commercial acolytes, the insurance firms, travel agencies, money exchanges and ticket offices. A third level of businesses is equally prominent and includes the plethora of cafés, bars, tavernas and gift shops, the merchandise of the latter – conveniently purchased with international credit cards – spilling on to the already choked pavements as colourful enticements to the hordes of passengers who disgorge from the large cruise vessels.

But it is the local port activities that give Piraeus its distinctive atmosphere and

53

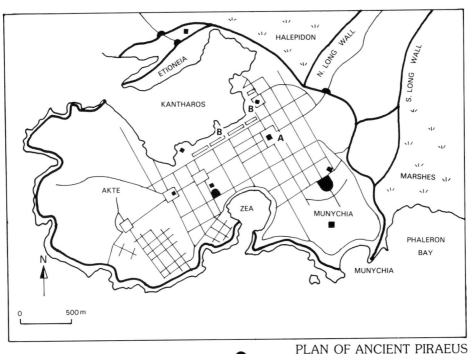

PLAN OF ANCIENT PIRAEUS

FORTIFICATION AND GATE   THEATRE

STREET AND SQUARE   **A**   HIPPODOMEIA

TEMPLE OR PUBLIC BUILDING   **B**   EMPORIUM

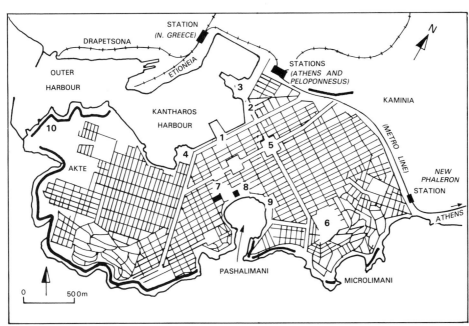

PLAN OF MODERN PIRAEUS

1. AKTI MIAOULIS
2. AKTI POSIDONOS
3. KARAISKAKIS SQUARE
4. CUSTOMS HOUSE
5. KORAI SQUARE
6. CASTELLA
7. ARCHAEOLOGICAL MUSEUM
8. MARITIME MUSEUM
9. CANARIS SQUARE
10. TOMB OF MIAOULIS

ANCIENT WALLS

personality, distinguishing it from its other large Mediterranean rivals such as Marseilles and Genoa or, for that matter, Naples and Barcelona. Its animated quaysides, notably Akti Miaoulis, Akti Posidonos and the area around Karaiskakis Square, resemble a huge marine station where long lines of ships' sterns proudly advertise their island destinations. Vessels of all sizes and ages blast and hoot as throngs of disembarking passengers collide with departing masses surrounded by material cargoes of the most diverse (and often improbable) kind.

Kantharos is one of Greece's great population mixing-points and the scene of both noisily ecstatic reunions and tearful farewells. It presents a frenetic cross-section of the Greek nation and, indeed, of its foreign visitors – lone travellers and three-generation-strong family groups, children in tantrum, cloth-capped farmers, jean-clad youth, black attired grannies, soldiers, sailors and welcoming females, dark suited officials clutching document cases, contented-looking priests, superior sun-hatted matrons, dapper sea captains, serious-faced nuns, foreign back-packers and grease-smeared engineers. Weaving their passage through such human claustrophobia are pedlars proffering a seemingly inexhaustible range of wares – sesame rolls, pistachio nuts, flowers, cheese pies, newspapers, *souvlakia*, children's novelties and lottery tickets. If anything else is needed for the journey, there are the pavement kiosks, those typically Greek institutions that have one of their densest concentrations along the Piraeus waterfront. Yellow-hutted miniscule markets, they seem to stock everything the traveller might have forgotten – soap, aspirin, sunglasses, razor blades, combs, sticking plaster, ballpoint pens and disposable lighters. They also sell postcards, cigarettes, confectionery, stamps, magazines, biscuits and newspapers, while many of them also act as telephone booths – probably the least private in the world.

Among the many feelings, emotions and moods that permeate the Kantharos quaysides, that of impatience, bordering on frustration, is particularly obvious. It stems largely from the fallibility of Greek shipping schedules and the difficulty of obtaining accurate, up-to-date information on sailings. The Greeks are conditioned (though anything but calmly) to anticipate such problems, and the visitor is in no position other than to tolerate them, especially when the standard official response to any questions or complaint is, at best, a nonchalant shrug of the shoulder accompanied by some vague, usually evasive reference to the publicized timetable being inaccurate. Invariably it is, for schedules are often changed at very short notice and cumulative delays are almost inevitable with vessels that serve a complicated inter-island itinerary. Problems are further compounded by the fact that ships and ferries are owned by a large number of individual private companies, and an employee of one line will be unable (often unwilling) to give information in respect of a rival company's movements. For all wishing to embark on a Greek island voyage, therefore, it is vital to check and re-check all advice received, fellow travellers often being of inestimable value in such situations, especially the Greeks themselves, who are masters at the art of forcibly extracting information. The port police usually know what ships are expected and when others are leaving, but a reasonable knowledge of the Greek language is needed if the visitor is to be fully confident of the information given.

Should delays prove unavoidable, there can be no better place than Piraeus to wile away one's waiting hours interestingly. Luggage can usually be left at a café or taverna where the visitor has eaten or plans to eat later after a walking tour of this largely peninsular and hilly city. Many guidebooks are guilty of dismissing it as a necessary functional adjunct of Athens when, in fact, it is a city in its own right, though one that for many years has been physically joined to the Greek capital by vast residential and manufacturing suburbs – the modern equivalent of the famous Long Walls built in the fifth century BC to turn Athens and its newly founded commercial port-city and naval base into a single, connected, fortified entity.

The site of Piraeus was once a hilly island separated from the Attic mainland by salt marshes now occupied by the suburb of Neon (New) Phaleron. It was here, along its great bay, that the Athenians beached their triremes which were visible from the walls of the Acropolis, some five kilometres to the north. In 510 BC Hippias began to fortify Piraeus – part of the present Akte peninsula – but it was Themistocles, the great statesman and creator of the Athenian fleet, who fully recognized its commercial and strategic importance. In 470 BC he instituted an ambitious programme of public works which included heavily defended port installations and the Long Walls project.

Though Athens and Piraeus were effectively turned into a single fortress, they were cities of greatly differing characters. In the planning sense, in spite of its uneven topography, Piraeus was given a regular layout of streets, a pattern based on a system evolved by Hippodamus of Miletus and extensively used by the Greeks in their new town constructions, particularly in their colonial settlements throughout the Mediterranean. Piraeus became the model city of the Greek mainland and one whose gridiron street structure stood in marked contrast to the narrow and irregular streets of Athens, the product of natural, often haphazard growth.

Then, as now, the harbour of Kantharos was divided between naval and commercial shipping, and the Themistoclean walls also guarded two smaller harbours on the opposite side of the peninsula – the land-locked Zea (modern Pashalimani) whose ship-sheds spread fanwise round the bay, and Munychia (now known as Microlimani – formerly Tourkolimani), which also housed triremes, the steep slopes above it once being crowned by the city's acropolis. Now known as Castella, the hill is entirely built over and is one of the most densely populated but also one of the most attractive parts of Piraeus. Its summit provides fine views of the city, especially its three harbours and the nearby islands in the Saronic Gulf.

ashalimani harbour,
iraeus, with Kantharos
arbour in the left
istance

Following the defeat of Athens in the Peloponnesian War, the Spartans forced the Athenians to pull down their fortifications. Piraeus, however, having developed as an important maritime centre in its own right, recovered and prospered until the year 87 BC, when the Roman general Sulla ruthlessly sacked the port. In Strabo's day the former great trading city was little more than an impoverished coastal village, and Pausanias devoted only a few pages of his famous *Guide* to a description of some of its points of interest. Though Piraeus apparently enjoyed a revival between the third and fifth centuries AD, it receives no more than passing mention during the Middle Ages, the Venetians referring to it as Porto Leone (from the marble lions that stood at the entrance to Kantharos) and the Turks as Aslan-liman. In the mid seventeenth century Piraeus was visited by G. Wheler, who commented in his *Journey to Greece*: 'The town that was here in former times is . . . utterly ruined and deserted . . . the only building that now remains is a kind of warehouse to receive merchandise and to gather customs and taxes.'

The modern revival of Piraeus stemmed from Athens' new role as capital of independent Greece. Between 1840 and 1870 its population grew slowly from 4,000 to 11,000 but between 1907 and 1920, as Greece's territorial area increased, the population of Piraeus expanded from 75,000 to 133,000. Many of its re-settlers were from the Greek islands, and they brought with them their inbred trading instincts which proved invaluable to the port's economic reconstruction. But after 1922 Piraeus and Athens received the brunt of the Asia Minor refugee problem, the concomitant of the Balkan Wars and the Treaty of Lausanne, by which Greece was obliged to receive the large Greek populations that for centuries had occupied Turkish lands.

Today the movement into the Athens-Piraeus conurbation is economically rather than politically motivated, for compared with the rest of Greece, and particularly the islands, the capital appears attractive in terms of job opportunities and social and entertainment amenities. There is certainly no dearth of the latter but, for the many thousands of Greeks who annually flock to Athens-Piraeus in search of employment, a large proportion find that the streets of the capital are paved only with the albeit attractive marble from the local Attic quarries. Piraeus itself is currently suffering from what is a worldwide excess in shipping tonnage. Greece's merchant fleet is one of the largest in the world yet, at present, some twenty per cent of the country's 334 Greek-owned ships are laid up, the majority off Piraeus, though the port has not lost its vitality.

Unlike Athens, few grand monuments from Piraeus' past have survived, yet there are enough venues of interest, albeit scattered and engulfed by modern building and industrial development, to appeal to most history buffs. Piraeus was savagely

Sorting the supper at
Pashalimani, Piraeus

bombarded by both the British and the Germans during World War II when the
port was at the forefront of these opposing forces' plans for control of southern Greece
and the Aegean. Considerable excavation work was undertaken in conjunction with
the town's urban renewal, and archaeological societies remain vigilant in recording
and preserving all that remains and is newly discovered of its past. Of the famous
Long Walls, only small sections survive, though their old alignments are followed
by the direct modern road (Odos Piraeus) and the electric railway to Athens. The

most extensive fortifications can be seen skirting the western and southern sides of the Akte peninsula between Kantharos and Pashalimani. These are remnants of the walls built by Cronon in 394–391 BC, the older Themistoclean circuit, encompassing a smaller area, being built over.

Under water in Pashalimani harbour are ancient ship-shed structures, close to which is a Hellenistic theatre where folklore concerts are staged. Adjacent to it is the modern archaeological museum containing one of the best-laid-out collections of exhibits in Greece. Its many interesting local finds include a remarkable series of ancient statues of superb craftsmanship unearthed by chance in 1959 when workmen were digging a sewer. They comprise a bronze-helmeted Athena draped in a full-length robe, a handsome Hellenistic maiden, an Artemis with quiver and arrow, and a superb stylized *kouros* (young man) in perfect state of preservation and now christened the Apollo of Piraeus. According to experts, these statues were stored by the Romans after Sulla's attack, the intention having been to ship them to Italy. Why this never took place can only be a matter of conjecture.

Also at Pashalimani is the Greek Maritime Museum where a large collection of models, paintings and relics trace the history of the country's shipping from antiquity to modern times. Of great interest are detailed tactical explanations of famous naval battles, and a strong emphasis is given to the exploits of Canaris, Miaoulis and other famous admirals of the War of Independence. The former is honoured in the name of the large square with open-air cafés on the western side of Pashalimani, whilst the tomb of the latter occupies the north-eastern tip of the Akte peninsula at the entrance to Kantharos's outer harbour.

If the museums and classical associations of Pashalimani fail to interest the visitor, there is still much to see and experience in its waterfront activities, which are a blend of traditional pursuits and modern, expensive pastimes. Here locals of all ages fish for their lunch or supper from harbour walls, while the dextrous fingers (and toes) of professional fishermen mend the nets of the caiques moored at the quayside. The contrast is to be found in the large up-to-date marina, where certain berths are reserved for the luxury yachts of Greek and foreign tycoons. Hissing and phutting down to Pashalimani comes the canary yellow trolley-bus from central Piraeus, which stops at Canaris Square, Pashalimani's popular meeting-place where, during summer evenings, its relatively inexpensive cafés and tavernas are thronged with local inhabitants as well as Athenians in search of cool breezes.

But by far the most picturesque harbour of Piraeus, and by comparison with Pashalimani decidedly up-market, is Microlimani. At certain times of the day, particularly before the restaurants and tavernas that completely encircle it are open for business, it is reminiscent of an intimate Aegean port. At lunchtime the restaurants,

whose tables approach the very edge of the yacht-filled quayside, rapidly fill with businessmen, high-ranking civil servants, politicians, sometimes film stars and other representatives of Athens-Piraeus *haute couture*. Microlimani has more of a popular appeal at night, though visitors should be warned that its sea-food specialities are not cheap, and fancy prices are charged for drinks accompanied by any form of live entertainment.

As for the kind of 'entertainment' that might be expected to lurk in backstreets of any international port, the contemporary version Piraeus has to offer is decidedly tame. Not so, apparently, a few decades ago, when the area behind Akti Miaoulis, and also the port-front itself, had sleazy cafés and tavernas peopled by hard-drinking bosuns' mates and ladies of the night. Though much romanticized, this image of Piraeus was made famous by the film *Never On Sunday*, which is said to have been partly responsible for the city-fathers' successful attempt to clean up the 'red-light' district. Certainly the port still has many 'Ilya look-alikes', but the so-called 'night-clubs' are mostly clip-joints, curtained to the street and with little promise behind other than loud music and expensive drinks. It might be noted that there are no streets in Piraeus (or in Athens for that matter) that blatantly purvey sexual wares in the fashion common to, say, Hamburg's Reeperbahn or even London's Soho.

By far the most popular night-spots – and this applies throughout Greece and its islands – are the cafés and tavernas. The Greek name for the former is *zakharoplasteion*, often made all the more formidable to visitors who like to test their mastery of Greek pronunciation by the addition of the prefix *galakto*. 'Café' is not

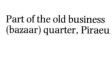

only a diminutive but also a gross generalization for this Greek institution – an establishment selling a wide range of alcoholic and soft drinks, coffee, ice-cream, cakes and puddings and confections, the *galaktozakharoplasteion* also specializing in dairy produce and breakfasts. There are numerous cafés in Piraeus, and the visitor will have no difficulty in distinguishing them from the *kafeneia*, the traditional home of Greek (Turkish) coffee and still very much a preserve of males, who tend to use them as local club houses for animated discussions, business appointments and games of backgammon. In marked contrast the *zakharoplasteion* is the social gathering place for families and friends and during the summer months a visit is always preceded by the evening *peripato* or *volta*. This is a particularly popular pastime on Sundays when it might seem that the entire population of Piraeus is occupied in strolling its streets, squares and harbour-sides, parading itself as much as enjoying the night air.

Piraeus is also well served with restaurants and tavernas, the latter being the most characteristic type of Greek eating-place. Nowadays, however, the distinction between taverna and restaurant proper is somewhat blurred, for there are *'de luxe'* tavernas (such as those at Microlimani) which are more sophisticated and expensive than the lower-grade restaurants which often carry a limited range of dishes. The fare of most tavernas is also usually limited to a few specialities prepared by the owner or his wife, the atmosphere informal and the service often slapdash and erratic. But for those who visit tavernas, the food is not the prime objective but merely one of a number of ingredients that combine to make an enjoyable evening spent in the company of family and friends.

Many tavernas have live music, and a number at New Phaleron, undistinguished in their appearance but welcoming visitors, have colourful, animated atmospheres derived from their largely impromptu concerts. The bases of these are improvizing instrumentalists and lusty sounding (and usually robust) females who perform an energetic repertoire into the morning hours. The distinctive sound in much of Greece's popular music comes from the *bouzouki* – not unlike a mandolin – whose plaintive tremolo sound complements the melancholic libretti of many Greek songs whose themes dwell on love, grief, death, unfaithfulness and tribulation.

The Phaleron tavernas and others scattered throughout Piraeus are the very places to witness those chauvinistic dances said to be the product of the Greek male's desire for self-expression. Few sights are more incongruous than the impromptu appearance of some burly, unshaven 'artiste', moved by the music (and by the ouzo and retsina), performing a complicated dance with the style, grace and agility of some international ballet star. Such dances involve an intricate sequence of bending and leaping, not least the *rebitika*, performed almost to the point of acrobatics, its gestures more than suggestive of sexual rites. Equally virile, though danced by two or three performers, is the *passapiko*, whilst the *tsiphteli* is usually attempted only by the least inhibited (or most intoxicated), for this is a kind of solo male belly-dance of undisputed Eastern origin.

Despite its function as a busy arrival and departure centre, Piraeus is not particularly blessed with a surfeit of good hotels. The big hotel concentration is in Athens, and accommodation at the port can cause something of a problem, especially for those using it as a stop-over between one island line and another. It is useful to remember that many ships into the Aegean tend to leave roughly at the same time, the most popular departure times, if schedules are running to form, being midday and what the Greeks would call mid-evening – that is, 20–22 hours. It is possible, therefore, to arrive in Piraeus in the morning, visit its attractions, eat, drink and then, if stamina permits, catch an evening ship to another destination. This is not what most people would call 'island-hopping', and it cannot be denied that a major part of the Greek islands experience is picking up ships at less frequented havens, but for islands relatively close to Piraeus, using the port as a shuttle base can prove advantageous to those on tight schedules, for it is often quicker to return to it and then strike seaward again.

No matter what class of accommodation is purchased, it is vital to arrive at the ship early, or be ready to board delayed vessels with little thought for Anglo-Saxon manners. Jostling with Greek grannies is considered fair game and a challenge, for

these otherwise meek, benign and friendly creatures resort to every queue-jumping trick and tactic. Berths and cabins on the larger vessels (such as those that ply to Crete) are frequently overbooked, and the rule is simply that of possession being 'ten-tenths' of the law. Most Greeks, however, head for the saloon accommodation, which quickly becomes the scene of a mini battlefield in the fight for space. Bags, bundles and tired, peevish children are strategically positioned with the objective of acquiring as much seating as possible, certainly enough to accommodate a size-able matron, who, immediately the engines start, vows that prostrate is the only position that will safely see her (God willing!) to her destination. She and numerous others, thanks to the heat and over-indulgence before embarking, will be among the first victims of seasickness, the symptoms often reaching an acute stage before the ship has left the protection of the breakwater. When seas are particularly rough, the air is filled with cries to the Virgin, the saloon floor becomes awash with earlier taverna meals, and those with travel-sickness pills, usually the unaffected tourists, find themselves hailed as maritime messiahs.

Hardened travellers, the graduates of experience, will opt for deck travel where the air is cool (often cold at night) and a grandstand view is provided of mysterious islands and partially hidden harbours. Yet on busy island routes deck travel also has its problems, for space is again ruthlessly partitioned in a manner reminiscent of land claims in some gold-rush fever. The Greek objective is to set up camp for

Brightly-coloured boats
adorn the harbour at
Aegina

A summer rainstorm
threatens Poros

The church and lush
garden of the Panayia
monastery on Calauria
(Poros)

The town of Hydra focused
on its busy waterfront

the duration of the voyage. The longer the journey, the more permanent the camp appears with all its vital paraphernalia. Territories are claimed by laying down blankets whose boundaries are respected by rival groups. However, as the journey gets underway, protectionism invariably relaxes as inquisitive conversations are started, and the proffering of a slice of melon from a formerly stern-looking frontier guard is a sure indication that a peaceful co-existence has been ratified.

A graphic description of a Greek boat journey is given by Henry Miller (*The Colossus of Marousi*), and many of his observations are still applicable to a modern Aegean odyssey.

> 'The wind was up and the boat was pitching and tossing. . . . In the rear of the boat the steerage passengers sprawled pell-mell over the deck, their possessions spread out around them, some snoozing, some coughing, some singing, some meditating, some arguing, but whether asleep or awake all joined indiscriminately one to another and giving the impression of life. Not the sterile, sickly, organized life of the tourist third class such as we know on the big ocean liners, but a contaminating, infectious, pullulating, beehive life such as human beings ought to share when they are making a perilous voyage over a great body of water.

Things have not really changed since Miller wrote these lines.

4

The Argo-Saronic Islands

The busiest and, in many ways, the most efficient of the shipping lines out of Piraeus are those that serve the islands of Salamis, Aegina, Poros, Hydra and Spetses. Collectively these and a number of tributary islets are known as the Argo-Saronic group, from their position in the Saronic Gulf and their proximity to the rugged Argolid coast of the Peloponnesus.

The Gulf is one of the Mediterranean's most used waterways, for as well as funnelling Aegean and Levantine traffic into Piraeus, it also receives, via the Corinth Canal, vessels from the Ionian Sea and the Italian ports of the Adriatic. Salamis and Aegina are close enough to Athens-Piraeus to act as commuter islands, whilst all members of this group are popular for day and weekend excursions by residents of, and visitors to, the Greek capital, a pastime further facilitated by a hydrofoil service from Piraeus that more than halves the journey time taken by conventional shipping. At weekends, especially in summer, the Argo-Saronic islands can be unbearably crowded, and visitors are advised to plan their itineraries when there is less demand on accommodation, tavernas and cafés.

In recent years some of these islands have been firmly placed on the international package-holiday map, a development viewed with more than a tinge of selfish sadness by those who knew them in their more authentic, unspoilt state. Up-market bars have replaced many of the traditional ouzo houses where small pieces of charcoal-grilled octopus accompanied every glass; discothèques are now common institutions, and many of the *zakharoplasteia* charge fancy tourist prices. Yet, away from their café and gift-shop-studded waterfronts, these islands are not expensive tourist-traps, for the discriminating Athenian weekenders have a beneficially moderating influence on prices and standards. Should the tariffs of 'harbour view' establishments appear inflated to visitors on carefully budgeted finances, there are plenty of backstreet eating and drinking venues where charges can be as much as fifty per cent lower. This is a general, though by no means infallible, rule-of-thumb guide worth remembering for all tourism-conscious islands.

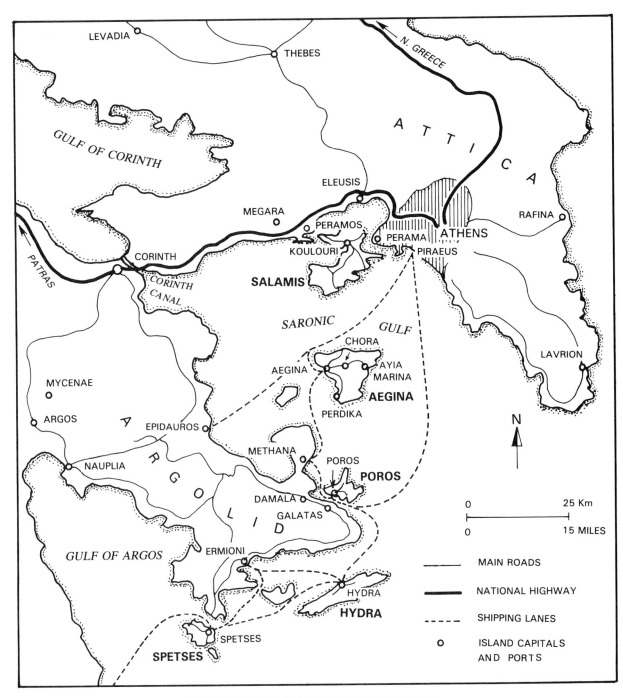

THE ARGO-SARONIC ISLANDS

Each of the Argo-Saronic islands has its own character and appeal, the latter stemming either from historical associations (for example, Salamis) or from the sheer charm of the situation and architecture of their small port capitals. Some might argue that their easy access to and from Greece's major centres of population deprives them of that special insular atmosphere common to their cousins further into the Aegean. The influence of Athens-Piraeus is certainly apparent, but no more than in some British contexts where, for example, the Clyde islands of Arran, Bute and the Cumbraes are conscious of their links with Glasgow, or the Isle of Wight with Portsmouth and Southampton.

Parts of Salamis might well be regarded as an appendage to the industrialized Attic mainland, but as for Aegina, Poros, Hydra and Spetses, the visitor will quickly fall under their island spells while, at the same time, taking comfort in the fact that the services and amenities of the Greek capital are close at hand. The narrow channel that separates Poros from the Peloponnesian coast is, for many, another advantage, since the island acts as a convenient base for day excursions to some of the Argolid's famous archaeological sites, such as Troezen, Epidauros and Mycenae. Spetses, too, the most distant of these islands from Piraeus, is but a short journey from the southern Argolid coast with its expanding holiday industry and roads to the afore-mentioned sites and to the historic town of Nauplia, the country's old provisional capital following independence.

Rocky-browed Salamis

The initial part of an Argo-Saronic journey is anything but romantic, though it is not without interest. The ships take a south-westerly route as they head for Aegina, passing the scrubby hills of Salamis beyond which rise the higher summits of the Attic mainland. The largest island of the Saronic Gulf, much of the life of Salamis is linked to the industrialized Bay of Eleusis, and it is not served by the vessels that frequently ply to Aegina, Poros, Hydra and Spetses. Motor-launches reach it from Piraeus, but the main access point is Perama, technically a western suburb of Piraeus, where flat-bottomed ferries operate a shuttle service across the narrow strait to Paloukia, Kamatero and Selinia. Perama is an important shipbuilding centre where small yards increasingly contribute to the renewal and expansion of Greek coastal tonnage, particularly passenger boats and car ferries, the lifelines of the islands.

Although geographically interesting and rich in historical associations, it would take many a glass of ouzo for visitors to see scenic beauty in the island's landscape. The present state of its dry, drab, denuded hillsides, reaching 402 metres in Mavrovouni, combines with the industrial vestiges of the mainland to depress the

spirits of all but the most ardent of Philhellenes. Irregularly crescent-shaped, the island effectively seals off the great Bay of Eleusis around whose shore is Greece's heaviest concentration of industry – shipbuilding and ship-repairing, cement-making, iron and steel foundries, distilling and soap-making. Fumes and smoke belch from a score of chimneys to drift out to sea, this air pollution being complemented by the oil-slicked waters, the product of a wide assortment of naval vessels, cargo boats and trawlers that cram the bay and flaunt the image of Greece as a major

ollection of antiquities
n the old city of
amis

shipping country. On the island itself a rash of functionally built modern housing, a quarantine station and a closely guarded arsenal do little to temper its tawdry image. With some justification, therefore, it has been said that of the offshore islands Salamis is probably the best known among those who have never visited Greece and the least known among those who have.

The basis of the island's fame and importance in antiquity was the wealth of natural harbours that bite deep into its bafflingly complex coastline, and its value as a major naval and commercial base was responsible for the protracted disputes over the island's sovereignty between Athens and Megara. On the insistence of Solon, Salamis was annexed by Athens in 612 BC, and it remained a tributary territory throughout the period of Athenian supremacy.

In 480 BC the island took its place irrevocably in world history with the famous Battle of Salamis, in which the combined fleets of the Greeks – though greatly outnumbered – defeated the vast Persian forces under Xerxes. From their victory over the valiant Spartans at Thermopylae in central Greece, Xerxes' army had advanced on Athens, and Herodotus records how they sacked and burned the city. Athens, however, had been evacuated, its men having withdrawn to Salamis, whilst its women, children and elderly were despatched to Troezen on the Peloponnesian coast opposite Poros. The exact location and the precise details of the battle have long been debated by scholars but, basically, the Persians' defeat was the result of their inability to manoeuvre their ships in the constricted waters off the island. Aeschylus' dramatic account of the scene in *The Persians* speaks of 'ships turned turtle, and you could not see the water for blood and wreckage'. The Persians are said to have lost two hundred ships at Salamis, compared with the Greek loss of less than forty. Tradition records that Xerxes witnessed the massacre of his men from a silver throne on the slope of Mount Aigaleous which overlooks the straits between Perama and Salamis. In his 'Isles of Greece' Byron was unable to resist six taunting lines that refer to the effective removal of the Persian menace from the Greek seas:

> A King sate on the rocky brow
> Which looks o'er sea-born Salamis;
> And ships, by thousands, lay below,
> And men in nations; all were his!
> He counted them at break of day –
> And when the sun set, where were they?

Nothing but memories exist on Salamis to attest to its vital role in this great naval contest, and what classical remains do exist are in a poor state of preservation.

The original capital was in the south of the island and faced Aegina, but the

The Temple of Aphaea,
Aegina, one of the most
perfectly developed late
Archaic temples in Greece

Athenians chose a new site on the Ambelaki peninsula, where traces of the Acropolis can be seen, though most of the city's remains are now submerged. Officially carrying the name Salamis, the island's modern capital is better known as Koulouri and lies at the head of a deep bay on the west coast. It has retained something of its original domestic architecture, with many of its houses painted mostly in blue roughcast. Nearby is the monastic church of Faneromeni, famed for its fresco of the Last Judgement, the work of the seventeenth-century painter Mark of Argos. This monastery is an important place of pilgrimage, especially during Easter and 4 September, when the religious celebrations (*panagiri*) attract many visitors, Athenians in particular, who arrive from the mainland in their boatloads.

Feast days, it should be noted, play a major role in island, as indeed in all Greek life, for in addition to Lent, Easter, Whitsuntide, Christmas and the various days that honour the Virgin, there is a lengthy catalogue of local celebrations that honour a village church or saint. These festivals are usually colourful and authentic occasions offering a blend of religious observance, folk-dancing and general merriment that often last for a number of days. On these days it may interest visitors to know what is going on, either in order to join in the festivities or to steer clear of public transport which is always overtaxed despite extra services.

Aegina – Piraeus' 'eyesore'

With Salamis to the right, the ships out of Kantharos first negotiate an open roadstead congested with tankers and other large vessels unable to find accommodation in the Piraeus harbours. Aegina, a fairly large (85 sq km), triangular island, looms ahead, the ship first doubling the low and sandy cape of Plakakia before reaching the island's port, a picturesque collection of blue-domed churches and pink- and ochre-washed buildings. On the northern mole where the ship docks is the twin-domed Cycladic-style church of Ayios Nikolaos whose main roof is barely high enough to accommodate its worshippers. Aegina town's narrow streets and winding back alleys house numerous small shops and businesses, and its attractive houses and slightly pretentious neo-classical public buildings give it a most distinctive air. Along the waterfront, cafés and tavernas shelter under brightly coloured canopies and awnings, their local dishes, by Greek island standards, being extremely good. Aegina is a fairly prosperous island, growing vegetables, vines and fruits, but its speciality is pistachio nuts, firm favourites with Greeks on all occasions.

Lying athwart the Saronic shipping lanes, Aegina became one of classical Greece's most powerful and prosperous city states, one that was often in conflict with the Athenians, who, with some malice, christened it 'the eyesore of Piraeus'. The Aeginetans controlled an extensive trading network between southern Greece and the northern Aegean and had colonies in Italy, Egypt and around the shores of the Black Sea. The island's coinage was accepted throughout the ancient world, as was its system of weights and measures. The ancient city had two ports, a commercial one used to this day, and a military one which Pausanias refers to as the 'secret port', not because it was hidden but on account of its narrow navigable entrance between submerged rocks, the access channel known only to Aeginetan sailors.

Beyond the location of the 'secret port' is the low hill of Kolona, named after the sole surviving column of a classical temple dedicated to Apollo. In 455 BC the Athenians defeated the Aeginetans, and during the Peloponnesian War the island was evacuated. Following Sparta's victory over Athens it was repopulated, but no longer was it to play a major role in Greek affairs, at least not until 1828, when Capodistrias established at Aegina the first seat of government of independent Greece, before the capital, in the following year, was transferred to Nauplia. Many of Aegina's public buildings date from this period and include the town hall, a number of large churches, a museum and many pretentious villas. In 1829 the first coin of modern independent Greece was minted in Aegina; on its face it sported a phoenix, the symbol of Greek national revival and one that has subsequently been used by many a government, democratic and military.

On the other side of the island, facing the coast of Attica and overlooking the sandy beaches and hotel complexes of Ayia Marina, are the ruins of the Temple of Aphaea. Unlike Apollo's sad sanctuary, this is one of the best preserved of Greek temples and an important tourist attraction. Aphaea appears to have been a local deity, possibly equivalent to Artemis, and her temple is a graceful Doric structure built in the sixth century out of local limestone and standing some 300 metres above sea-level. It has six columns on its short, and twelve on its long side, and its attendant buildings, whose structures are visible, include various altar precincts and priests' quarters.

The other major attraction of Aegina is Palaea Chora, the island's old inland capital six kilometres from Aegina town on the road to Ayia Marina. It was here that much of the island's post-classical history was enacted, but all that remains of the town – built to be safe from attacks from the sea – are thirty-two well-presented churches and chapels dotting the old rocky hill site. They are of exceptional interest to students of Byzantine ecclesiastical architecture, and some of them contain carvings and restored frescos. This part of the island is particularly attractive in spring, when the hillside is ablaze with wild flowers and aromatic plants – honeysuckle, thyme, wild roses, mauve sage, cistus and garlic. From Palaea Chora paths lead to the summit of the gracefully shaped Ayios Ilias, which at 534 metres provides splendid views, especially at sunset, over the entire Saronic Gulf. The climb can also be made from Perdika, an unspoiled village on the island's southern coast, where there is some modest accommodation and a number of traditional tavernas specializing in fish and octopus dishes.

Poros – the neck of the womb

On leaving Aegina the ship usually heads for Methana, a rugged peninsula connected with the Peloponnesian mainland by an isthmus only a few hundred metres across. The small town and port of Methana, shrouded by the eroded slopes of Mount Khelona (749m), is a popular spa with three springs, one hot and two sulphur – the latter accounting for its nickname *Vromolimni* ('stinking shore'). It is here that many Athenian matrons, clad in bright frocks and large sunhats, disembark, for the baths, run by the National Tourist Office, are recommended for the treatment of skin diseases and rheumatism. The ship now threads through a picturesque narrow channel close to the rocky Argolid coast and enters the Bay of Poros, which has the appearance of a calm and exceptionally beautiful lake surrounded by pine woods, olive trees and citrus groves, all punctuated at irregular intervals by large Italianate poplars.

The town of Poros, a pyramid of white houses, seems to float on this inland sea and is separated from the mainland and the village of Galatas by only 370 metres of water. 'Poros' means both 'strait' and 'ferry', and where the ship docks along the town's café-studded waterfront a line of small open boats wait like a marine taxi-rank to transfer those passengers heading for the Peloponnesian shore. Henry Miller was intoxicated with Poros and its setting, claiming that to sail slowly past its houses was to 'recapture the joy of passing through the neck of the womb . . . a joy almost too deep to be remembered' (*The Colossus of Marousi*).

Poros is really two islands. The one on which the town is built is a small, rocky offshoot called Sphaeria, now linked by a narrow causeway to the larger pine-covered Calauria, whose interior is largely uninhabited. Calauria's many shingle coves and a few small sandy beaches have, however, recently become the concern of tourist speculators whose new hotels and villa complexes now increasingly dot the southern coast. Such modern developments contrast with the traditional red-tiled cubic houses of Poros town, whose narrow, shaded streets wind up and around its hilly site. One vantage point is crowned by a clocktower whose reliable chimes (the bane of the light sleeper) can be heard on the mainland. Behind it a jumble of residences rises higher to a disused windmill which offers exquisite views of Calauria, the Saronic sea lane to Hydra and the Argolid coast whose impressive mountain chain is known locally as the '*Koimomeni*' – 'sleeping lady'. In the enclosed

bay below is the town's most prominent building, the naval training college, a Greek Dartmouth, off which is moored the historical battle-cruiser *Averoff*, which distinguished itself in the Balkan Wars. The nautical air of Poros adds considerably to the animated atmosphere of the town's numerous water-front cafés, bars and tavernas. The willingness of cadets and petty officers to display their dancing skills, especially when tourists are present, means that impromptu shows are very much a feature of Poriot evenings.

The island has few cars and only one, inevitably overcrowded, bus that shuttles between the harbour, the hotels and the island's monastery, beautifully situated on pine-covered slopes overlooking the sea. Behind it a path (and now a road) leads to the scant remains of the Temple of Poseidon, the symbolic centre of the oldest Greek maritime confederation. Formed in the seventh century BC and known as the Calaurian League, its members included Athens, Aegina, Troezen, Epidaurus, Ermione and Orchomenos in Boeotia.

The best views of Poros are obtained from the small cafés of Galatas, which is also the mainland bus terminus for Nauplia, Epidaurus and Methana. From here, too, local excursions can be made to the incredibly beautiful Lemonodassos or Lemon Forest (seen and experienced at its best in spring), and to the picturesque mountain village of Damala, which stands close to the site of ancient Troezen, the reputed birthplace of Theseus and the location of the Phaedra and Hippolytus epic. In March 1827 Damala was the scene of the Third Greek National Assembly at which Capodistrias was elected the Greek president.

Seafaring Hydra

One hour by ship from Poros (three hours from Piraeus) is the long, mountainous and largely barren island of Hydra. It appears uninhabited until the ship turns sharply into a semi-circular natural harbour around which an amazingly picturesque town rises amphitheatrically into the hills. Compared with the rugged, bare cliffs that surround it on all sides, the town is a riot of colour, for its brightly painted houses and large mansions are topped by bright red tiles above which rise the ornate belfreys of its many gleaming white churches. Hydra is one of the great visual experiences of the Greek islands and, not surprisingly, its attractiveness has made it a mecca for artists and film directors who, together with yachting enthusiasts and sun-worshippers (though it is poorly endowed with beaches), transform it in summer into a cosmopolitan and somewhat overtly pretentious community.

The cannon that guard the harbour mouth recall the time when Hydra was famous for its ships and sailors for, as in many Greek island communities, barrenness and the seafaring tradition have tended to go hand in hand. The island quickly developed a remarkable capability for adventurous, often piratical trading, earning for itself the title 'Venice of the Aegean'. It had, in fact, been one of the small ports in the Venetian empire chain, and its vessels plied the waters of the Mediterranean and Black Sea and even traded as far west as the Caribbean and the coasts of South America. During the Napoleonic Wars a profitable contraband trade developed as Hydra's ships ran the British blockade, and by the time of the War of Independence the island had reached the peak of its maritime prosperity. Of its estimated population of 28,000, almost half were seafarers, and Hydra boasted some 120 ships.

Manned by their merchant-corsairs-cum-admirals, the island's fleet played a major role in winning Greece's independence. It was from Hydra that the raiding parties of Tombasis and Tsamados sailed, supported by their own personal fortunes and the wealth of other trading families, such as Koudouriotos, Voulgaris and Bourdouris. But the island's hero was undoubtedly Andreas Miaoulis (1769-1835), who defeated the Turkish fleet on a number of occasions and supplied the besieged mainland town of Missolonghi. To the Greeks Miaoulis was their Nelson, though a better comparison would be with the earlier privateering activities of Sir Francis Drake. Yet even great admirals are not infallible, and in 1831, in the political confusion that surrounded the war's initial success, Miaoulis, using a fire ship (see page

78

Part of the inner harbour, Hydra

144–5), by accident ignited the Greek fleet anchored off Poros. He died, aged sixty-six, in Athens and is honoured each June in the *Miaoulia*, a festival when, for one day at least, the town's visitors are subordinated to the pride of Hydra's illustrious past.

Hydra's commerce rapidly declined with the changing conditions of trade that accompanied the advent of the steamship and the opening of the Corinth Canal, the latter favouring the rise of Piraeus. Its former glory is, however, reflected in the town's architecture, for the large mansions of the old magnates occupy superb cliff settings above the harbour. Now museums or hotels, they contain rich legacies acquired as a result of trade – Italian paintings, porcelain, Venetian glass, fine tapestries and mahogany furniture. In their heyday these mansions, some of them complete with water-cisterns, storehouses and even bakeries, were also designed as miniature fortresses, capable of resisting prolonged siege.

On Hydra there are no cars and no roads to speak of. Bicycles are impracticable, and transport is by mule or on foot. Walks through the town's alleyways and winding stairways are as attractive as they are strenuous, but the views from the hillpaths and along the cliffs are particularly rewarding. It is somewhat unfortunate that the island has now gained the unenviable reputation of being a Saronic Mykonos,

attracting more than a fair share of pseudo-intellectuals as well as the less orthodox fringe. It is inevitable that such an ethos inflates prices, and those requiring a less lively and expensive nightlife are well advised to stay on one of the neighbouring islands from which a day trip to Hydra can be easily made, not least on the fast hydrofoil service – the 'Flying Dolphin'.

Pine-clad Spetses

Compared with the stark and rugged island of Hydra, the pine-covered island of Spetses presents a gentle, soothing landscape and, despite its popularity, the atmosphere of its main town and port is more tranquil and down-to-earth. Situated at the entrance to the Gulf of Argos, it is the last port of call on the Argo-Saronic run, though motorboat services link it with the fast-developing resorts on the south-western shores of the Argolid. Spetses is another island of hardy sailors, formerly rivals of the Hydriots, and their equals in bravery during the War of Independence. The heroic deeds of its sea captains are also now part of local folklore, not least the exploits of Lascarina Bouboulina, among whose distinctions was the fact that she was a *kaptetanissa*, a woman commander. She valiantly led a number of land and sea battles against the Turks, but then was assassinated, and the whole of the Argo-Saronic coast remembers her strength and fortitude. Bouboulina's statue in the mainland town of Nauplia is romantically flattering, though many of her personal exploits are exaggeratedly recalled with that savage chauvinist humour not uncommon to the Greek male. It is said that she could outdrink any man, and so lacking in feminine graces was this nineteenth-century Amazon that she seduced her lovers at gunpoint. An annual regatta in September commemorates the part Spetses played in the war, the island's tactics having been planned in the small harbour square still ceremoniously guarded by cannon.

This square, with its numerous cafés and tavernas, is the social mecca of the town, and close by are a few discothèques and a couple of open-air cinemas. Many attractive old houses make up the main body of the town, including some substantial mansions set in colourful gardens. Like Hydra, the island has no cars, but there are (infrequent) buses, mopeds and bicycles, although Spetses is small enough to be walked around and across. Its low, formalized hills are richly clothed in pines, and there are countless rocky inlets, coves and beaches, excellent for swimming and often deserted. Interesting excursions can be made to the ruins of two early Christian basilicas on the south-east coast. Visitors who wish to travel the island in leisurely, if expensive luxury can avail themselves of the many horse-drawn carriages which add greatly to the pervading sense of old-world charm.

Despite its increasing popularity as a package-holiday destination, especially for

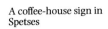

A coffee-house sign in
Spetses

the British, Spetses is a tasteful resort and one heavily patronized by affluent Greeks, particularly the yachting fraternity. Significantly, the islet of Spetsapoula, to the south of Spetses, is owned by the Niarchos shipping family, thus continuing the tradition of the Argo-Saronic islands as the home of both maritime magnates and minions.

Large waterfront villas at Spetses currently let to visitors

Euboea and the Sporades

'Sporades' means 'scattered', a term that might be used to describe a number of the Aegean's island groupings. In fact, it is often applied to the Dodecanese, but here the qualifying 'southern' is added, in order to distinguish them from the 'northern' Sporades, lying in the west central Aegean, off the coasts of Thessaly and northeast of the large insular region of Euboea.

Skiathos, Skopelos, Alonnisos and other lesser members of the group belong to the mainland *nomos* of Magnesia and are administered from Volos, a busy port, commercial and industrial centre. From it ships sail to the Sporades, with the exception of Skyros, though intending visitors from the Athens area can sail from Ayios Constantinos, a small port on the Boeotian coast, the route skirting the attractive wooded shores of northern Euboea. Skyros, the farthest of the Sporades from the mainland, is administered as part of Euboea, and ferry services link it with Kimi on Euboea's east coast. A complex of boat services makes island-hopping easy within the Sporades, and many of the vessels are large, comfortable and modern. Skiathos also has daily flights to and from Athens, which makes it a popular island resort and week-end playground for many of the well-to-do of the Greek capital.

In fact, all the main islands now attract ever-increasing numbers of visitors, and each has its own individual attractions in terms of tourism. Skiathos is undoubtedly the most popular, sophisticated and cosmopolitan, and Skyros the least commercially developed, though it too has greatly expanded its facilities in the past decade.

Euboea – the 'Mainland' Isle

Of the Greek islands, Euboea (3,658 sq km) is second only to Crete in size and, like the latter, is long, narrow and mountainous. It extends in a north-west to southeast direction for some 179 kilometres off the eastern coasts of Attica and Boeotia and the southern coast of Thessaly, continuing into the Aegean the geological structure and general topography of these mainland regions. Many tend to disregard

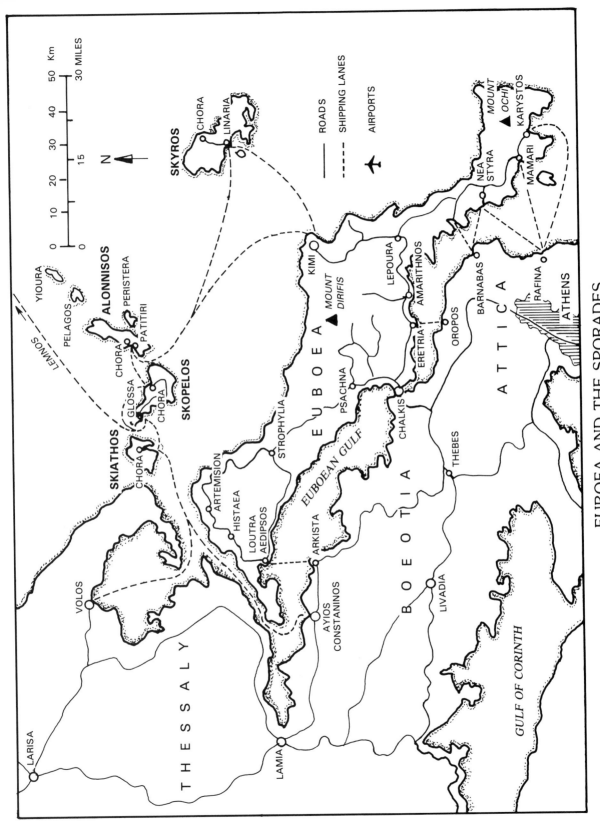

EUBOEA AND THE SPORADES

its insular characteristics, for at Chalkis, the island's sizeable capital, a swing-bridge links it to the mainland, spanning the Evripos Channel, at this point only sixty metres wide. This is a treacherous stretch of water with a strong tidal race in which the current direction changes eight (some say ten) times a day – a complex version of the English Solent-Southampton Water. Tradition has it that Archimedes, who, amongst other scientific problems, had grasped the mechanisms of water displacement, failed to comprehend this marine phenomenon (and it remains a mystery). It is said that, in desperation, he contemplated drowning himself in its channel, but he met his end when the Romans took Syracuse, foiling his work on catapults and grapnels as aids to the city's defence.

Perhaps it is the relative ease of access and the lack of a senses-setting sea journey (though numerous short ferry crossings also link it with the mainland) that has dulled Euboea's attractiveness as an Aegean destination. Certainly there are parts of the island, particularly Chalkis and its hinterland, that remain 'mainland' in spirit, and until recently most of Euboea's visitors have been Athenians on weekend trips in search of short periods of relaxation away from the summer heat, noise and congestion of the capital. Currently, however, foreign visitors are beginning to 'discover' Euboea, and the island is now exploiting its image as an Aegean island. Much of the new holiday accommodation has gravitated to Eretria and Amarithnos (southeast of Chalkis) and to a few other locations close to ferry connections with the mainland.

In one sense Euboea's size is advantageous, for though it lacks the more intimate atmosphere of lesser Aegean islands, it provides large areas that are totally umcommercialized. Long sandy and secluded beaches fringe its coasts, and inland fertile plains give way to wooded hills and mountains that are wild and unspoilt. Much of the island remains a rural backwater, one of its most attractive parts being the environs of Mount Dirifis (1,745m) where Euboea reaches its maximum width of fifty kilometres.

The main gateway to the island, and a strategically important town throughout history, Chalkis (35,000 inhabitants) makes no claim to being picturesque. Noisy, dusty and architecturally ugly, its role is that of an agricultural, manufacturing and communications centre. By Greek standards, it keeps early hours, though some cafés and restaurants err towards nocturnalism. Most of these are located along its modernized waterfront, where the townsfolk congregate during evenings. The few vestiges of Chalkis' past – and it has a lengthy pedigree, being the mother-city of many Greek colonies – are found in its archaeological museum.

In antiquity Chalkis was famous for the manufacturing of bronzes ('*chalkos*' means 'bronze') and for its exports of weapons, votive tripods and vases. The archaic settlement lay east of its modern counterpart, and there are remains of an acropolis on the lower slopes of Vathrovounia. The classical city of Kanethos is buried beneath the modern town. Relics from the Middle Ages can be seen in a restored Turkish mosque which has an attractive marble fountain, and close by is the Byzantine basilica of Ayia Paraskevi which in the fourteenth century became a Crusader cathedral. The mainland suburb, across the Evripos Channel, is guarded by the Karababa, a seventeenth-century Turkish fortress whose walls offer good views of the whole town. From the railway station a regular diesel service links Chalkis with Athens.

Chalkis is the centre of the island's bus services which run to all other towns and villages and most places of scenic and historic interest. Some parts of Euboea are, however, inaccessible to vehicular traffic, especially the precipitous east-central coast, and motorists should be warned that side roads and tracks marked on maps are no guarantee of passability.

The main island roads lead to Kimi on the west coast, to Karystos in the extreme south-east and to Histaea and Loutra Aedipsos in the north-west. The latter is a long trek of some 153 kilometres over roads that are being improved. It makes a scenically rewarding excursion for any difficulties encountered, for after Psachna it heads through the island's northern interior with dense woodlands, mountain vistas and deep ravines. Climbing the eastern spur of Kandilion, a long range that shields the view of the Euboean Gulf to the west, the road reaches some 700 metres to provide extensive retrospective views of Chalkis and the Evripos and, eastwards, across the main island chain to Skiathos and Skopelos. It now descends through an impressive valley, passing through Prokopion (a village noted for its handicrafts), to a large, plane-shrouded lowland, richly cultivated and opening to the east coast and the village of Mantoudi. Continuing upward again, a branch road at Strophylia leads to Limni, an attractive settlement on the Euboean Gulf. It has a good beach shielded by pinewoods, and is a resort of artists. Nearby is the Galataki monastery, the oldest on the island, built on the site of an ancient temple of Poseidon. The road from Strophylia, now extremely difficult, traverses the wild north-eastern corner of Euboea to Cape Artemision and the ruins of a temple of Artemis. Off this coast in 480 BC the first and indecisive battle was waged between the Greek and Persian fleets, the latter based on the harbours of the Trikeri peninsula on the mainland opposite.

South-westwards from Cape Artemision is Histaea, a small picturesquely sited town overlooking a well-cultivated plain. Ancient Histaea was a Thessalian city which Homer describes as 'rich in vines', though its inhabitants were expelled by the Athenians who founded the nearby colony of Oreos, represented today by a

The splendour of an Aegean sunset – Apollo's nightly spectacle

An itinerant watch-repairer, Alonnisos

From its waterfront, the town of Skopelos clambers up and around an amphitheatre of rock

small village. In its square is a statue of a Hellenistic bull recovered from the sea in 1965. The Venetian fort occupies the site of the old acropolis which protected the ancient harbour. This part of the island is rich in antiquities.

South from Oreos, overlooking a sheltered appendage of the Euboean Gulf, is Aedipsos, one of Greece's most ancient spas. Its hot springs contain chlorine and their waters are recommended for rheumatism, arthritis, sciatica and other related ailments. The ruins of a Roman bath, said to have been patronized by Augustus, Hadrian and Sulla, are close to the spring of Ayios Anargyros. Modern Aedipsos remains a popular spa and has a number of hotels, some open throughout the year. A car ferry provides access to the Boeotian harbour of Arkitsa where buses leave for Athens. Aedipsos also has a boat service from Chalkis, usually a daily caique that operates only during the summer months.

The southern journey from Chalkis to Karystos takes about the same time to accomplish as the northern – by bus an exhausting three hours. Once the drab manufacturing suburbs of Chalkis are abandoned, the road passes orchards and olive groves to reach Eretria, once one of the most important maritime states in Greece and a great rival of Chalkis. Systematic excavation of its site by the Swiss

89

Archaeological School began in 1964, though much of it is covered by the modern town whose dusty streets are punctuated by the ruins of temples, baths, tombs and agora buildings. The old acropolis lies to the north, from where there are views extending across the Euboean Gulf to the plains and mountains of Attica. Eretria is also known as Nea Psara after the refugees from that island settled here in the 1820s. At nearby Malakonta Beach, a thriving holiday complex is served by the ferry that links this part of the island with Oropos on the Attic coast.

Continuing to hug the shore, the road reaches the beach and bungalow resort of Amarinthos before heading inland to Aliveri, an old red-roofed settlement which houses the workers of the lignite plant that helps serve Athens with electricity. Here taxis can be hired to the ancient city of Dystos, whose ruins command a hill overlooking a marshy lake whose shores are the haunt of snakes. At Lepoura a north-east branch road leads through hilly terrain under vineyards and orchards to the small town and port of Kimi, finely situated on a ridge with views across to the island of Skyros. Famed for its bold merchant sailors during the War of Independence, Kimi deserves exploration, its main focus being a small square with a church that fills with locals in the evening enjoying its cool sea breezes. From its port, Paralia, the boats sail for Skyros, the daily bus from Athens, via the Oropos ferry, taking up to four hours.

Continuing south-eastwards from Lepoura, the road crosses the island's watershed to provide spectacular views of the coast with its irregular promontories and small islets. Nea Styra is a pleasant fishing village which has recently developed as a holiday centre, its counterpart, further on, being Mamari, with ferry connections with Rafina. A few kilometres beyond Mamari, and also linked to Rafina, is Karystos, an attractive port and summer resort popular with Athenians. It is a good centre for exploring the surrounding villages – Myli, with its lush vegetation and waterfalls, being particularly attractive. Great rocky outcrops dominate this part of the island and, rising above them, Mount Ochi (1,398m) provides views of Skyros, the Cyclades and Attica.

If climbing and hill-walking interest the visitor, Euboea has unlimited possibilities. Its highest summit, Mount Dirifis (1,745m), can be approached from a number of directions, and for the less adventurous the ascent is greatly simplified by a road that leads to the village of Steni on its south-eastern slopes – though even from here, with mules and a guide, the climb takes up to five hours. Gradually the deciduous woodlands change to pines at higher elevations and then to mountain scrub. The views from the summit are magnificent, particularly out to the Aegean, where much of the atmosphere of Greece's 'mainland' island most definitely belongs.

Traditional Skyros

Situated forty kilometres to the north-east of Euboea and some sixty kilometres to the south-east of Skopelos and Alonissos, Skyros is the most remote island of the Sporades group and, as such, is distinctively different in character. Now, however, it is reached by more regular shipping services from Kimi, for in 1980 the Skyrians formed their own ferry company to supplement what, especially in winter, were infrequent sailings operated by the Loucas Nomicos line which primarily serves the other Sporades. The Skyros Shipping Company's *Anemoessa*, makes at least one daily crossing in each direction between the island and Kimi, which means the Skyrians can visit Chalkis and some mainland destinations without the former necessity of an overnight stay. Yet, despite these improvements, Skyros still remains an isolated community, backward in terms of the services it can offer and suffering from the draining social and economic effects of depopulation – one of the reasons why the islanders have recently looked in the direction of tourism, though at present the industry remains embryonic.

One of the most striking characteristics of Skyros is its landscape contrasts between the well-wooded and cultivated north (highest altitude 370m) and the

e white cube-houses of
yros town occupy the
pes of an imposing crag

south, which, especially in summer, is an area of brown, stony, olive-strewn slopes. The latter, whose highest point reaches 792 metres, is strongly reminiscent of those features common to the Cyclades, and the traditional architecture of Skyros – flat-roofed, cubist buildings – also underlines its transitional character between that of the Sporades and the Aegean islands to the south. Southern Skyros is the home of the island's famous wild ponies, a unique small breed said to be found nowhere else in the world and indigenous to the island since earliest times. In danger of extinction, they have recently come under Greek government protection and are now seen only at annual summer shows organized by the islanders.

The island's physical differences are further enhanced by the large natural harbour of Kalamitsa in the south-west, which, with its smaller counterpart in the north-east, the more exposed Bay of Achilles, separates the island into almost equal halves, the low-lying isthmus between these sea incursions being barely five kilometres in width. At the head of Kalamitsa is Linaria, the island's sheltered ferry port with its basic complement of a few cafés, some tavernas, a number of tourist shops and a ticket office. From the port the island's only tarmac road, in places barely wide enough for vehicles, crosses to the north-east of the island to the capital, Skyros town, or Chora as it is known, sheltering behind a massive rocky crag over-looking the sea. [It should be noted that the term *Chora* is often used interchangeably with the official names of Greek island capitals, especially where the latter, as in Skyros, carry the same names as those of the islands.] Chora is built amphitheatri-cally around the slopes of an acropolis on which the Byzantines and Venetians built a fortress – the Castro.

Homer described the ancient town as 'steep', and this might well have been Plutarch's 'high cliff' from which the local king, Lycomedes, pushed Theseus to his death. This supposed incident provided Kimon with a reason for conquering the island in 476-475 BC, after which Skyros remained under Athenian domination until the Macedonian period. It is said that Kimon discovered the remains of Theseus and took them to Athens, where a temple was built (not yet discovered!) in the hero's honour. Another story connected with ancient Skyros relates to Thetis, who, to prevent her son Achilles being enlisted for the Trojan War, hid him, disguised as a girl, among the daughters of Lycomedes. It was the wily Odysseus who dis-covered him and promptly took him to Troy, where he was killed prior to the city's capture by the Greeks.

Chora is by far the most unspoilt town in the Sporades and one bursting with character. It is a labyrinth of stepped streets and alleyways that follow no particular pattern other than that imposed by its cliff-top site. Scattered amongst its haphazard collection of flat-roofed cubist houses are stone-tiled whitewashed churches, the

Only animals and
pedestrians can master the
steep lanes and alleyways
of Skyros town

93

largest belonging to the monastery of St George, downslope from the Castro. Further indigenous charm is provided by the islanders' costumes – the old men in black caps, baggy breeches, black woollen gaitors and the island's sandals, while many women still wear yellow head-scarves and richly embroidered skirts, but these are now seen at their best only during festivals. Conspicuous sights are women hand-weaving garments and men making sandals, though leather is now being replaced by soles made from old motor tyres!

But the most famous products come from the island's wood-working shops, which produce carved chests, tables and low chairs, the decoration strictly following the Byzantine tradition. Such ornate carving can be seen in many of Chora's old homes, a common feature being the decorated wooden balustrade that cordons off an upper floor. The Faltailtz Museum, housed in one of the town's old mansions, has an attractive display of folk art, reputed to be one of the best in the Aegean. It includes early examples of carved furniture, rich embroideries, copperware and local costumes, and one section of the museum is set out as a traditional island home with walls decorated with colourful textiles and hammered copper plates, and shelves laden with hand-painted ceramics. Other interesting features include masks and costumes used during the annual carnival – a colourful though somewhat sinister procession. Compared with the Faltailtz, Chora's archaeological museum is a rather staid institution with displays of Mycenaean relics, classical sculpture and Roman artefacts.

Richly decorated ceramic plates are among the many traditional handicrafts of Skyros

The focal point of Chora, especially during evenings, is Brooke Square, named after the poet Rupert Brooke, who lies buried on the island. His bronze memorial – a naked youth, cast in the heroic style and symbolizing 'Immortal Poetry' – gazes immodestly out to sea, a pose that still causes the local matriarchs to avert their eyes! Brooke's valedictory sonnet, 'The Soldier', anticipated his death abroad, though it was fate rather than preference that singled out Skyros as his final resting-place: the poet died from blood poisoning aboard a French hospital ship, *en route* to Gallipoli, but anchored off the bay of Tris Boukes in the south-west of the island. The date, appropriately, was 23 April, 1915 – St George's Day – and a convenient olive grove became that 'corner of a foreign field that is forever England'. His grave remained largely untended until 1960, when the Royal Navy decided to restore it. Taxis take interested visitors to the spot, though it can also be reached by boat from Linaria. The Skyrians have adopted Brooke as their own personal English poet, pointing out that the Byron cult is shared by many places in Greece.

Alonnisos – A Tale of Two Villages

'Character' rather than 'charm' describes Patitiri, the small, expanding port-village of Alonnisos, a long, narrow island to the east of Skopelos. Patitiri is almost entirely the creation of the last twenty years and is now the centre of the island's growing tourist industry, though one that is insignificant compared with that of Skiathos or even Skopelos. The port is dominated by a huge breakwater and jetty which accommodate surprisingly large ships, whose arrivals and departures are among the few events that break the soporific *mañana* (in Greek, *avrio*) atmosphere that permeates both the port and the entire island. Patitiri has an apology for a beach and only the semblance of a waterfront with some unpretentious tavernas, a few cafés and one or two gift shops whose faded postcards and dusty textiles suggest that those who come to the island belong to the die-hard escapist brigade whose last thoughts are of writing home or browsing for souvenirs.

Leading inland is Patitiri's main street with a collection of basic shops and a popular bakery also used as a communal oven by the local housewives. The street leads to Votsi, now linked to Patitiri as a result of the spate of new residential building that began in the mid-sixties when an earthquake damaged the island's old hill village, 200 metres above sea-level and known as Idiodromia, but also as Alonnisos. Many of its inhabitants were housed between Votsi and Patitiri, though some left the island for destinations elsewhere in Greece. For a period Idiodromia was practically deserted, but its traditional stone houses were subsequently seen as cheap propositions for foreigners seeking second homes in the Aegean. Though hardly authentically Greek, the village now has a new lease of life, albeit confined largely

to the summer months. Germans, in particular, have renovated the old homes that form a closely packed settlement served by steep alleys and stepped lanes. Taking advantage of the seasonal trade, some islanders have re-opened a few shops and cafés, the latter being welcoming sights to those who have walked to Idiodromia along the old mule-track from Patitiri. There is an alternative track for vehicles, and they meet in an open area in front of the village, where a series of large stone threshing-floors recall the old agricultural character of this interesting hill village.

From Idiodromia a steep track leads down to the rugged west coast with its isolated coves and, at Vrisita, one of the island's few sandy beaches. Though having few roads suitable for motorized transport, Alonnisos is a hiker's paradise, for a complex network of shady tracks leads through farmlands and along wooded slopes to sheltered and deserted pine-fringed bays. The east coast is popular with boating enthusiasts, for the off-shore island of Peristera shelters an extensive stretch of water suitable for a range of marine sports. Boat trips can be made to Peristera and to other neighbouring islands to the north and east – Pelagos, Yioura, Piperi and Psathura – all uninhabited except for seasonal grazing animals and their tenders.

The ruins of a large city lie submerged at Psathura, and scholars have tentatively

hill-top settlement of ·dromia (Alonnisos) ·ins much of its old ·racter and ·osphere

linked it with the Halonnesos of antiquity. Its ownership was a bone of contention between the Athenians and Philip of Macedon, and one of the extant orations of Demosthenes deals with the conflict. Off Alonnisos itself, there are two other sub-merged cities – one at Kokkinocastro on the island's east coast and another, further north, at Ayios Dimitrios, beyond which the island is scarcely inhabited. These ruins speak of the greater importance of Alonnisos in the past, in marked contrast to its present 'away from it all' character. As yet its numbers of visitors are not enough to disturb the peace of this island retreat – not even the growing influx that patronize the holiday village of Marpounta, a few kilometres from Patitiri on the island's extreme southern tip.

Shaded Skiathos

Although 'Skiathos' means 'Shadow of Athos', other Aegean islands are closer to the great Holy Mountain of the Chalkidiki peninsula and, hence, offer more spectacular views of it. Some 150 kilometres of open sea separate Skiathos from the mountain, yet such is the visibility in Greek waters that the 2,033-metre-high peak is frequently seen from the island's main vantage points.

Though it cannot claim to be as picturesque as some of the other Sporades, Skiathos is, nonetheless, a most attractive island, and in summer it is by far the busiest, when its population (the islanders number around 4,000) more than quadruples. Its proximity to the mainland, the presence of an airport handling scheduled and chartered flights, and a wealth of sandy beaches (there are over sixty, with Koukounaries justifiably claiming to be one of the best beaches in Greece) are some of the factors that account for its popularity.

Skiathos has a few up-market hotels, many smaller, more modest establishments, a number of service apartments, a lot of rentable villas and numerous private rooms for letting. Even so, during the height of season accommodation can be a problem, and this is one of an increasing proportion of Greek islands where camping on or near the beaches is discouraged by the authorities. The island's main centre is Skiathos town (Chora), the port for ships arriving from Volos, Ayios Constantinos and, via the other Sporades, Kimi. It is built on the site of the ancient city where the Persian king Xerxes, following the damage to his fleet caused by a storm off the Magnesian coast, used its harbours as a temporary ship-repairing base. On Lefteris, a rocky reef between Skiathos and the mainland, he built what is said to have been the world's first lighthouse for, as a safeguard against Athenian naval attack, he was anxious to move out his refurbished fleet at night.

From the close of the classical era onwards, the scourge of many an Aegean island was piracy. For protection, coastal dwellers who had relied on seafaring as their livelihood sought more secure sites for their settlements. By the sixteenth century, the inhabitants of Skiathos had moved to an almost inaccessible settlement on the most northerly tip of the island. The majority of the Aegean islands had such strongholds, but few adopted the extraordinary protective measures of the Skiathotes, whose fortified rocky islet was reached by a strongly defended draw-bridge. With the liberation of Greece during the early nineteenth century, islanders throughout the Aegean returned to the old coastal locations, most of which had declined in status to dilapidated fishing havens. Hence the present town of Skiathos dates from the 1830s and expanded as the Castro became progressively depopulated. Today the latter is uninhabited but provides the reason for one of the most interesting and scenically rewarding excursions on the island.

By walking the mountain tracks, Castro is some three hours distant from Chora, though it is more easily reached by boat. The intrepid will opt for the trans-island route with the expansive views it offers, especially from the monasteries – Taxiarkhis, Evangelistra and Karalambous – picturesquely shrouded by forests. The vivid green of the pines that shade its tracks and lanes is the distinguishing feature of Skiathos. This makes walking practicable even during the heat of midday, though it is essential to take adequate provisions, for away from the beaches there are few refreshment facilities. The excursion to Castro – which once had twenty-two churches and over 300 houses – is one of many walking itineraries that Skiathos offers, and a useful guide detailing them is the popularly known *Blue Book* (ed. Jack Causton), on sale in the town's souvenir shops. It also has sections on folklore and festivals and an interesting chapter on villa development and the island's 'second-home' population.

Graphic insights of the past life of Skiathos can be gained from the writings of Alexander Papadiamantis (1851–1911), a native of the island and son of a priest. His novels centre around the lives of local seamen and farmers, and they remain popular throughout Greece. His memorial stands prominently at the entrance to Bourdzi, a former island, which now separates the town's two harbours. The older, south-facing one, Mandraki (also locally known as the Port of Xerxes), is largely reserved for fishing boats, and visitors may be lucky to witness the landing of sponges and the traditional methods used in their sorting and drying. Ferries, freighters and the increasing number of private yachts use the east-facing port, which has modern berthing and handling facilities.

From the sea, as the boats approach Skiathos, the town is a most attractive sight. Above the bright awnings of its waterside cafés and shops, the whitewashed, red-tiled houses cluster around two hills reached by narrow winding backstreets, many of them cobbled. From the smaller of the hills, on which stand a clock tower (most island capitals have one) and the chapel of St Nicholas, there are panoramic views,

A matriarchal presence,
Skiathos town

and another good vantage point is the church of Ayios Fanouris, a short walk to the west of the town. Skiathos is well served with restaurants and tavernas, and such is its current cosmopolitan character that down at the waterfront are self-service cafeterias, popular with visitors who would rather point to dishes than suffer the traumas of deciphering Greek menus. The latter, it might be added, are for effect only, for invariably most of the meals they highlight are unavailable, and a trip to the kitchen to view and smell the large cauldrons of the day's specialities is a much safer method of receiving what was originally ordered.

Like most tourist-conscious island capitals, Skiathos also has a number of so-called 'nightclubs', where drinks are double (at least) the normal prices. Dancing is to small bands or to discothèque music, but unless visitors are unable to survive without such entertainment, cheaper, much more authentic and atmospheric evenings can be spent in the backstreet tavernas, where there is Greek dancing to the music of the juke-box. There is also the cinema, whose programmes change three times (sometimes more) per week. Although films are not dubbed but have Greek sub-titles, the sound quality is invariably poor, reels are often out of sequence and such occasions are remembered more for the experience than for the impact of the film.

Serene Skopelos

Skopelos is larger and more rugged than Skiathos. When approached from the latter, its high, uneven ridge – the island's name means 'rocky' or 'cliff' – gives it the appearance of a different world. Yet Skopelos is more fertile than its neighbours and, unlike Skiathos with its traditions in seafaring, its economy has long rested on agriculture. It is this fact that underlies a major difference in its human character, for Skopelos lacks the impromptu friendliness of Skiathos, and Chora (Skopelos town), its main port, though attractive, has none of the exuberance of the Skiathote capital.

There appears to be much truth in Ernle Bradford's observation that communities whose livelihoods have come from the sea are far more gregarious and outgoing than those whose lifestyles are geared to the land. Whereas Skiathos warmly welcomes visitors, the people of Skopelos are more reserved and tend to keep tourists at arm's length. The reason might well be, of course, that Skiathos is now increasingly dependent on tourism, whilst Skopelos, like many an Aegean island, is faced with a dilemma. Its agriculture is not nearly as prosperous as it once was, and the islanders realize that a substantial income can be reaped from a tourist industry. But as yet they are rather reluctant to open their doors to what could be, in view of the island's attractiveness, a mass invasion. Here there are no oversized hotels, and what development has taken place in and around Chora has been tastefully done to merge into the town's fabric rather than to appear tasteless adjuncts. However, the visitor still gets the feeling of being something of an intruder, even at the popular waterfront cafés, where large television screens are turned pavement-wise to entertain a predominently local clientele.

If Skyros wins the title of being the most attractive of the Sporades capitals, Skopelos town must be a close runner-up. From a tree-lined waterfront, its houses and churches (there are some 360 of them on the island, and 123 in Chora) rise steeply into the hills. The townscape is one of uniformity, without monotony, for the mainly two- and three-storey homes, the majority gleaming white, have brightly painted doors and shutters. A few houses are colour-washed in pastel shades, and the roofs of the town alternate between red clay tiles and the older grey-green slates.

Slate from local quarries was once the ubiquitous roofing material until the earth tremors of the sixties led to the adoption of cheaper building materials.

Storage pots await shipment at the waterfront, Skopelos

The true character of the town is best appreciated by wandering its narrow, curving alleys and passageways – shaded, private worlds from which courtyards lead, choked with shrubs and flowering plants. Mingling with sturdy stone buildings are old Venetian-style homes with projecting upper storeys supported on wooden beams. Balconies of wrought iron, wood and, less pleasing, concrete (which trailing plants do their best to hide), are the summer 'sitting-rooms' of those content to watch the curious visitor in the streets below. At the top of the town the ruins of the Venetian Castro offer beautiful views across the bay, and the descent can be made by following a cascade of old, stone-built, slate-roofed Byzantine churches that mark the seaward edge of the town and precariously perch above a steeply cliffed and rocky beach. The ninth-century Ayios Athanassios is particularly interesting, its squat tower contrasting, as do those of its neighbours, with the more ornate belfreys of the latter churches scattered throughout the town.

Skopelos is an island that begs personal exploration. Inland, its dissected topography offers shelter to intensively cultivated valleys, their uppermost slopes forming pine-girded conical hills. Deciduous fruits, particularly pears and plums, are island specialities, the latter emerging as prunes from the local drying-ovens, though this industry is less important than formerly. Quinces, which are either bottled or made into jam, are also grown, together with table grapes, olives and almonds. It is as agriculturally rich as an Aegean island can be – a factor that most certainly explains its current policy towards tourism.

Many of the island's hills are crowned by small churches and chapels, whilst around the bay to the east of Chora is an interesting collection of monasteries perched high amid forests and offering beautiful views of the hills and coasts. A new motor track makes access easier, though the final assaults need to be on foot. Depending on the time of day and the numbers of visitors they receive, refreshments are usually proffered, particularly at the Evangelistra, run by a small number of elderly nuns, it being a fact of monastic life throughout Greece that young recruits now rarely replace the natural loss of old inmates. The Evangelistra monastery is 600 years old, and its small church, standing in an attractive floral patio, has an impressively ornate gold-painted altar screen. In order to help with its running costs there is more than a hint of commercialization at Evangelistra. Woven and embroidered goods are on sale, but whether these are the products of sanctified hands or those of the local prison internees is a question that need not sully the occasion of such a visit.

The island's main tarmac road that carries the scheduled buses links Chora with

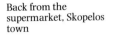

Glossa on the north-west coast. First, however, the road leads south and then west to Agnondas, which is situated at the head of a deep, beach-fringed bay. This is an auxiliary port used when blustery conditions prevent ferries docking at Chora. With its tavernas and cafés, Agnondas is a good base for a visit by fishing-boat to the attractive sandy cove of Limonari. Popular beaches are also found to the south of Chora, particularly at Stafilos and Velanio, the latter secluded by high cliffs and the resort of nudists – an unexpected scene for what is otherwise a somewhat staid island.

North-west of Agnondas the road to Glossa manoeuvres in switchback fashion the scenically rugged west coast, passing side-turnings down to the beaches of Panormos, Melia, Chovolo and Elios. A few kilometres beyond the village of Klima is the peaceful cliff-top town of Glossa, really an overgrown village, which does not cater for tourists. Yet, though lacking in sophistication, its collection of straggling streets and surrounding fields with an assortment of animals fully captures the farming atmosphere of Skopelos. Some of its houses tumble down the steep cliff face to Skala Glossa, where there is limited accommodation. This is a port of call for the ferries to and from Skiathos, the journey time taking only forty-five minutes, as opposed to $1\frac{1}{2}$ hours from Skiathos to Skopelos town. A good ploy when visiting the island is to enter by one of the ports and leave from the other, thus economizing on time otherwise taken up by backtracking.

6

The Cyclades

By far the best known of the Greek islands, either as a result of their history or on account of their current popularity as holiday destinations, the Cyclades are a close collection of some thirty-nine central Aegean territories, the largest having daily ferry links with Piraeus or with Rafina on the east coast of Attica. A complex and useful set of services also operates from Syros, the main port, biggest commercial town and adminstrative capital of these islands, and many regular schedules continue to the eastern Aegean islands and to destinations in the Dodecanese. Island-hopping is greatly facilitated by the local boat services that link the smaller islands with their larger neighbours, and throughout the summer months the frequency of ships and boats is greatly increased to meet the demands of what is an exceptionally heavy influx of visitors. The three Cycladic airports are on Mykonos, Milos and Santorini and are principally served by Greek domestic lines from Athens.

The ancient Greeks spoke of the Cyclades as 'the wheeling ones' for they saw them as encircling the small, sacred island of Delos, the birthplace and cult sanctuary of Apollo, the Greek sun-god, popular protector of light and also of the arts and medicine. Perhaps more so than in other parts of the Aegean, it is the intense quality of the Cycladic light that first captures the visitor's attention, for this is no ordinary light but a clear, almost unreal illumination that in summer beats fiercely on these sun-parched insular domains. Wherever the eye turns, it is brilliantly reflected – from the white cubic houses, the domed and arcaded churches, the ornate dovecots and the solid, sentinel windmills, while even paths and alleys, dutifully whitewashed, contribute to its brilliant, at times blinding, severity. The great visual contrast in these islands is between the gleaming whiteness of the towns and villages and the dry, brown, stone-dyked countryside – lean and haunting landscapes that harbour in their folds the patches of rich green cultivation, the gold of secret sandy coves and the sparkle of farmsteads protected from the seasonal winds that chop the encircling seas into countless small mirrors of irridescent qualities. Early morning, when the dark Cycladic seas are calm, is the time to witness one of the Aegean's

THE CYCLADIC ISLANDS

greatest natural spectacles, the arrival of Apollo's illuminating and warming rays that stealthily creep over mountains, hills and promontories in diligent search of every shadowed recess. This is the hand of Homer's 'rosy-fingered Dawn' which he further likened to 'Apollo's golden chariot winging up over the steep countryside, making the bare peaks shine like crystal above the cold violet valleys and the still dark sea'.

Such is the character of much of the Cyclades' commercialized tourism that few summer visitors experience this moving, natural *'Son et Lumière'* spectacle. Yet they are fortunate, for the theatrical drama is even more splendid at sunset when the Cycladic skies, tinged first with shades of improbable red, gradually darken to purple and then to a blue-black canvas, the backdrop for myriads of stars and a powerful golden moon whose shimmering reflection over the waters pales the glimmer of the magnesium lamps that pin-point the fishing-boats already hard at work. One might forgive the proprietors of the popular clubs above the harbour at Ios for commercializing the Cycladic sunset. For some two hours, from around 7 p.m., they feature classical music for those wishing (at a price) to witness Apollo's nightly departure. Thereafter the music switches to the latest disco records – for some a far too abrupt rift for the senses. Such, however, is the contemporary character of these islands – ever changing, yet ever the same.

Escapist Andros

Geographically, the northern islands of Andros, Tinos and Mykonos (to the south-west of which is the famous Delos) are the continuations into the Aegean of the rugged mass of Euboea, whereas Kea, Kythnos, Serifos, Sifnos and Milos are extensions of the Attica promontory. To the south and east are Syros (around which, despite the ancient belief, the majority of the Cyclades circle), Paros, Naxos and Amorgos, and south again are Ios, Sikinos and Santorini – beyond which lies open water as far as the northern shores of Crete.

The second largest of the Cyclades, Andros (380 sq km) is also wooded and well watered with large areas under vineyards. Traditionally it is the home of sailors and shipowners, many of whom built large mansions on the island, chiefly in and around Andros town (Chora) situated on the east coast. The Rafina ferry calls at the small west coast port of Gavrio, where the island's longest road runs southeastwards, via Batsi with its modest tourist development, to Vorthi, the junction for Chora. The island's main antique ruins are at Palaeopolis, a settlement that was abandoned in medieval times following its repeated sacking by pirates. Here can be seen the remains of an acropolis, temples, theatre and stadium.

Andros is visited more by Greeks than by foreign tourists, the former tending

e dovecots are
acteristic features of
Andros landscape

to gravitate to the island in July and August. For the remainder of the year it is a restful, escapist place, and Chora is an attractive capital, as is the island generally, with its green hills, neat villages, fortified monastery and numerous white dovecotes that were introduced to the Cyclades by the Venetians.

Pious Tinos

The distinction of being the longest Venetian-ruled Greek territory belongs to the island of Tinos, for the Ghizi family acquired it in 1207 and were not ousted until 1714. Consequently Tinos (and many of the Cycladic islands) has a substantial Catholic population, although the majority of the island's churches and chapels – there are said to be some 1,200 – are now Orthodox. The most famous of its orthodox sanctuaries is the huge white marble church of Panayia Evangelistra, which dominates the port capital and is visible for miles out to sea. It was built to house the icon of the Virgin (Panayia) discovered in 1823 and credited with countless miraculous cures. Thus, Tinos is the Orthodox equivalent of Lourdes, an island of pilgrimage, particularly around 25 March (Feast of the Annunciation) and 15 August (Feast of the Assumption) when many thousands of devout pilgrims seek spiritual uplift and relief from all manner of afflictions. The boats from Piraeus become extremely crowded, with whole families bringing gifts and offerings and many clutching giant Athens-bought candles, rather worse for wear after a hot and claustrophobic sea passage.

Two main streets lead from the port to the great church, one a broad processional way that ends in monumental steps, the other a narrower thoroughfare devoted to the sale of holy pictures, beads, candles, incense, medallions and other Christian bric-à-brac. This area of the town often has a heavy atmosphere and, except for those interested in Orthodox ritual, is best avoided during the major feastdays, for the sick and infirm who line the streets through which the icon is paraded – hardly visible for the gold, silver and precious-stone offerings that cover it – can be a heart-rending sight. Of the island's other religious institutions, the Kehrovouni Convent, above the town, was the retreat once used by Princess Andrew of Greece, the late mother of the Duke of Edinburgh.

But Tinos is not all sanctity and piety, for more recently it has been firmly placed on the tourist map. It now has a number of modern hotels and an active nightlife centred around its waterfront cafés and restaurants. The town's attractive new archaeological museum is well worth visiting, and a stroll through the backstreet alleyways behind the harbour will reveal many architectural relics (particularly iron balconies) of its Venetian past.

The mountainous Tinian countryside, with its terraced cultivation, also begs exploration. The island is said to have sixty-four villages, all gleaming white and many reached only by donkey tracks. Each is dominated by a church, though these are also isolated features of the Tinian scene, as are many of the island's 600 dovecots – square, crenellated towers, ornately decorated and with bell-turrets. From Tinos town (Chora) a good, if at times erratic, bus service leads to all the main island settlements and popular beaches, the most frequented of the latter being Ayios Focas to the east of the harbour. The climb of Exoburgo (553 m), the island's highest point, offers extensive Cycladic views in addition to its ancient and medieval ruins.

Capricious Mykonos

There can be few greater Aegean contrasts than those between the summer atmosphere of Tinos and Mykonos. Whereas the former has a strong stake in the things of the spirit (which are, however, not beyond the clutches of commercialization), the latter is nowadays unashamedly embroiled in worldly pursuits and not averse to purveying the things of the flesh. 'Cosmopolitan', 'flamboyant', 'self-indulgent', 'avant-garde' and 'permissive' are but a few of the adjectives applicable to its summer crowds – the pilgrims of pleasure who have created in the island's attractive white town, and on its sun-drenched sandy beaches, an Aegean St-Tropez, where anything goes, particularly sexually. Mykonos is not an island for the conformist or the puritan, neither is it a venue for 'family' relaxation. It seems to go out of its way to shock, though, interestingly, the locals have learnt to accept or, at least, turn a blind eye to the often revealing happenings on this most un-Greek of the Greek islands.

The concomitant of the island's popularity is its exceptionally high prices, and those on tight budgets should give it a wide berth. Unfortunately Mykonos is the main means of access to Delos, which, for many, is one of the chief reasons for visiting the Cyclades. Yet the large number of ships that call at Myconos means that it is possible, by staying one night, to visit (albeit briefly) the town and take the caique service to Delos – weather permitting, for in summer the short crossing between the two islands is frequently precluded by the ferocity of the *meltemi*. The other major problem is the shortage of summer accommodation, though the casual visitor is often left wondering how many beds are actually slept in at night, for this is a nocturnal island whose cafés, clubs and discothèques close nearer to dawn than midnight.

The Mykonos summer 'carnival' is enacted in a town setting that ranks as one of the most attractive in the Greek islands, though parts of it are superficially shrouded by the neon and other garish advertising trappings of commercialization. However, away from its waterfront (presided over by the town's mascot – a solicitous

The Paraportiani church in Mykonos town is an inspired creation in plaster and lime

Drying the nets at Mykonos

Delos – the parched and
naked heart of the Aegean

The monumental remains
at Delos span the period
from the second
millennium BC to Roman
times

Mykonos: an idyllic
setting for a cosmopolitan
summer society

pelican) and the main streets behind it, it is still possible to walk through cool, flower-filled lanes and alleys, shaded by cube-shaped whitewashed houses, windmills and dovecots and pink and blue domed chapels with ornate belfreys. The town's most unusual church is the Paraportiani, which is really a collection of chapels built in juxtaposition and also one above the other, this whole curiously complex structure being one of dazzling whiteness, as, indeed, is the entire town. Wandering its backstreets is a lesson in disorientation, though eventually (usually unexpectedly) the waterfront is reached with its continuous line of cafés, tavernas, gift shops, expensive boutiques, banks and shipping offices. West of it is the square of the Three Wells (Tria Piyadia), which is close to a small cove offering a good view of what is locally called Venetia – a collection of old houses with overhanging wooden balconies rising straight out of the sea. To the south-west is the famous hill of windmills, some restored and working to the stiff *meltemi* breezes. Other windmills in the town's upper parts are excuses for exploration, the reward being majestic views over the entire townscape, its harbours, the sea and distant tawny islands.

Mykonos is justly famous for its beaches, the majority involving bus-trips from

113

the town. Usually crowded, they cater for all shades of nudity and sexual leanings. Away from its coast the island in the summer months can be unbearably hot, windy and dusty. Enclosed by stone walls, the parched fields are of a uniformly ochre colour, and between them winding paths lead to farmsteads, chapels and small villages that nestle below rocky profiles. Depending on the time of day, farmers laboriously work their fields with the help of a resigned-looking mule or donkey. Such scenes have little changed from the Reverend Charles Robson's description of Mykonos in 1628: '. . . a barren iland of small extent . . . wholly inhabited by poore Greekes . . . the barrennesse is much helped with the industry of the people, forcing corne out of rocky mountaines, scarce passable to men'. This, the other side of Mykonos, is a far cry from the commercialized bustle of the town and the idling existence of the sun-worshippers.

Colour-washed churches and chapels punctuate the alleyways of Mykonos

Delos – Apollo's Isle

The Mykonos caiques that ply the waters to Delos land their passengers on the shores of yet another different Cycladic world, basically an uninhabited domain that leaves an unforgettable impression on visitors. In spring it is clothed and coloured with an abundance of wild flowers, but in summer it is a treeless, naked isle, rocky, arid and mercilessly scorched by the sun. At first the extensive ruins of the great cult and trading city, themselves the colour of parched soil, evade the eye, and it is only gradually that the visitor becomes aware that much of the island is a vast out-door museum, the product of some of the earliest and most detailed archaeological excavations in Greece – and the task of reconstructing the fascinating story of Delos still continues.

Other than the advantage of centrality within the Cyclades and, hence, the southern Aegean generally, there are few other geographical factors that account for the siting and growth of a great city on a small, resourceless island. It is in the realms of mythology, chiefly the Homeric *Hymn to the Delian Apollo*, that one must turn for other reasons. Leto, being with child by Zeus, had sought in vain to find a refuge in which to bear her offspring. Every realm, it appears, had refused her sanctuary on account of their inhabitants' anticipation of the wrath of Hera, the legitimate spouse of Zeus. Ultimately Leto found refuge on a floating, rocky island which Poseidon, taking pity on her, anchored to the sea bed. Here on Delos Leto bore to Zeus the twins Apollo and Artemis and, according to legend, the prophecy about the island's future began to be fulfilled: 'You shall not . . . be plentiful in cattle, nor shall you bear vines or see the growth of numerous plants; but you shall possess temples of Apollo . . . and the whole world shall assemble here to sacrifice . . . for it is by the support of another that you shall nourish your inhabitants, since there is no fertility in the soil.'

As it transpired, the Apollo cult quickly grew to prominence on Delos, and the island was to gain material profit as a major eastern Mediterranean emporium and also prestige from its religious significance. Little wonder that it was coveted by the Athenians, who claimed some right to it on account of the tradition that Theseus, on his return from Crete, had stayed on Delos and established the Delian Festival. In the fifth century BC Delos became the head of the Delian Confederacy, a maritime league under the effective control of Athens, but in 454 BC the Athenians carried off the league's treasury. Some decades later the Delians established their independence, having 'purified' the island and passed a law forbidding that anyone be born or die on it. Its renewed prosperity attracted merchants and shipowners form all parts of the eastern Mediterranean who built large villas and residential quarters. They also brought with them their own cults and faiths, transforming the island into a remarkable cosmopolitan community. The Romans were to inherit the wealth of Delos and, to develop it commercially, they made it a free port, a move that was largely responsible for the character of the trading district to the south of the area of the great sanctuaries. Above all Delos developed as a major Mediterranean slave-market. A succession of plunderings weakened the island both economically and politically, and when Pausanias visited it in the second century AD it was inhabited only by the custodians of the otherwise deserted sanctuaries. As throughout the ancient world, the old cults suffered from the competition of Christianity and, although attempts were made to re-establish Delos in Christian times, it never regained any religious prominence.

Unless the visitor is content to be overwhelmed by the ruins and enjoys wandering at will around monuments in various stages of excavation and restoration, a guide-book with a detailed plan is essential, and some previous background reading is also advantageous, for the Mykonos caiques allow but a few hours stay on the island. Whether armed with a plan or not, the easy ascent of Mount Kynthos (112 m) should be made for a bird's eye view of the ruins which, from this vantage point,

The 'Avenue of the Lions'
Delos

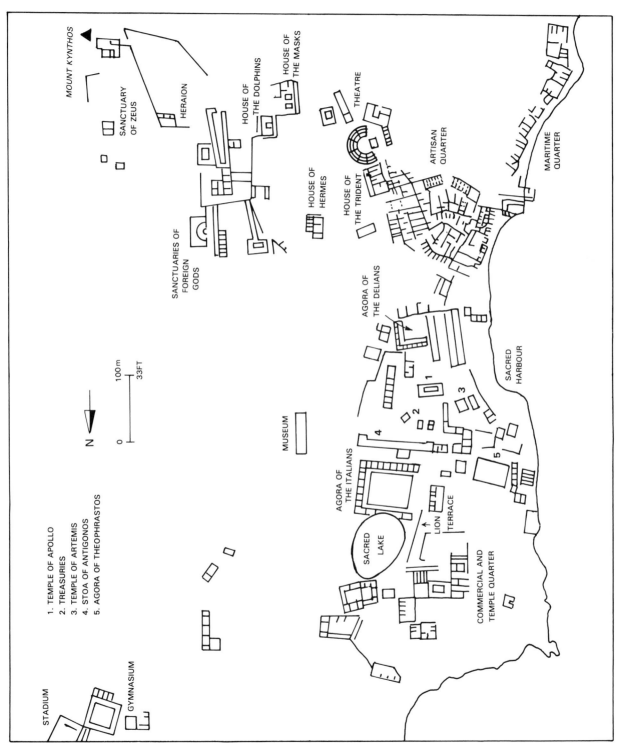

DELOS

STADIUM

GYMNASIUM

1. TEMPLE OF APOLLO
2. TREASURIES
3. TEMPLE OF ARTEMIS
4. STOA OF ANTIGONOS
5. AGORA OF THEOPHRASTOS

N

0   100 m
          33 FT

MOUNT KYNTHOS

SANCTUARY
OF ZEUS

HERAION

SANCTUARIES
OF
FOREIGN
GODS

HOUSE OF
THE DOLPHINS

HOUSE OF
THE MASKS

HOUSE OF
HERMES

THEATRE

HOUSE OF
THE TRIDENT

ARTISAN
QUARTER

MARITIME
QUARTER

AGORA OF
THE DELIANS

SACRED
HARBOUR

MUSEUM

AGORA OF
THE ITALIANS

SACRED
LAKE

LION
TERRACE

COMMERCIAL AND
TEMPLE QUARTER

1
2
3
4
5

are easily distinguishable in terms of their functional quarters. It is unfortunate that day-time visitors to the island miss the Delian sunset – a spiritual experience well worth the expense of an overnight stay in the small state-run hotel.

The remains of many of the city's large, luxurious villas occupy the upper part of the site, and the majority have taken their names – House of the Dolphins, House of the Masks, House of the Trident – from their rich floor mosaics. Close-by are the remains of the 43-tier theatre, and this area was also colonized by various foreign sanctuaries such as those of Syrian deities and those built by the Egyptian Ptolemies. The large agoras and stoas, marking the centre of the international trading quarter, occupy the area between the grand residences and the main sanctuaries to the north, and here the remains of the classical guildhalls are also found. In many ways, however, the artisan and working-class quarter is of greatest interest, for numerous humbler homes have been laid bare, revealing in full their plans and sanitation facilities. A maze of narrow paved alleys links these homes, providing visitors with the rare experience of walking along the actual pavements of classical streets. But the most photographed part of Delos is the famous processional way flanked by a line of heraldic beasts (the 'lions') in Naxian marble, dating from the seventh century BC. They look towards the Sacred Lake (filled in in 1925–6 on account of the danger from malaria) where the palm tree traditionally marks the spot of Leto's labours, which instigated the remarkable Delian story.

Syros – Cycladic Capital

What Delos stood for in antiquity, Syros stands for today, the nerve-centre of the Cyclades, though its role as a shipping and commercial centre has been greatly eroded by the competition of Piraeus. By Greek island standards, however, its capital, Ermoupolis, remains an impressive sight, especially when approached from the sea, and it retains many tell-tale signs of its greater economic importance, not least its ship-building and ship-repairing yards. Modern Syros is primarily a nineteenth-century neo-classical town, focussing on its animated waterfront and, behind it, a large town hall, the administrative centre of the Cyclades, which is also a museum, although not a particularly interesting one, for the modern town is built over its ancient predecessor and there have been few archaeological finds.

Upslope, Ermoupolis divides as two prominent urbanized hills, one (105m high) crowned by the island's principal Orthodox church, dedicated to Anastassis, the other (180 metres), known as Ano Syros, leading in a series of steeply stepped lanes to the Catholic cathedral of St George. Ano Syros represents the medieval town and recalls the time when, from the Fourth Crusade until 1566, the island belonged to the Duchy of Naxos, thus inheriting a sizeable Roman Catholic population. As

a result, Syros (and other Cycladic islands) was protected by France during the Ottoman period, and it remained neutral during the War of Independence, providing a refuge for Greeks who had escaped the massacres on Chios and Psara. These new arrivals were largely responsible for the development of Ermoupolis around the slopes of Ano Syros. Meaning 'Town of Hermes' (the god of commerce), Ermoupolis rapidly became Greece's largest nineteenth-century port, as its many grand commercial buildings testify. The town has comfortable hotels and a plethora of good restaurants and cafés. No one visiting Syros should fail to sample the island's speciality, *loukoumia* (Greek 'Turkish Delight') which comes in a variety of colours and local flavours.

Many dismiss the island's interior as uninteresting. Certainly it is largely arid, but the southern part is more fertile, the local villagers growing vegetables and tending vineyards and olive groves. An interesting excursion is to the Cycladic site of Chalandriani, whilst there are many sheltered bays with small fishing villages overlooking quiet beaches. Those who venture no further than the Ermoupolis waterfront miss much that is authentically Greek and rapidly vanishing in the more tourist-conscious islands.

119

The Western Acolytes (Kea, Kythnos, Serifos, Sifnos, Milos)

As noted, the western Cycladic islands of Kea, Kythnos, Serifos, Sifnos and Milos continue the structural trends of Attica into the Aegean. Closest of the Cyclades to the Greek mainland, Kea's claim to historical fame is that it was the birthplace of Simonides and Bacchylides, lyric poets of the sixth and fifth centuries BC. This has not proved enough of an incentive to send international tourists flocking to the island, although the Greeks have long discovered its relaxing atmosphere and take full advantage, on weekends in particular, of the many sailings from Piraeus, Rafina and Lavrion. Korissa, also known as Livadi, is the main port on the island's north-west coast and is linked to Kea, the main settlement, which lies some two kilometres inland. The latter is basically a sizeable agricultural village surrounded by terraced fields, though it occupies the site of ancient Ioulis and has a Venetian castle whose grounds have recently acquired a modern hotel. Across the bay from Korissa is Voukari, a small fishing village close to the excavations at Ayia Irini, a Bronze Age settlement that prospered *c.*2000-1200 BC. This will essentially interest the experienced archaeologist, though the novice will certainly appreciate what, to date, has been dubbed the oldest Greek temple.

Kythnos, rocky and barren, is chiefly visited for its spa at Loutra, whose waters are reputedly good for rheumatic ailments. Here the island's few small hotels are concentrated, but more recently holiday villages have begun to colonize the good beaches. As yet there is little organized entertainment, except for the local festivals, which are lively and colourful occasions. The island's capital, Kythnos (Chora), is an attractive collection of houses and churches that straggle the barren slopes of a hill. It is linked by road to Loutra in the north and the coastal settlement of Driopis in the south. However, the boats from the mainland, via Kea, use the small port of Merihas in the centre of the west coast. Kea has many churches with interesting frescos, and its monasteries contain a wealth of old icons.

Another rocky and hilly island, but with two well-watered and fertile valleys, Serifos supported a much larger population when its iron-ore and copper mines were fully working. The effects of its earlier extractive industry have marred certain sections of its landscape, though its villages remain largely unspoiled and typically Cycladic in appearance and atmosphere. Livadi, the port, and Chora, the capital, are the main settlements, the latter perched some 300 metres on and around a steep hill laced by narrow lanes leading to cubic houses and numerous churches, the village being overlooked by a row of windmills. According to mythology, Serifos was the island where Danaë and her son Perseus were washed ashore in a chest, and it was also one of the adventure grounds of Theseus, who used the severed head of Medusa to turn King Polydeuces to stone. The site of the ancient town of

Serifos is thought to have occupied that of the present village of Megalo Chorio, but there is no evidence to support this theory. The island has many isolated coves and sandy beaches and is a popular destination for water-sport enthusiasts, particularly skin-divers. One of its main sites of historical interest is the sixteenth-century Taxiarchon monastery, which has a valuable collection of Byzantine manuscripts. The island's oldest church – AD 950 – is in the village of Panayia to the north-west of Chora.

Siphnos, a most attractive island, has also been famous for its minerals, in this case lead, silver and gold, which were worked to exhaustion in classical times. By Cycladic standards it is also well watered and agriculturally productive, its terraced cultivation extending up the slopes of a central peak that reaches 694 metres. The industrious islanders have long been famous for their handicrafts, and they continue to produce pottery, basketwork and woollen products. The main harbour is at Kamares on the west coast, which is linked with the twin villages of Appolonia and Artemona – names that recall the island's association with the Apollo and Artemis legends. Both settlements rise in a series of terraces, their flat-roofed white houses being linked with many precipitously steep lanes and alleyways. Castro, occupying the site of ancient Siphnos, is another picturesque village with a ruined Venetian castle and many old churches. Throughout the island the countryside is dotted with small chapels, dovecotes and, interestingly, some forty Hellenistic watch-towers that recall the time when the island's economy was geared to its rich mineral reserves. Many of the island's beaches are accessible only on foot, though Platy Yalos, boasting the longest beach in the Cyclades, is a rapidly expanding summer resort.

The prehistoric importance of Milos and the archaeological significance of the Phylakopi excavations have already been referred to (page 33). The island's cultural prominence continued into classical times and later, another of its main historical attractions being the Christian catacombs, located near Trypti and unique in Greece. Also dating from Roman times is a well-preserved theatre that sometimes hosts summer plays. But Milos is remembered chiefly for its statue of Aphrodite – the famous Venus de Milo that now graces the Louvre – accidently discovered in 1820 by a local farmer. The first description of it indicates that its right arm was still intact and that the hand held up an apple – symbolizing, perhaps, the very apple presented to her by the shepherd-boy Paris in the divine beauty contest held on Mount Ida. Such was the physical attractiveness of the statue that many nations clamoured for its possession, and a fight actually broke out when Venus was being loaded on to a French ship. It appears that this fracas was responsible for her further dismemberment, and the fated limb has never been found.

Milos is an island of volcanic origin, as proved by its colourful and contorted rock formations, its obsidian and bentonite deposits and a number of hot springs. Its coastline is particularly rugged, and a great natural bay almost divides it in two. Adamos on the north-east side of the bay is the island's port and area of main tourist development. From it a four-kilometre-long road climbs to Plaka, or Milos, the capital, beyond which is Profitis Ilias (773m) crowned by the ruins of a Venetian fort and the small hamlet of Castro, an old and now largely depopulated hill settlement. The views are magnificent and, on a clear day, extend as far south as the mountains of Crete.

Naxos – Ariadne's domain

The largest island of the Cyclades, Naxos (428 sq km) is where the ungrateful Theseus abandoned Ariadne, despite her invaluable help in his escape from the Knossos labyrinth. Mountainous but well watered and fertile (the west coast in particular), the island was known to legend as Dia, and here the spurned Ariadne might well be forgiven for turning for solace to the wine-loving Dionysos who, according to Ovid, 'did both comfort her and take her to his bed'. The Athenians again made much of their claim to the island on account of its Theseus connections, though the Apollo cult was strong enough for Naxos to assert its Cycladic independence. Adjacent to Naxos town is the islet of Palatia, thought to have been the site of Ariadne's palace, but the prominent ancient gateway and other ruins are the remains of a sixth-century Apollo sanctuary, the god's name being further commemorated in Apollona, a large seashore village forty-two kilometres from Chora (Naxos town).

The importance of the island in classical times was chiefly related to its large marble quarries and to its school of sculptors. Near Apollona is an ancient quarry in which lies an unfinished archaic statue 10.45 metres long. Contrary to popular belief, it is a representation not of Apollo but of Dionysos, another patron of the island. Other ancient quarries can be visited at Melanes and Potamia, where there are also unfinished statues indicating that the classical sculptors worked their potential masterpieces close to the source of their raw materials. From Chora to Apollona is an excursion of great scenic variety offering impressive views of Mount Oxia (1,003 metres), which dominates the island's austere mountainous region. Circuit routes are possible and take in magnificently situated hill villages, those of Sangri and Khalki having many old churches, the latter settlement also preserving the remains of Marco Sanudo's castle and those of a number of fortified towers in which the islanders formerly took refuge from corsairs.

Sanudo acquired Naxos in 1207 and was the first Venetian Duke of the Archipelago with jurisdiction that encompassed the entire Cyclades. At Chora his major

The township of Kea, surrounded by its terrace fields

The Piraeus ferry approaches Milos

A parched summer
Cycladic landscape

fortress, though little is left, dominated the town which was built within a walled enclosure. Sections of the latter survive, as do many medieval *palazzi* preserving the coats of arms of their original inhabitants – for example, the Barozzi and Sommapirra families. The same compound houses a Roman Catholic cathedral and an Ursuline convent, though as elsewhere in the Cyclades the Catholic population has greatly declined, and Chora is also the seat of a Greek Orthodox Metropolitan. The island is not fully geared to the demands of visitors, but Naxos town has some comfortable hotels, and accommodation is also available in private houses. There are some superb beaches, good tavernas and a welcoming population – few better reasons for visiting the island. In addition Naxos is efficiently served by daily ships from Piraeus, whilst other lines link it with the majority of the Cyclades islands, with some connections, via Ios and Santorini, to Crete.

Paros – the marble island
Lying close to Naxos and clearly visible from its western coasts, the beautiful island of Paros attracts a large number of Greek and foreign visitors. Oval in shape, with a single central mountain mass, an undulating plain rings its shores, many parts

of it being extremely fertile, with olive trees cloaking the terraced fields that support vineyards, grains and vegetable crops. In antiquity the island, like Naxos, was renowned for the quality of its marble, particularly the translucent variety known as Lychnites ('lamp-lit'). Many an acclaimed piece of classical and earlier sculpture was executed in white Parian marble, and such was the industry's importance in Roman times that it was made a state or imperial monopoly. The famous quarries, some of them underground (technically making them mines), are situated a few kilometres south-east of Paros town (Paroika), close to the village of Marathi. Deserted since ancient times, these quarries have briefly come to life whenever there has been special need for quality monumental stone – they provided, for example, the marble for Napoleon's tomb in Paris.

The island takes its name from the semi-legendary Paros of Arcadia, and its history details the general chronology of events that influenced the Cyclades as a whole. Although little is known of the ancient city (for its site is occupied by Paroika), the story of Paros can be pieced together from the well-displayed exhibits in the town's museum. It houses a good collection of early Cycladic idols, but one of its main treasures is the Parian Chronicle, or at least a fragment of it (for the major portion is in Oxford's Ashmolean Museum), which details Greek 'history' from the time of the first Attic king, Kercops (c.1582 BC), to the year 264 BC. There are plenty of examples of sculpted objects from Parian marble, including exhibits from the excavations of the Delian – a sixth-century temple dedicated to Leto and her children Apollo and Artemis – which can be reached in an hour's walk from Paroika. Near it are the remains of a sanctuary of Aphrodite, both sites providing memorable views over the northern Cyclades.

The town of Paroika is particularly attractive, having something of the charm and atmosphere of Mykonos and, nowadays, almost as many visitors. Near the harbour, where the Piraeus and inter-island ships dock, is a spacious square with cafés and tavernas, and from it leads the main street, a narrow, busy collection of shops, banks and travel offices. On either side narrow lanes and alleyways pass dazzling white buildings with blue and green shutters, bougainvillea-decked walls, colour-washed churches and flowered courtyards. The narrowest lanes lead to the ruins of the medieval castle, itself occupying the site of the ancient acropolis whose masonry was incorporated in the fort's thirteenth-century walls. The town's other eminence carries the typically Cycladic church of Ayios Constantinos, attractively arcaded and blue-domed, its stout walls descending to the sea. Here there are remains of another of the island's ancient temples.

Paroika's main church, one of the largest in the Cyclades, is the massive Panayia Ekatontapyliani. Its 1960s restoration gives it, at least on first sight, a deceptively modern appearance when in fact parts of its structure date to the fifth and sixth centuries AD. One story refers to it as having been founded by Helena, the mother of the Emperor Constantine, whereas another says it was commissioned by the Emperor Justinian and its designer was the architect responsible for Constantinople's Santa Sophia. Twice wrecked by earthquake, the church underwent a tenth-century restoration and there have been many additions since, including some in the Baroque style. Unlike most island churches, the great basilica has been stripped of its former white plaster rendering to reveal in its masonry patterns its complex building history. The interior is splendid and consists of chapels, crypts, baptistry and some ancient columns. It has rich altar screens, a bishop's marble throne and many valuable icons and other works of art. '*Ekatontapyliani*' means 'with a thousand gates', a description that applies not to the church itself but to its reputed wonder-working icon of the Virgin.

Paros has an efficient bus service with routes that follow the coastal road circuit in clockwise and anti-clockwise directions from Paroika. Request stops link the visitor with many attractive beaches, and all principal villages are accessible by

The town and beach of
Paroika, Paros

public transport. Most visitors to the island stay in and around Paroika, though Naoussa to the north-east, situated at the head of the island's major bay, has rapidly gained in popularity on account of its authentic fishing-village atmosphere and accessible sandy beaches. Other good beaches are found at Aliki and Drys in the south of the island, though for the ultimate in escapism a trip to Antiparos is recommended. This islet off the main island's south-western coast is served by motorized caiques from Paroika and Pounda. It offers a small village (also called Antiparos), good fish tavernas, water sports and the interest of a large grotto where nature's hand has produced some incredible stalactite and stalagmite shapes.

Ios, Sikinos and Amorgos – the 'dry' islands
Midway between Paros and Santorini, and linked to both by ferries, the popularity of summer-parched Ios began some twenty years ago in 'flower-power' times, when ever-increasing youthful factions descended on the (then) largely unprepared islanders. But it was not long before the locals 'got their act together' as a spate of new cafés and tavernas gravitated to the island's beaches and 'rooms to let' signs appeared in the small port and throughout Ios town. Development has been such that the former 'back to nature' image has advanced to a stage where tour companies now offer package deals in comfortable hotels and beach-bungalow complexes. The progression was inevitable, for the island's multitude of swimming coves, accessible beaches and attractive Cycladic landscape could not have remained 'undiscovered' for long.

Approaching from the sea, the island's brown, rocky form is visually relieved by the gleaming white complex of Ayia Irini, domed and belfried and standing on a headland on the south side of the bay. The small port now boasts many hotels, and others line the road to Chora, the village-capital that straggles the slopes of the island's principal valley. Overlooked by a line of windmills, it stands on the site of the ancient settlement whose stones and pieces of sculpture were used in the construction of Ayia Ekaterini, the principal church. Attractive, if at times strenuous, walks can be made from Chora through landscapes of olive groves, terraced vineyards and church-dotted hills. At Plakoto on the north coast is the supposed tomb of Homer, the story being that the poet was shipwrecked here. Close by is the Kalamos monastery, which commands impressive views.

Local boat trips can be taken to the sandy bays in the south and south-west of Ios and motorized caiques also run to Sikinos, one of the smallest of the inhabited Cyclades. Its northern shores are devoted to olives, figs and vines, but the rest of its domain is barren. Above the steep northern coast, at an altitude of 280 metres, is the island's main settlement, Sikinos, overlooked in true Cycladic fashion by a ruined medieval castle. Sikinos appears to have played little part in Aegean history, and the same can be said of the equally rocky Folegandros to its west. From an elevation of some 200 metres the latter island's main settlement overlooks the small anchorage of Karavostasis, infrequently served (as is Sikinos) by vessels of the Piraeus-Santorini line.

Due east of Ios the curiously shaped Amorgos marks the extremity of the Cyclades group and acts as something of a transitional territory between the latter and the Dodecanese. Basically it consists of three interconnected peaks which provide a sinuous island with a coastline of extreme irregularity. Despite a shortage of water and extensive areas of barren land, the island supported three ancient settlements whose modern equivalents are the villages of Arkesini, Aighiali and Katapola, the latter, at the head of a large bay on the north coast, being the main port. A six-kilometre-long road links it with Chora, its old capital, which like many in the Cyclades, was a former stronghold of the Dukes of Naxos. Chora commands views along the island's north and south coasts, and a steep descent from the village leads to the monastery of Panayia Khozoviotissa, shielded by an immense shoreline cliff. Founded in 1088 by the Byzantine Emperor Alexis Comnenos, it contains another of the Aegean's miraculous icons – and there are numerous precious gifts to attest its powers.

Volcanic Santorini

In the *Timaeus* Plato left to posterity a graphic description of Atlantis, a utopian-style city-state suddenly destroyed as a result of some great cataclysm. The geographical whereabouts of this domain were not given, and the reasons for its disappearance are tantalizingly vague. The ensuing centuries have produced a wealth of theories suggesting its possible location and the causes of its destruction, but the majority of these speculations can only be termed improbable fantasies.

The great age of archaeological discovery in Greece, led by such scholars as Schliemann and Evans, renewed scientific interest in Atlantis, for the excavations at Troy, on Crete and at Mycenae had firmly established legend and fact as compatible bedfellows. The cataclysm capable of destroying a complete civilization was not the main problem, for Evans had already argued that the enormous eruption of Santorini had been the major cause of the decline of Minoan Crete, and throughout the southern Aegean there is further evidence of islands and cities suffering from extensive tidal and seismic damage at a time that coincided with the Santorini explosion – that is, *c.*1450 BC. Initially the question was whether Atlantis referred to Crete, though the thorn in this theory was Plato's description of his city-state as circular in shape. Attention turned to Santorini itself, really a group of islands, the largest

Naxian serenity belies th island's rich and eventfu history

128

In the nineteenth century Ermoupolis (Syros) was the largest Greek port

Colourful bags and dress are tempting 'buys' throughout the islands

SANTORINI

CAPE
MAVROPETRA

THIRASIA

OIA

PHIRA

KAIMENES

ASPRONISI

PYRGOS

ANCIENT THERA

PERISSA

CAPE
AKROTIRI

AKROTIRI

EMBORION

N

CAPE EXOMYTI

0   5 Km

0   3 MILES

forming a huge semicircle of land open to the west and enclosing a vast bay, the
ancient volcano's collapsed crater. That Santorini, prior to the eruption, had been
circular, is geologically and topographically proved by the smaller islands of Thirasia
and Asponisi, the outer remnants of the once larger island of some 150 square
kilometres. The massive explosion, estimated as being far more powerful than that
of Krakatoa in 1883, had obliterated its earlier form – but had it also destroyed
a long-established island civilization?

This question was answered from 1967 onwards, when excavations carried out
under the direction of Spyridion Marinatos at Akrotiri in the south of the island
gradually brought to light what had been a prosperous Minoan town – a 'second
Pompeii' it was called – which had been engulfed by volcanic material from the
1450 BC catastrophe. The theory that Santorini and Atlantis were one and the same
was supported by the findings of the geologists and seismologists. In 1966 an American research mission systematically studied underwater formations around the
island, using instruments of great precision. What they discovered were four circular
ditches which had surrounded the island prior to the eruption, compacted layers
of lava and ash, and evidence of a submarine lake beneath the accumulated layers
of volcanic material. The ditches were of particular significance, for they bore a

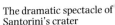
The dramatic spectacle of Santorini's crater

close resemblance to the moats and defences said to have encircled Atlantis. Many remain unconvinced that Atlantis has been found or, for that matter, that it had really existed. What has certainly been proved is that Santorini, prior to the monumental eruption – which altered the course of southern Aegean history – was a flourishing and prosperous place, having strong Cretan contacts but also a distinctive culture of its own.

Many centuries elapsed before the island was re-occupied, and it came to be called 'Kalliste' ('the most beautiful') and, significantly, 'Strongili' ('round'). The name Thera, by which the Greeks know the island today, relates to a Spartan hero, though it subsequently came under Athenian domination and, following the dismemberment of the Alexandrian Empire, the Egyptian Ptolemies made it an important religious and military base. The remains of the ancient city (not the Minoan one), with its temples, sanctuaries, agora and theatre, occupy a rocky hill above the coastal village of Kamari in the island's south-east. Here the ruins also include those of the Roman, Byzantine and medieval periods, the latter relating to Santorini's incorporation within the Duchy of Naxos. Its name, Santa Irene, dates from this period, as does the Roman Catholic element in its contemporary population.

As in prehistoric times, the island's documented history has been troubled by volcanic and seismic forces, as the often smouldering mass in the caldera and the presence of earthquake scars make clear. In 197 BC the islet of Palaeo Kaemene

130

('the old burnt one') surfaced out of the drowned crater. In 1570 Mikra Kaemene appeared, and between 1707 and 1711 Nea Kaemene, which in 1925-6 merged with the other volcanic islets. Nea Kaemene remains an active vent, its last violent eruption in 1956, combined with earth tremors, causing considerable damage to the island's settlements, particularly Phira, the capital, perched precipitously on its volcanic ridge with a commanding view of the entire Santorini archipelago.

Ships arriving at Santorini sail into the caldera and pass close to the Kaemenes before unloading their passengers onto the small boats that land them at Skala. This miniature port (some vessels dock at Athinos, to the south) is situated at the base of an awesome cliff, 300 metres high, colour-banded with red and pink tufas, grey and black basalts and yellowish-white pumice. It represents a sectional remnant of a mountain that once reached some 1,500 metres. Crowning it are the brilliant white homes and churches of Phira, which is linked to its harbour by 587 stone-ramped, zigzagging steps built for mule and donkey access. It is foolhardy to attempt them with heavy luggage: the animal taxis will almost certainly reach the town before the exhausted foot-climber. Fortunately, for the timid,

e Kaemenes at
ntorini are still
lcanically active

inter-island boats also now dock at Athinos, where a bus and taxis ply to and from Phira.

Phira has been completely rebuilt since its 1956 destruction, its traditional architecture being preserved as far as possible. Most of it is still confined to its precarious site, though the town has also expanded to the gentler slopes of what was the old volcano's outer rim. Phira's streets, alleys, homes and churches make it a photographer's paradise, as do the views across the town into the caldera and along the great cliff edge in the direction of Oia, another perched settlement at the northern tip of the volcanic crescent. Phira has both a Greek Orthodox and a Roman Catholic cathedral, together with a Dominican convent and French-run schools. Its small museum is devoted mainly to island artefacts of the Greek, Roman and Hellenistic periods and includes an impressive collection of geometric and red-black figure vases of the fifth century BC. There are plans to open a new museum next to the Orthodox cathedral which will display the finds from the Minoan site at Akrotiri. Inevitably, many of these artefacts have found their way to the National Musuem in Athens, where they can obviously be appreciated by a much larger audience. The housing of priceless Minoan finds at Phira has also been criticized on account of their dubious safety in this seismic-torn island.

The situation of Phira between the crater edge and the island's gentler slopes to the east and south is another of Santorini's many visual surprises. Here the rich volcanic soils have long supported sizeable villages whose livelihoods come chiefly from vegetables and vineyards, the latter luxuriously clothing this undulating region that terminates in a series of popular beaches. Perissa, with its large circular church, and Emborion, are authentic villages largely unaffected by the island's recent fame, and Pyrgos is a particularly attractive settlement with a Venetian fort, cobbled streets and a number of large mansions. From it visitors should make the rewarding climb of Profitis Ilias, the island's highest point with magnificent views. The crowning monastery has a wealth of treasures: wood paintings, parchment documents and numerous icons, including one of Elijah, the monastery's patron. It is also possible to visit the kitchens and the basement caverns lined with bones said to be those of departed monks. This macabre sight is soon tamed by the traditional farewell offering of sweets and *tsikoudia*, a strong liqueur made from local vine leaves.

In order to appreciate fully the physical and historical impact of Santorini, visitors should spend time at the Akrotiri excavations and, if they have the nerve, take a boat trip to the lunar-like terrain of the Kaemenes. The faint-hearted, unwilling to set foot on active terrain, will still gain much insight as to the precarious existence of the Santorini islanders from sailing around these contorted volcanic shores that epitomize both fascination and danger. The latter also stalked the excavation work

Santorini's volcanic soils provide rich terraced farmlands

at Akrotiri, the collective tragedy of that settlement being personalized by the accidental death of its discoverer, Marinatos, while working on the site. Its unearthing and conserving proved a difficult and precarious task, for its buildings, some of them three storeys high, had bulging walls kept in place only by the pumice, lava and other materials that had accompanied the eruption. Accidents were common, and it seemed fitting that Marinatos should be buried in a house close to where the tragedy happened.

As at Pompeii, the evidence suggests that the Minoan inhabitants of the doomed city left in a hurry, for no skeletons have been found nor much in the way of jewellery and other precious items. The heavier and less important objects and furnishings were left intact – for example, a kitchen stove was discovered in almost workable condition, with every pot, pan and utensil in place. Entire dwellings have been unearthed to reveal an abundance of fittings and also the remnants of frescos which, like those from the Cretan Minoan sites, have been expertly pieced together. Some of the now famous frescos (displayed in Athens) include those of a naked youth carrying bunches of fish, two boys boxing and a detailed representation of a naval expedition. No palace complex has been found at Akrotiri, although a number of large mansions have been unearthed. The suggestion is that the city was ruled as a plutocracy by merchants and shipowners, a condition that would seem to fit the utopian image given to Atlantis by Plato.

7

The Eastern Islands

Unlike the Cyclades, Sporades and Dodecanese, the islands of the eastern Aegean, which hug the coast of Turkey, have never acquired any collective or group title. This is partly a reflection of their separate histories but is also related to the fact that their larger territorial areas have endowed them with strongly individual identities that make comparisons between them extremely difficult. What they do share, however, is their close proximity to the western shores of Turkey, of which they are geographically a part. Sometimes they are referred to as 'Greece in Asia', and for much of their history they have had closer links with Asia Minor than most other Greek islands. This fact largely explains the situations of their capital towns which, rather than facing into the Aegean, gaze instead across narrow straits to the rugged Turkish mainland.

Today the geographical position of the eastern islands raises some sensitive political issues, for, as noted, the seas that surround them form part of a larger disputed zone coloured by both Greek and Turkish claims to deepsea and continental shelf oil rights. Thus the islands of Samos, Icaria, Chios and Lesbos, together with Lemnos, Samothrace and Thasos to the north (and the same can be said for many of the Dodecanese), are potentially volatile territories, which explains the strong Greek military presence in this part of the Aegean and also the modern airport installations on the larger islands. On the domestic front the regular daily flights from Athens to Samos, Chios and Lesbos has naturally improved accessibility, but these islands have long been served by shipping lines from Piraeus and by a less frequent route, though one particularly useful to island-hoppers, that traverses the entire Aegean from north-west to south-east, linking Salonica with Rhodes via the main eastern islands and lesser ports of call.

Samian Wine
Closest of the Aegean islands to the Turkish coast and linked by boat to Kusadasi (from where the ruins of ancient Ephesus can easily be reached), Samos is a large, mountainous, well-wooded and fertile island, once called 'the Isle of the Blessed'.

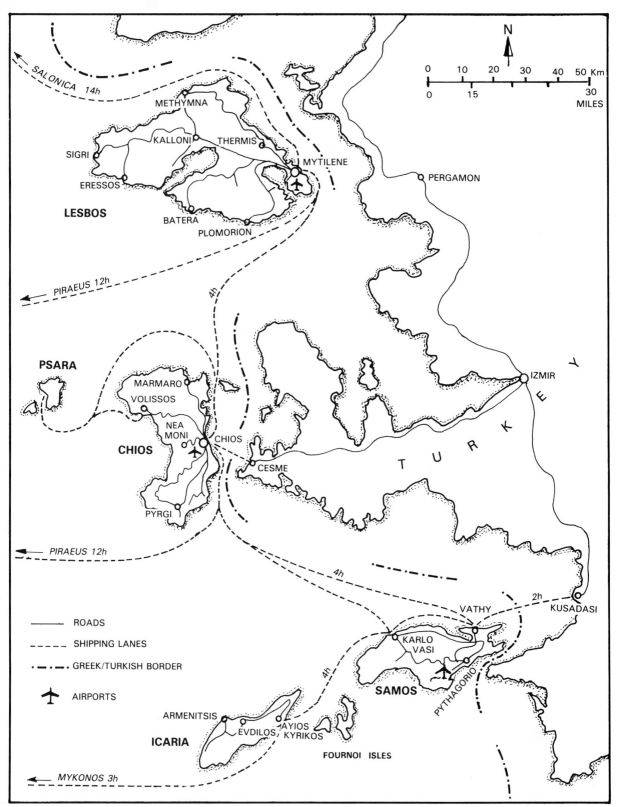

THE EASTERN ISLANDS

Its rich agriculture continues to give it an air of prosperity, an impression enhanced by its vivid green forests which extend high along the slopes of the island's east-west mountain chain that culminates in the summits of Kerketeus (1,440m) and Ambelos (1,161m). This range unfolds to the island's coasts, the north being rugged with steeply descending cliffs, whilst southwards a rippled landscape, well watered and productive, ends in a series of sandy bays and sheltered harbours. These lands are clothed with olives, tobacco crops, grains, vegetables and the island's famous vineyards that have made the name Samos a byword for wine since ancient times.

According to tradition it was Dionysos (the Roman Bacchus) who taught the Samians the skills of wine-making, in return for the help they had given him in driving off the Amazons, who appear to have amused themselves by taunting and ridiculing the inebriated god. The islanders have not forgotten his instructions and devote large areas of the humid plains, sheltered from winter winds, to vine cultivation. Throughout history the grape harvest has been instrumental in restoring the Samian economy, not least after 1943 when the island was devastated by the German bombardment that preceded its temporary occupation. Samian *moschato* (muscat) is a sweet red wine with a high reputation in Greece and abroad. There is also a dry Samian wine and a number of less sweet reds, and though some may not

general view of Samos

be available locally, the visitor will have little trouble in complying with Byron's exhortation to 'Fill high the bowl of Samian wine.'

As well as its connections with Dionysos, Samos in antiquity was associated with the goddess Hera, originally a pre-Hellenic deity who later became firmly absorbed into the Olympian pantheon through her stormy marriage to Zeus. Early Pelasgian settlers were responsible for introducing the Hera cult to Greece, and there is a story that Angaeos, one of the Argonauts, built her first temple on Samos at Kolonna on the island's south coast. Here, at the mouth of the River Imbrasos, the early colonists found a wooden image which they recognized as Hera, and the succession of altars and shrines that came to mark the spot were later replaced by a large stone temple designed in 570-550 BC by Rhoikos and Theodoros. When it was destroyed by fire, an even larger edifice, measuring 112 metres by 55 metres, was commissioned by Polycrates, and though it failed to rank among Antipater's seven ancient world wonders, it achieved fame with the Greeks as being the largest temple they ever built.

The Heraion was one of a number of great buildings and engineering feats sponsored by Polycrates, the so-called 'Tyrant' of mid-sixth-century BC Samos who, gaining control from the local landed gentry, established the island as a major naval power and cultural centre. His strongly fortified capital (modern Pythagorio) was described by Herodotus as 'the first among all Hellenic and barbarian cities', and from it, in a splendid palace occupying the lower slopes of Ambelos, he entertained the kings and princes of the eastern Mediterranean. The city also attracted distinguished artists, architects and poets, and among the later was Anacreon, a lyricist concerned mainly, at least according to the surviving fragments of his work, with the pleasures of love and wine – probably Samian. Many of the local artists found an outlet for their work in the statues that lined the eight-kilometre-long Sacred Way that led from the capital to the Heraion.

There are many remains in and around Pythagorio to attest to this great period of Samian history. Formerly called Tigani, this small, attractive town, situated on the island's south-east coast, was renamed in 1955 in honour of the great philosopher and mathematician Pythagoras, a native of Samos but an émigré to Croton in southern Italy. The ancient harbour works, the line of the old walls and the theatre are of considerable interest, but what speaks volumes for the organizational efficiency of Polycrates' dictatorship was the Tunnel of Eupalinos, an underground aqueduct that ran for one thousand metres through the hills to bring water to the city. The tunnel, which is said to have taken fifteen years to complete at the cost of many hundreds of lives, was also built as an escape route and was used as such during the Persian king Darius' attack on the city.

With the increasing influence of Christianity, the cult of Hera on Samos declined, as did others in the pagan world, and during the Byzantine period Samos was graced with a large number of churches, many of which can still be visited. Following a brief period under Latin rule, the island fell to the Turks in 1458, and in the centuries that followed, migration and depopulation were endemic. Enough zealous Samians remained, however, for the island to play a leading role in the Greek War of Independence, and such was the dogged resistance of Lycurgus Logothetes and his followers that 'to go to Samos' became a proverbial Turkish expression to signify

al market-day on
nos

certain slaughter. In an effort to appease the islanders, the Turks declared Samos an autonomous principality under the rule of Greek 'princes' appointed by the Porte, the first of whom was Stephanos Bogoridas (1834–59). But the striving for union with Greece continued and a rising organized by Themistocles Sofoulis brought this about following the decisive battles off Vathy in 1912.

Vathy, also known as Samos, was made the new island capital in 1834. Its name means 'deep', for it lies at the head of a long, narrow bay, the port being functional rather than attractive. Away from the harbour it focusses on a public garden around which are grouped the town hall, the post office and the museum containing relics from the island's main excavations. On a hill to the south of the bay is Ano Vathy, a most agreeable suburb whose elevated position provides impressive views of the harbour town and the Asia Minor coast beyond. Rising in a series of terraces, its attractive red-tiled houses (many of them handsome mansions whose structures incorporate the free use of wood) are linked by narrow alleys and often precipitous stairways. Its age-old charm begs exploration, and the visitor will be rewarded at almost every turn by authentic, often intimate, insights into Aegean town life. Yet in midsummer both the port and this older quarter can be unbearably hot and exposed to debilitating north winds. At this season Samos has far more relaxing places to stay in, though the recent popularity of Pythagorio has led to the inevitable inflation of its hotel and taverna prices.

The less comfort-conscious traveller should take advantage of the island's circular road, which, west from Pythagorio, after the junction for the Heraion, leads to Chora, a traditional hillside village (and one time island capital) where cheap, if unsophisticated hospitality can be found. Utilizing saddles between the main island peaks, the road then winds past monasteries, hilltop churches and sizeable villages, the latter perched on mountain spurs and surrounded by glistening groves of olives. Heading north, it reaches the coast at Karlovasi, the island's second largest town, where the Piraeus boats call before arriving at Vathy. The centre of an important vine-growing region, it is an ideal base for mountain walks, the goals being the number of monasteries that cling to the Samian heights. Unfortunately any lengthy sojourn at Karlovasi is somewhat marred by the pungent aroma of the local tanning industry.

Large sections of the coastal road from Karlovasi to Vathy run along precipitously high cliffs that shield small fishing hamlets and pebbly coves, while inland tracks lead past extensive vineyards and fruit orchards. The terraced farmlands that are precariously perched above the shore give way to pinewoods as Vathy is approached along the western side of its gulf. This round trip of Samos, from either Vathy or Pythagorio, can be comfortably accomplished in a day.

Elemental Icaria

South-west of Samos, past the irregular islets of Fournoi, is the exposed, weather-beaten island of Icaria. In all probability its name derives from the Phoenician '*ikor*', referring to the abundance of fish, but for the romantically minded the story that it commemorates the fated exploits of Icarus, son of Daedalus, will prove more acceptable.

The legendary craftsman-inventor, whose name also became synonymous with cunning, Daedalus is said to have moved from Athens to serve in the palace of the Cretan King Minos, at best a troubled ruler and certainly where his wife Pasiphae was concerned. A woman of unexpected whims and unbridled passion, she found herself love-smitten for a bull which Poseidon had sent to the island for sacrifice. To appease her unorthodox desires, Daedalus engineered a hollow wooden cow with which the bovine suitor mated, unaware that the willing Pasiphae was hidden inside. From this unnatural union the Minotaur was born, and Daedalus is also credited with the construction of a labyrinth in the Knossos palace where this beast, half man, half bull, was hidden.

Such was the total dependence of Minos on the resourcefulness of Daedalus that the inventor was placed under a kind of palace arrest. Anxious to procure an escape for himself and his son, he set about the construction of wax and feather wings and drilled Icarus in the principles of aeronautics, stressing that every caution should be taken to prevent the apparatus overheating. The escape flight of Daedalus was a great success, and he first landed at Cumae on the Bay of Naples before proceeding to Sicily. But for Icarus, over-confidence and youthful daring brought catastrophe. Forgetting his father's instructions, he flew too close to the sun, whose heat melted the wax, and the wings disintegrated, plunging Icarus into the Aegean, where he drowned. Daedalus returned to bury his son on the island nearest to where the accident had happened – thus Icaria was named and also the Icarian Sea, as this part of the Aegean is still called.

Nowadays people rarely drop out of the sky over Icaria, for it is one of the few large Aegean islands (255 sq km) without a commercial airport. Neither is it as well served by shipping as neighbouring Samos or the Dodecanese to its south, and during the winter months access is often difficult, for its exposed position subjects it to high winds and seas that are among the roughest in the Aegean. Summer winds also blow; these are warm and only slightly temper a dry heat that makes 'siesta' a by-word, and 'shade' a synonym for 'sanctuary'. Yet Icaria is well watered and shares the greenness of the other eastern islands, its fertile soils supporting many small villages dependent on orchards, vineyards and vegetable gardens.

After Mykonos, the Samos-bound ships from Piraeus follow Icaria's southern

coast, which extends in a north-east to south-west direction for some forty kilometres, much of it rocky and steeply cliffed. The backbone of the island is a ridge known as Atherus, which reaches 1,030 metres in the south-west. Occupying its slopes is the coastal village of Manganitas, the island's most isolated settlement, reached only by mountain tracks or a daily caique from Ayios Kyrikos. A warm welcome awaits visitors to this and other Icarian villages, the local inhabitants appearing somewhat bemused by the fortitude of those who make such seemingly unnecessary journeys. Wandering through Icaria, however, or taking the battered bus to Armenitsis on the north coast, the intreprid are rewarded by some amazing coastal views, the discovery of deserted coves and splendid vistas of verdant hill country – all, as yet, largely untouched by tourism.

Ayios Kyrikos, the little capital and island port, lies at the centre of the southern coast. It has barely a thousand inhabitants and is not a stage set for tourists, though it does have a few hotels and rooms to let. Most visitors to Icaria make for Therma, a waterfront village whose medicinal springs are patronized by a fair proportion of elderly Greeks, the sufferers from rheumatism, arthritis and gout. Its history as a health resort stretches back to antiquity, and there are ruins scattered around that date from this period. In summer, provided the weather is favourable, boat trips can be made from Therma to the island of Patmos, the northernmost member of the Dodecanese group.

Classical and medieval ruins, together with deserted settlements, indicate that Icaria was an island of greater importance in earlier times. Interesting excursions can be made to the old acropolis of Drakanon near the north-eastern tip of the island, to the tombs at Katafigion and to the remains of the old city of Oinoe near Kambos. The Byzantines rebuilt the latter, calling it Doliche, though it acquired the local name Palatia on account of its many fine buildings. Byzantine presence is also indicated by the tenth-century castle of Nikaria which stands on high ground to the south of the attractive north-coast village of Evdilos, where there are also good beaches.

Like so many of the less prosperous Aegean islands, Icaria has suffered from the debilitating economic and social effects of out-migration. During the summer months, however, the tables are briefly turned when many exiles return for a hectic round of family visits and celebrations. A good time to be on the island is 17 July, a date which commemorates the islanders' defeat of the Turks. Visitors are usually hospitably invited to sample the traditional fare of goat's meat, country soup, freshly baked bread and local wine.

The Trials of Chios

There are parts of all countries which appear to have suffered more tragedy and tribulation than is perhaps the national norm. Chios is a case in point, for the history of this island reads as a catalogue of misfortunes and disasters that have included wars, invasions, earthquakes, insurrections and savage reprisals. Empires defended it against predators and pillagers, the opposing forces both recognizing the strategic worth of its situation close to the Asia Minor coast and commanding north-south sea lanes at a point where the Aegean basin narrows at its centre. It might be expected, therefore – especially in a country where the element of fatalism frequently surfaces and pervades – that Chios would exhude an atmosphere that could only be described as 'heavy'. In fact, the opposite is the case, the islanders being solicitous and outgoing, more concerned with the problems of today's living than dwelling on the traumas of their past. Having said this, however, one cautionary note is needed, for modern Greek shipowners, following the traditions of the past, have chosen the island as an exclusive retreat and exercise their powers to prevent Chios from developing into a tourist mecca.

Somewhat scenically disappointing for its size (842 sq km), Chios does have some spectacular countryside, for the island is traversed from north to south by a rugged range of limestone mountains that reach a maximum height of 1,297 metres. Much of the island's attractiveness, however, lies in its well-cultivated valleys, where citrus fruits, vines, olives, mulberries, cotton and vegetable crops are grown in fields and gardens enclosed by high walls. But the product traditionally associated with the island is mastic gum, extracted from a variety of lentisk which covers large areas of the island's south. When Chios passed to the Genoese in the fourteenth century, the mastic trade was monopolized by the Giustiniani family and was subsequently strictly controlled by the Turks, for the product was much valued in Constantinople, not least among the ladies of the harem – who probably chewed it as much out of boredom as to sweeten their breath!

Chios had fallen to the Ottoman Turks in 1566 and, despite uprisings and reprisals, enjoyed a degree of autonomy and a general period of prosperity by supplying the Seraglio with the fruits of its fertile soil. The great tragedy came during the early stages of the Greek War of Independence when the Samians induced the Chiotes to join them in revolt. In the following year (1822) the Turks inflicted a dreadful revenge, slaughtering some 25–30,000 islanders and enslaving an estimated 45,000. It is said that sack upon sack of human fragments were proudly sent to the Sultan in Constantinople, who further decreed destruction of the island's crops and villages, though not those of the south. Some years after the massacre the American poet George Hill described the effects of the orgy of ruin as a 'heart-sore sight' and damned the Turks in fourteen moving lines, the last of which read:

> Yet here the Moslem, dull, as in a waste,
> Like tiger, from the relics of his prey
> Unroused, by no avenging weapon chased
> Heeds not the spring flower's bloom, nor blithe bird's lay.
> The ground is red with blood whereon he kneels to pray.

The massacre served as a theme for artistic exploitation by a whole generation of romantic poets (e.g. Alfred de Vigny and Victor Hugo) and painters. Though bitterly attacked on their artistic merits, a series of grisly canvasses by Eugène Delacroix successfully moved western opinion in support of the Greek cause, as did the premature death in 1824 of Byron in the camp of the Greek insurgents at Missolonghi.

The destruction of Chios was the work of Kara Ali, who was subsequently killed in the same waters aboard his flagship. The hero of this battle, and one of the great military leaders of the Greek struggle (see page 45) was Constantine Canaris, a native of the small island of Psara, some twenty kilometres to the north-west of Chios. Canaris became famous throughout Europe for perfecting the use in battle of fire-ships. These were expendable vessels whose insides were daubed with pitch, turpentine and sulphur, as were the riggings. Appearing at night from the numerous secret creeks that festoon the Aegean, these ships were steered down on enemy vessels and their powder trains set alight, leaving the Turks to fight both fire and sea. One such missile destroyed Kara Ali's ship and, with it, almost all the Turkish captains of the fleet as they gathered aboard to celebrate the end of the Ramadan. This major Greek success had a demoralizing effect on the Turks, who again took to bloody reprisals, destroying Psara and most of the islanders on 21 June 1824. This event is lamented by Dionysios Solomos (1798–1857) in a short poem which J. N. Mavrogordato has translated:

> On the island's blackened stone
> Glory paces all alone,
> Thinking on the shining dead
> Wears a garland on her head
> Of the little that is found
> Green upon the wasted ground.

Despite the eastern islands' early and active support of the Greek cause, the Turks were able to hang on to them, and not until 1912 were they united with the mother country. The intervening period on Chios was marked by a series of earthquakes, the great tremor of 1881 causing further physical damage and the loss of more lives estimated in the region of 3,500. Many of the Chiotes who had escaped the Turkish massacre had settled in other parts of Greece, notably Ermoupolis, or in foreign ports such as Marseilles, Palermo, Leghorn and London, where some of the island's old leading families re-established themselves as merchants, continuing overseas one of the traditional activities of their native island.

As for Canaris, he subsequently had a number of terms in office as prime minister of independent Greece, though sadly his home island received few honours for the part it played in the country's emancipation, and Psara, today, remains poor, isolated and lacking in even the most basic of facilities. It can be reached only by motorboat or caique from Volissos on the north-west coast of Chios, and visitors will need to seek private accommodation in the small village 'capital' in the bay on the south coast, below a medieval castle. Save for a few monks in a monastery on the north coast, the village houses the island's entire population – a mere 600.

Facing Turkey's rugged Karaburna peninsula (some ten kilometres distant), along which, from Cesme, a modern highway leads to Izmir, the town of Chios (known as Chora) straddles the site of an ancient predecessor, the proud claim being that this is the capital of the island where Homer was born and where the *Iliad* and *Odyssey* were written. This tenacious local belief derives solely from a reference in the Homeric *Hymn to Apollo* to 'the sightless man of stony Chios'. Perhaps it can be accepted that Homer was blind but there is much speculation as to who he was, where he lived and the dates of his life, the latter being variously placed between 1050 and 850 BC. The island was certainly an established centre of commerce and culture when Homer is said to have written his epics, and accepting the island as the poet's birthplace, rather than the claims of such rival contenders as Athens, Rhodes, Salamis and Smyrna (Izmir), at least provides some air of romance when approaching Chora from the sea.

The town's initial prospect is that of a drab, nondescript and not unduly animated port, despite its history of seafaring and the fact that many of Greece's leading shipping magnates hail from the island. First impressions of its centre conjure up even less excitement, for Plateia Vounakis contains a hybrid mixture of architecture, and its western part is taken up by a bare, dusty municipal garden with an obligatory statue of Canaris. Opposite is an undistinguished mosque-turned-museum with a motley display of exhibits including indifferent copies of paintings portraying the island's tragic past. Yet it does contain a good collection of locally discovered antique vases and some other interesting yields from island excavations. Despite their somewhat dowdy appearance, the cafés of the square are worth a visit for they specialize in oriental pastries, a rich range of Greek (Turkish) Delight and the island's renowned preserved fruits, mastic products, local wines and ouzo.

The most atmospheric part of Chora is the old Castro quarter lying within the walls of the Genoese fortress that still proudly displays the names and arms of the Giustiniani family. The grand, though dilapidated Genoese residences (occupied and partly reconstructed by the Turks) speak of the fourteenth century as one of the most prosperous periods in the island's history. The Castro's narrow streets also contain a ruined mosque and small prison where Bishop Platanas and seventy-five leading Chiote citizens were hanged, almost as a Turkish *hors d'œuvre*, before the main massacre meal. The streets of the Castro lead up to the site of the ancient acropolis, which affords marvellous views of the island's east coast and, beyond the narrow channel, the mountain peninsulas of Turkey.

There is another building in Chora that deserves at least passing acknowledgement. Its upper floor houses a folk museum with a colourful collection of local costumes, while below it is the Korais Library, first founded in 1817 and re-opened in refurbished premises in 1978. A native of Chios, Adamandios Korais (1748–1833), ranks as one of Greece's greatest scholars who, after studying medicine at Montpellier, settled in Paris in 1788, where he formed close contacts with other men of letters. In France at this time revolutionary fervour ran high, though Korais was a contemplative scholar who had little respect for insurrectionary factions. A

'The Baptism of Christ': a detail from an 11th century mosaic in the Monastery of Nea Moni, Chios

prolific writer, editor and translator, he laid stress on Greece's classical heritage and sought to bridge the gap, which had widened over the centuries (not least under Turkish occupation), between the written Greek and spoken, demotic languages. This proved to be more than a mere academic exercise for, as in other Balkan countries, codifying the language was a powerful factor in the birth of the new Greek nation. Korais set himself the task of restructuring a literary Greek language which combined the best elements of the ancient and modern tongues, removing in the process all foreign accretions. The result of this systematization was *katharevousa*, a purified, largely artificial language which, though adopted as the official form after liberation, was unfortunately little understood at lower social levels. Korais bequeathed his own library (including works on Egypt given to him by Napoleon) to Chios, and the collection was further enlarged in 1962 by the library of Philip Argentis, the London scholar and philatelist. With over 140,000 volumes, the Korais library is the third largest in Greece.

A good local bus service, albeit suited to the needs of the islanders rather than those of visitors, links Chora with the island's main points of interest. Unlike Samos and Lesbos, however, there are few adequate circuit routes; rather the routes fan out of the capital in all directions, thus necessitating a duplicated return journey.

An outstandingly attractive excursion is to the eleventh-century monastery of Nea Moni, a complex of buildings magnificently situated amid the rugged central mountains. The seven-kilometre-long road ends at the colourful village of Karyes, from which the monastery is reached by an exhilarating walk along a pine-fringed track. Founded by the Emperor Constantine IX Monomachos to house a miraculous icon found by some hermits, the monastery became prosperous and is famous for its simple but elegant church mosaics depicting scenes from the life of Christ. Of its other buildings the seventeenth-century refectory has a large stone table running the length of the hall, with specially cut niches for cutlery and napkins. Around it the monks must have dined in relays, for Nea Moni in its heydey had hundreds of inmates. Today it is run by a handful of nuns (technically making it a convent) who conduct modestly dressed visitors on a lengthy tour of its buildings. A brief pause is made at a chamber crammed with skeletons – the remains of islanders massacred by the Turks, on this occasion in 1882.

If the macabre fascinates, take a further walk into the mountains to the largely ruined hill village of Anavatos. Here Chiote women and children are said to have hurled themselves to their deaths from a cliff rather than expose themselves to the savage hands of the Turks. Only a few families now occupy this settlement, but their welcome is warm and the views are breathtaking.

In marked contrast to the wild mountain scenery of the island's interior are the tamed and fertile lands which stretch from Chora to the south coast. The road leads first to Cambos, the name referring to the extensive plain which, in effect, is a vast orchard filled with all kinds of fruit trees. Here old country houses, walled and surrounded by gardens, bear the coats of arms of the original Genoese aristocracy. When Osbert Lancaster (*Classical Landscape with Figures*) visited them in 1946, they were shuttered and their gardens overgrown. Many have now been renovated and their high walls obscure all but the tops of ornamental trees. However, the mansion of the Argentis family is open to the public and provides a remarkable insight into the aristocratic lifestyle of Chios many centuries ago.

Beyond Cambos the dark green hues of the terebinth lentisk increasingly dominate the cultivated landscape. This is mastic country, whose production is based around old fortified towns and some twenty villages collectively known as Mastichoria. Though indigenous to many parts of the Mediterranean, it is only on Chios (and here only in the island's south) that its resin (masticha) is tapped. The trees are gashed by a special tool in May-June, and harvesting takes place in late summer. Once mastic was used in the production of varnishes and, as noted, provided the earliest form of chewing-gum, but its trade suffered greatly at the hands of cellulose and Messrs Wrigley of the United States. Chios mastic is now used to flavour alcoholic drinks (particularly a spirit with the potency of ouzo or the Cretan raki) and sticky, jelly-like jams traditionally served on a spoon at the bottom of a glass of water – in Greek called *ypovrychion* ('submarine'). Island shops also sell other mastic confectionery.

Such was the importance of the mastic trade that the southern villages were spared the horrors of the 1822 massacre. Their farmers were also freed from statute-labour and taxes and, unlike their northern compatriots, the villagers were allowed to ring their bells, a fact that might well explain the great number of churches in the Mastichoria. During harvest time many measures were enforced to safeguard the crop, the Turks elaborating on the old Genoese system of maintaining walled villages with watchtowers manned by armed guards. Some of the settlements are still enclosed, and with their narrow gateways and winding alleys they retain a picturesque quality. Pyrgi (25 kilometres south of Chora) claims to be the most traditional and attractive settlement on the island. Its name, meaning 'tower', refers to the old Genoese keep that rises from its centre around which a labyrinth of narrow lanes, spanned by earthquake-protection arches, lead to small squares and numerous churches. Many of its houses are decorated in *sgraffito* – intricate blue and grey designs either scratched into the stone or scooped out of the cement and plaster-rendered walls. Adding further to the local colour are the native costumes of the women. Although not as common as they once were, the big kerchief, fringed

A street in Pyrgi, the mastic 'capital' of Chios

on one side, which covers the head, distinguishes a married woman (coloured or patterned) from a recently widowed (black) and a widow of long standing (white). Many have commented on the un-Greek look (if there are such things as standard Greek features) of the inhabitants of Pyrgi, but theories that they and other villagers in this part of Chios are descendants of Saracen marauders is pure romantic licence.

Other notable old settlements are Olimbos and Mesta, the latter, the one-time mastic capital, having narrow cobblestone streets which huddle below the former protection of a fortress. It is in the process of restoration, and some of its old buildings have been turned into traditional guest houses for visitors to this part of the island. Mesta is a suitable base for visiting the ruins of Emborio and Kato Fano, both sites excavated by the British School in 1951–4. Situated on a promontory of the south-east coast, the Bronze Age settlement of Emborio, a commercial rival of Troy, was destroyed by fire, but its site was re-occupied and remains from the archaic, classical and Roman periods are scattered over a wide area. At Kato Fano, near the fishing village of Ayia Pantes, are ruins of a temple of Apollo which mark the site of ancient Phania, a city that existed as early as the ninth century BC.

Northwards out of Chora two main routes offer further interesting excursions. The one to the north-west circuits Mount Aipos and passes the eighth-century church of Ayios Isidoros before dropping down to the coastal lowland dominated by the Genoese castle of Belisarius at Volissos. The village itself, a compact collection of colour-washed houses, was once the home of the Homeridae, a clan claiming descent from Homer. From its small port the boats leave for Psara, while westwards the road ends at the monastery of Ayios Markellas, where there is a good sandy beach and extensive views across the island.

The more direct route north from Chora leads to Kardamila and Marmaro, passing first through the villa suburb of Vrontados, on the northern outskirts of which is the so-called Stone of Homer, also known as *Daskalopetra* (Teacher's Stone) by its association also with St Peter. It is nice to dream that the *Iliad's* opening lines – 'It was Apollo, Son of Zeus and Leto, who started the feud . . .' – were first fashioned at this spot, yet this great block of dressed stone, situated on a spur, can probably lay little claim to literary inspiration, since opinion connects it with a country cult associated, perhaps, with Cybele, the mother goddess.

Further north is the fishing village of Langada on the Gulf of Delphinion, named after the fortified Athenian city that occupied this coastal lowland and looked across to the escapist islet of Inoussa (access from Chora). The road now climbs to Kardamila, a picturesque village whose port is Marmaro, noted for the skill and daring of its sailors. Here on the island's rugged north coast are good beaches and tavernas specializing in sea-food and local wines – a place to rest and contemplate the singular character of Chios.

Those Lesbian Women

To much of the world the world 'Lesbian' carries a distinct connotation derived from the supposition that Sappho, the celebrated lyric poetess of Lesbos, wrote passionate verse to, and about, her female friends and charges. Only fragments of her work survive, for the church in Constantinople banned and burned her poems, but one complete ode and stanzas from other poems make it clear that her principal theme was love, expressed always with natural simplicity, sometimes with tenderness, sometimes with passionate fire. Little is known about her except that she was born of aristrocratic parents and was a friend of Alcaeus, another lyric poet of Lesbos, author of hymns to the gods and songs of war and love, of which, again, only fragments survive. Many of the stories relating to Sappho are apocryphal, not least the tale that in middle age (and contrary to her rumoured reputation), her amorous desires were directed towards a handsome boatman named Phaon, who, by rejecting her advances, forced her to leap to her death from a sea cliff at Lefkas. In truth, both Sappho and Alcaeus, in consequence of political troubles, appear to have left Lesbos for Sicily and to have died there.

Yet, by gleaning the ancient sources, it does seem likely that on Lesbos Sappho was mentor to groups of girls and young women who had dedicated themselves to the cults of Hera and Aphrodite, the former the champion of women and marriage and the latter of beauty, love and reproduction – often debased in Greek literature to sexual gratification. Lesbian women, many of whom might have been temple conscripts, were renowned for their beauty and desirability, and in the *Iliad* one of the conciliatory sops which Agamemnon offers Achilles is 'seven women . . . Lesbians, whom I will choose for their exceptional beauty'. There are also references to Lesbian beauty contests, and Alcaeus describes a parade 'where Lesbian girls go to and fro with robes, being judged for their beauty, while the marvellous sound of the loud cries of women echoes round them every year'.

The descendants of noble, land-owning families, both Sappho and Alcaeus were critical of the political changes that were affecting Lesbos and the Greek world in general. The transition from feudal control to a system fashioned on democratic principles was not a smooth process but one marked by internal strife which on Lesbos centred around the conflict between the cities of Mytilene and Methymna. In such times of crisis it was not difficult for an ambitious politician with military influence to seize power, provided he had the support of the poor and discontented who, until then, had been subjected to the feudal influence of the aristocracy. By breaking the power of the landed classes and by encouraging industry and foreign trade, such a 'tyrant' could institute revolutionary changes. Hence what Polycrates did for Samos was matched on Lesbos by the rule and reform of Pittacus, who put an end to internal dissention and laid the foundations of Mytilene's commercial and cultural prestige in the Levant. A powerful fleet and wide mercantile interests were matched with a high standard of education, and Lesbos became particularly noted for the comparative freedom of its women in the realms of politics and the arts. Along with such contemporaries as Solon of Athens, Cleobulus of Rhodes and Periander of Corinth, Pittacus was considered one of the Sages of Greece, whose maxims, inscribed on the front of Apollo's temple at Delphi, were 'Know Thyself' and 'Nothing in Excess'. Alcaeus and, one assumes, Sappho were protagonists of Pittacus. A graphic picture of the political intrigue at this time is given in Peter

Flowering bougainville adds further charm to streets of Paros

A coastal windmill catches the Aegean breezes at Paros

A small Santorini chapel resplendent in the midday sun

Storehouses and homes are easily cut into Santorini's volcanic layer

Women harvesting the olive crop on Lesbos

Green's *The Laughter of Aphrodite*.

The contribution of Lesbos to Greek scholarship was to continue for a number of centuries, another famous native of the island being the philosopher and scientist Theophrastus (*c.*322–288 BC) who succeeded Aristotle as head of the Peripatetic School in Athens.

Lesbos was to suffer the same fate as most of the Greek islands close to the Asia Minor coast. It fully experienced the repercussions of the Persian and other wars in classical times and was later embroiled in the power politics waged between Byzantium and the trading states of medieval Western Europe. Venetians, Genoese,

A view of Mytilene, the capital and main port of Lesbos

Franks and Catalans all recognized its strategic, commercial and agricultural worth and contested for its possession. But during the fourteenth century, it enjoyed a period of untroubled prosperity, for it was given to Francesco Gattelusio, a Genoese adventurer, who had helped John Palaeologos regain the Byzantine throne. This important Aegean trading possession was terminated in 1462 when the island fell to the Turks and, despite attempts to overthrow Ottoman sovereignty, it continued, at least nominally, a possession of the Porte until 1912.

The third largest of the Greek islands (after Crete and Euboea), Lesbos (1,630 sq km), also known as Mytilene, after its main town, has been likened to a giant jigsaw piece searching to complete the pattern of the irregular Asiatic coast from which it was spawned. Imaginary lines drawn from the apexes of its three broad promontories would simplify it to a regular triangular form, yet massive land-locked gulfs – Kalloni in the south-west and Yera in the south-east – cut deeply to produce an insular shape of great irregularity. Around the shores of its gulfs extensive lowlands are guarded by mountainous blocks whose volcanic rocks – basalts, tufas, trachytes and conglomerates – denote crustal instability, an activity by no means extinct as the incidence of earth tremors and the presence of numerous hot springs bear witness. The island's strata have been weathered to produce some fertile soils which support a luxuriant vegetation and, where cleared, fields of wheat, cotton, tobacco and, on higher slopes, vineyards and olives. The island supports some 97,000 inhabitants, though, despite its rich agriculture and industries that include olive-oil refining, tanning, soap manufacturing and textiles, the rate of emigration is heavy.

Much of the island's industry is concentrated in and around Mytilene, the capital of the island, with a population of around 24,000. Boldly facing the Turkish coast, the town rises up-slope to overlook its harbours and the isthmus that joins it to the mainland promontory on which its castle stands, built by Gattelusio in 1373 on the site of an older Byzantine fortress. Fragments of masonry incorporated in its walls and towers are also a reminder that this was the site of the ancient acropolis. A pine-fringed path leads to the strongly fortified entrance, which displays the heraldic arms of Gattelusio and his Byzantine princess. Within the walls are a number of defunct mosques and a Moslem *medersa* (theological college), and the castle's northern ramparts provide good views of the old harbour and the remains of its breakwater.

From its original island site, the ancient city expanded across the isthmus, the 'new' section being laid out on a grid-iron plan which, in part, is still followed by the streets of the modern town. To the west of the old harbour is the ancient theatre, whose original form was modified to stage Roman gladiatorial and animal spectacles. It is said that this theatre gave Pompey the idea of building the first stone amphitheatre in Rome. Also dating from the Roman period is a villa which now houses the town's archaeological collection and contains some rare Aeolian-type capitals and mosaics illustrating scenes from the comedies of Menander.

In Mytilene, however, it is easy to forget history, for the town itself, except for a marble statue on its waterfront honouring Sappho, appears adept at doing just that. This is a work-a-day island capital lacking pretension and sporting some incredibly ugly architecture, hardly softened by its two main churches – the cathedral of St Athanasios and the enormous Baroque-style structure of St Therapon on Ermou Street, the town's main business artery. Pulsating with an animation more typical of larger Levantine towns, it welcomes the 'holiday voyeurs' but they quickly realize that they are observing a busy *entrepôt* and administrative centre – a smaller, insular Volos, or another Ermoupolis which Mytilene's atmosphere most closely approaches. At one time many Greek island ports had such grass-roots determination, and former centres of indigenous commercial activity would probably welcome the opportunity to be less reliant on the ephemeral tourist trade. Not that Mytilene is entirely lacking in social graces, for its waterfront is the scene of nightly relaxation and is one of the town's *volta* venues, its participants rounding off their evening proceedings in the numerous cafés that offer oriental-style sweetmeats. The main street behind the waterfront is also lively at night, where the atmosphere is reminiscent of a crowded bazaar.

Although new accommodation has recently sprung up all over the island, the majority of hotels are in the capital and, providing one is not in search of a 'chocolate-box' setting (and is immune to noise), Mytilene, as the focus of island communications, provides an interesting and useful base for touring.

Yet, on seeing Methymna (Molyvos) on the island's north coast, visitors will almost certainly wish they had made this the target of at least a few days visit. Dominated by another of Gattelusio's castles, this attractive hill town has the added advantage of a long beach fringing the bay it overlooks. Much of its early history made it a commercial and political rival of Mytilene; today it is content to win this battle on the basis of old-world charm, for its steeply inclined streets are full of Turkish-style houses with corbelled walls, and its alleys are choked with a profusion of flowering plants. But reality strikes home in the lack of accommodation, for it is surprisingly uncommercialized and what little hotel space there is (and this also applies to private rooms), is usually the preserve of Greek and foreign writers and artists who seek inspiration in this exceptionally attractive place. Nightlife matches its *avant-garde* atmosphere, but like most Greek towns it tends to revolve around the many tavernas, some with terraces overlooking steep drops to the sea, others concentrating near the harbour, where there are impromptu concerts of Greek songs and dances. During the summer evenings the castle is floodlit and seems to float like some unreal theatrical backdrop above the town. The views from its battlements, especially at sunset, are magnificent.

There are two routes from Mytilene to Methymna, and both offer much that is of historic and scenic interest. After some twelve kilometres, the east-coast route reaches Thermis, where there are hot springs, ancient baths and the ruins of a temple to Artemis. Its origin as a spa dates back to *c.*2,750 BC when it appears to have been colonized from the Troad in Asia Minor before coming under Cycladic influence. The city was fully excavated in 1929–33 by the British School, which recognized fire as the cause of its abandonment, the till-then current hypothesis being that it was destroyed by Greek armies *en route* to the siege of Troy. Loutra Thermis now functions as a modern spa and also has good bathing-beaches. There are other ancient remains at Mistegna, and Nea Kidonia has a ruined castle, beyond which the road heads inland through rolling hills to Mandamados, whose church contains a black icon of St Michael carved in wood. Here a remarkable post-Easter festival takes place, involving the sacrifice of bulls, undoubtedly the survival of a pagan rite which is also celebrated in other Lesbian villages. After Kapi the road to

tive church relic
e of mastic

Methymna skirts high mountains to reach the north-west coast at the small fishing village of Petra. Methymna is situated a few kilometres to the north, and the return journey to Mytilene can be made by taking the road south from Petra to Kalloni, situated close to the gulf of that name.

Kalloni is the junction for a circuit route through the south-western lobe of the island where the traditional village of Eressos vies with Mytilene as being the birthplace of Sappho and Theophrastus. Its small port, Skala Eressos, has a large sandy beach, a small village square and some good tavernas. On the west coast is the promontory village of Sigri famous among palaeontologists for its petrified forest, the result of volcanic activity and the chemical effects of hot, mineralized water. An inland road leads north-eastwards, via Antissa, back to Kalloni.

Skala Kalloni, a few kilometres to the south, is a small sardine-fishing port, and samples are usually available at unpretentious tavernas that also specialize in a powerful, locally produced red wine. The alluvial lowlands around the head of the gulf are intensively farmed, and from it the road back to Mytilene skirts the prosperous hill village of Agiasos, whose central church attracts thousands of visitors on the Feast of the Dormition. Southwards the vista is dominated by Mount Olympos

Keeping the island's
produce fresh

(Prophitis Ilias) which, rising to 967 metres, is the island's highest point. Here extensive areas are under pine and chestnut, and the roads that skirt the mountain to Batera and Plomorion on the south coast provide great scenic rewards. But not Plomorion itself – though disappointment is greatly alleviated by the quality of the ouzo! From the Agiasos junction the return to Mytilene is made via the northern shores of the Gulf of Yera, where there are further hot springs. Many settlements fringe the gulf, including Perama, which announces itself well in advance by the pungent aromas from its tanneries and olive-oil refinery.

Getting around Lesbos presents no great problems, for its roads are kept in reasonable order, and its local buses, largely a fleet of bone-shakers, generally arrive on time – credit being due, no doubt, to the religious bric-à-brac that envelops their drivers.

8

The Northern Islands

Compared with its southern basin, the northern Aegean has far fewer islands, though those that punctuate its waters are, with some exceptions, sizeable territories. For the most part they are located in, or close to, what is known as the Thracian Sea, that stretch of water extending east of the triple-fingered Chalkidiki peninsula, west of the Turkish lands of Gallipoli and Phrygia, and south of the Greek coasts of Macedonia and Thrace. Through the latter, to the east of Alexandroupolis and following the Evros river, runs the Greek-Turkish border, which continues south-westwards into the Aegean to retain for Turkey the islands of Imbros and Tenedos that flank the entrance to the Dardanelles (the Hellespont). These islands are all Turkey managed to salvage from an entire archipelago once ruled by the Ottoman Empire.

The islands of the northern Aegean that belong to Greece are Lemnos, Thasos, Samothrace (Greek Samothráki) and Ayios Efstratios, though the latter is small (43 sq km) and isolated and receives few visitors. Its role in history has been a strategic one, for in both ancient and medieval times it was a base on the sea route that connected south-east Greece with the Hellespont. Part of this route is still followed by ships operating between Piraeus and Alexandroupolis which call, though rarely more frequently than once a week, at Ayios Efstratios, Lemnos and Samothrace. The Euboean port of Kimi also has links with Ayios Efstratios and Lemnos, and the latter is further served from the Macedonian port of Kavala. Being closest of the northern islands to the Greek coast, visitors to Macedonia and Thrace will have no difficulties in reaching Thasos, for regular ferries operate to the island from Kavala and Keramoti. Samothrace is more isolated and is best reached from Alexandroupolis, which has the advantage of being on the Salonica-Istanbul railway. The nearest station to Kavala is Drama, a town on the same railway line thirty-two kilometres to the north. Both Kavala and Alexandroupolis have airports with scheduled flights to and from Athens, but the only island airport in the northern Aegean is on Lemnos.

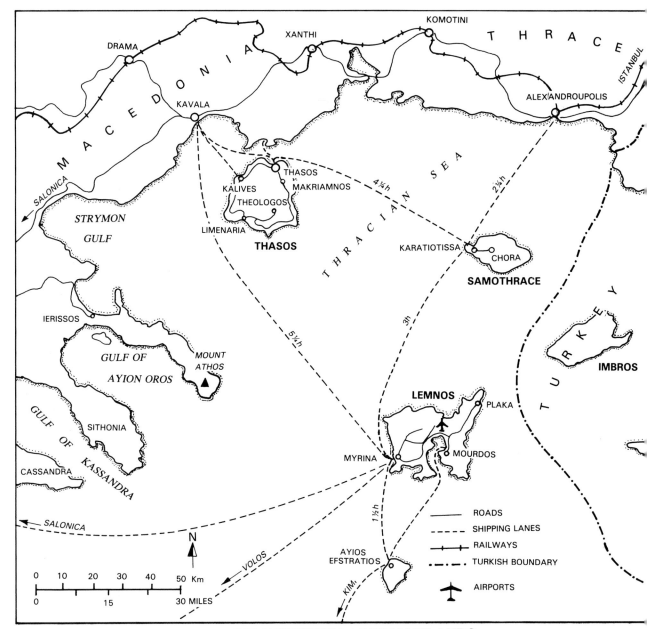

THE NORTHERN AEGEAN ISLANDS

Lemnian Earth

Despite air links with Athens and Salonica, Lemnos remains an isolated island lying off the main Aegean tourist routes. As such, it allows visitors the now rare opportunity of sampling a largely authentic Greek island lifestyle untainted by those often pseudo developments that in other parts of the Aegean are promoted as tourist attractions. Yet an island with a purely local infrastructure can present problems, and visitors to Lemnos might well encounter difficulties in finding suitable accommodation, a problem compounded by its skeletal bus service. Taxis are available, and hitching lifts is both acceptable and commonplace, though the latter demands considerable patience, for this basically agricultural island is decidedly lacking in vehicles with spare seats.

The lowest-lying of all the Aegean islands, Lemnos is hilly rather than mountainous, and largely bare of trees, due to the fierce winter winds that sweep down from the Dardanelles. Its sheltered areas are devoted to corn, tobacco, sesame and cotton, above which scrubby hillsides are the grazing grounds of sheep and goats whose numbers are said to be about six times that of the island's human population – some 18,000 inhabitants, currently inflated by a sizeable military presence at Mourdos Bay. This, one of the best natural harbours in the Aegean, bites deeply into the island and, with its smaller counterpart along the north coast (the Bay of Pournia), almost cuts the island into two unequal parts, the umbilical link being barely three kilometres wide. The importance of Mourdos Bay is readily explained in terms of another prime geographical factor – the central position of Lemnos in the northern Aegean, half-way between the Greek and Turkish mainlands and opposite the entrance to the Dardanelles. Through this natural waterway shipping has passed from time immemorial into the Sea of Marmora and, beyond, via the Bosporus, to the Black Sea. The site of an important city in Homeric times, Lemnos was later contested by Persians, Athenians, Spartans, Macedonians and Romans, the roll-call of conquerors and invaders continuing through to the Middle Ages when it was disputed by Venetians and Genoese, Byzantines and Turks.

Of the Aegean islands Lemnos had the distinction of becoming part of modern Greece as early as 1829, yet this status lasted no more than a few months, when it was exchanged with the Turks for Euboea, a much larger territory geographically closer to the heart of the expanding nation. Greece again acquired it in 1912, following which Mourdos Bay became the base in World War I of the Mediterranean Expeditionary Force from which Sir Ian Hamilton launched his attack on the Dardanelles in the Gallipoli Campaign conceived by Winston Churchill.

On 25 April 1915 an Allied force (predominantly British and Australian, but with French support) landed on the Gallipoli peninsula, their objective being to seize the ports that guarded the approaches to Constantinople and thereby to open up a route to assist Russia. The fleet floundered and nine months of fighting brought the Allied armies nothing but disease and death. The 19th Division of the Turkish Army was commanded by Mustapha Kemal Atatürk under the direction of the German General Liman von Sanders, this combined leadership breaking the Allied attack and forcing them to withdraw. Many of the dead were brought back and buried on Lemnos, and the largest of the military cemeteries, with some 900 graves, is located to the north-east of the town of Mourdos. At Portianos, on the west side of the inner harbour, are a further 350 graves. Mourdos also has a French memorial to their fallen (the graves were removed in 1922), and a further reminder of the ill-fated expedition is the so-called 'Pier of the Australians'. On a more successful note Mourdos Bay was the scene, on 30 October 1918, of the Armistice with Turkey concluded aboard HMS *Agamemnon*.

Mourdos itself is a disappointingly dull town, but from it the ruins of Poliochni can be visited by following a rough dirt road to the south-east coast. The principal finds from its excavations, and those from Hephaestia (see below), are displayed in Myrina, the Lemnian capital situated on the island's west coast. Poliochni was a city commercially linked with Troy, and presumably it represents the Homeric 'Lemnos'. As befitting an island that was a trade-bridge for centuries, the Italian School of Archaeology discovered in 1931–6 four superimposed settlements – two neolithic, one of the Copper Age and the 'latest' (and richest) belonging to the early Bronze Age. The site is somewhat overgrown on a windswept eminence overlooking the sea, and among its points of interest are ancient walls, the remains of dwellings, deep wells and baths reported to be amongst the oldest in Greece. South of Poliochni is a desolate landscape where extensive windblown sand has provided its name – Lemnos Sahara.

The main Lemnian city of classical and Hellenistic times, though one with pre-Greek origins, was Hephaestia. Its remains, close to the aptly named hamlet of Palaeopolis, are situated on the shores of the Bay of Pournia. The association of the island with Hephaestos (Roman Vulcan), the metalsmith and god of fire, is of particular interest. The son of Zeus and Hera, he is said to have been thrown out of Olympus during one of his father's frequent fits of rage. He was lamed for life by falling on what legend tells us were the jagged rocks of an actively volcanic island. Both the ancient writers and modern scientific research substantiate this view. Lemnos is said to have occasionally 'blazed' from its higher slopes, and Herodotus and Pausanias report that a small island known as Chryse, off the Lemnian coast, was swallowed by the sea as the result of some cataclysm. Significantly, underwater research in 1960 around the Charos Reef located the ruins of an archaic temple of Apollo that might once have graced ancient Chryse. The volcanic rocks of the island's eastern half, weathered to rich agricultural soils, together with the presence of hot springs, lend further support to the idea that elements of truth lie hidden in even the most romanticized of ancient stories.

Other strange episodes recorded in mythology might also reflect actual events in Lemnos' dim and distant past. The island appears to have been sacred to Hephaestos not only on account of its volcanic nature but also because of its early tradition in ironwork introduced by peoples from the north, the Dorians. The infamous 'Lemnian deeds' refers to an episode when the island's men were massacred, probably by these warlike invaders, though legend couches the circumstances in the most bizarre of tales.

In the *Odyssey* the minstrel to the court of King Alcinous relates the story of Hephaestos' marriage to the notoriously unfaithful Aphrodite and the way in which he traps her in a net when she is love-making with Ares. Indignant at the way the goddess had treated Hephaestos, the women of Lemnos refused to honour and serve her, but Aphrodite retaliated by conjuring a plague which gave the women body-odour and halitosis. Neglected by their menfolk, the women collectively resorted to mass murder, and were it not for the fact that the Argonauts dropped anchor off Lemnos (the odour scourge having apparently disappeared), the population of the island would have continued to decline. Here many ancient myths and folk-lore tales have obviously merged to produce a composite and complicated story which refers to heavy losses of the male population as a result of conquest by the ironworking Dorians and the subsequent cultural blending between indigenous islanders and newcomers.

At the core of these Lemnian stories is the Hephaestos cult of the 'earth fire' and the famous *terra sigillata* ('stamped earth') which in classical times was, for some reason, impressed with the head of Artemis. This medicinal earth, with a high percentage of silica – common to weathered volcanic deposits – was considered a trusty treatment for wounds, abrasions and snake-bites and was one of the reasons why Philoctetes, the champion Greek bowman of the Trojan war, was hastily despatched to Lemnos. He had developed a gangreous leg but was cured in time to return to the battle and fire the crucial arrow that killed Paris outside the Trojan walls. On a specified occasion each year this Lemnian earth, under the strict supervision of a priestess, was dug from a specially guarded mound near the modern village of Kotchinos on the island's east side. Galen, the great medieval physician, attended a similar ceremony and reported that only one wagon-load of the precious substance was removed each year. Dr John Covel also witnessed the procedure and described in his diary (1664–77) how 'Women drink it to hasten childbirth, and to stop the

rina, the Lemnian
ital, viewed from its
netian castle

fluxes that are extraordinary; and they count it an excellent counter-poyson, and
have got a story that no vessel made of it will hold poyson, but immediately splinter
in a thousand pieces.' On 6 August – the Feast of Christ the Saviour – the ceremony
of digging Lemnian Earth is still performed, under the vigilance of an Orthodox priest.
It can be bought locally at the island's pharmacies and certainly takes the sting
out of bites!

Hephaestia was excavated by the Italian School of Archaeology between the wars
to reveal a large necropolis, various sanctuaries and a theatre that had been remod-
elled by the Romans. A little to the north, at Chloe, the ancient port of Hephaestia,
are the remains of a Cabeirion (a cult centre of non-Hellenic deities) which might
be older than that of Samothrace. It was extensively redeveloped in Hellenistic times,
and the large foundations of its initiation halls and other ritualistic buildings suggest
that it did, in fact, compete in prestige with the Sanctuary of the Great Gods (see
page 174–7). The remains of a Roman-style basilica attest to Hephaestia's role as
an important Christian centre in Byzantine times, but in 1204 the city fell to the
Venetians, and during the next century it was wrecked by a landslide and
abandoned.

For a time the medieval castle of Kotchinos controlled the island before its administrative centre of gravity, shunning the great bays, moved to Myrina (also called
Castro) on the west coast. This is now the main port of Lemnos and, on arriving
by sea, visitors might well be forgiven for deciding to move no further than the
capital and its immediate surroundings, for Myrina is one of the most attractive
small towns in the Aegean and exudes an atmosphere of light-heartedness found
nowhere else on Lemnos. There is charm in the stone-paved streets, floral alleyways
and weather-beaten homes built by prosperous seamen, and the entire town is
dominated by a well-preserved Venetian castle that separates a long sandy beach
in the north from the harbour area to the south. Protected from prevailing winds,
the latter is surrounded by restaurants and cafés which offer the island's excellent
fruits, locally produced yoghurt and tempting array of pastries. A number of modest
hotels and a newer, up-market bungalow complex make Myrina an attractive and
relaxing place to stay. South-west of the town the scenery is the most pleasant on
Lemnos, for this is wine-growing country centred around Thanos, and there are
also good beaches. The whole of the island's west coast looks across the Aegean
to the majestic prospect of Mount Athos, sixty kilometres distant. The finest views,
especially at sunset, are provided from Myrina's castle.

The tranquil charms of
Thasos

The Green Circle of Thasos

With the beauty and variety of its scenery, its plethora of fine beaches, interesting antiquities, picturesque mountain villages and excellent accommodation, Thasos is a materialization of most people's pre-conceived ideas of what a Greek island is all about. It has the added advantages of an efficient tourist infrastructure, friendly and helpful islanders and a road system with regular bus services that ring the island. In total, it is one of the most appealing of the Aegean islands and extremely popular with motorists and campers from northern Greece and those from other parts of western Europe who enter the country via Yugoslavia. Now firmly established on the package-holiday map, the island has not been vulgarized by commercialization, and though the capital, Thasos town (also known as Limenas or Limen), is more costly than places further removed from the ships and ferries, even here visitors are respected and not taken advantage of.

Essentially circular in shape, Thasos is mountainous and of volcanic origin. Mount Hyparion (1,203 metres) forms its geographical centre, and its slopes are deeply gashed by torrent courses that radiate to the island's coasts. These valleys are thickly wooded with pines, firs, chestnuts and planes, an indigenous vegetation that is Macedonian-Thracian rather than Aegean, for Thasos experiences relatively damp and cool winters and is subject to frequent summer thunderstorms. Lumbering has long been one of the traditional occupations of its hillside villages, and its volcanic rocks contain zinc, iron, antimony and silver deposits. In antiquity gold was also worked, but supplies were soon exhausted; not so its famous marble quarries, which are still in production. Where the river courses meet the sea, small alluvial plains have been built up to provide land now under cultivation with wheat, tobacco and vegetable crops, interspersed with vineyards and olive groves. Bee-keeping is also a flourishing activity, and samples of Thasos honey can be bought locally or eaten in the cafés with yoghurt and, at breakfast time, with bread.

Thasos town, situated on the island's northern coast, is a curious jumble of modern buildings and archaeological ruins. The remains of temples, theatres, gates, basilicas and walls (many occupying back gardens) happily co-exist alongside modern housing, tavernas, cafés and administrative buildings, a situation similar to that in Kos town in the Dodecanese. Like its modern counterpart, the centre of the ancient town occupied a coastal tract beyond which steep slopes led up to the acropolis from whose ruins a good general view of the town's form and situation, ancient and modern, can be obtained. A tour of the ancient ramparts is highly recommended, though it involves a strenuous hike of some five kilometres past the remains of twelve towers that defended gates. As has so often happened, the *bas-reliefs* and items of sculpture (in this case protecting deities) that adorned these gates have found their way to Greek mainland, French and Turkish museums, the exception being a satyr on the main landward gate. Excavation of the ancient site began in 1862, and further work after 1910 was undertaken by the French School of Archaeology which has published an indispensable guide to the site. The prosperity that was able to maintain the city's great defences was continued into the Hellenistic and Roman periods, and further cultural overlays were added by Byzantine, Frankish and Turkish occupation. The little museum has proved incapable of accommodating the great wealth of monumental sculpture, which now overflows from the main building into its garden.

Many famous classical personalities were drawn to the commercially rich city of Thasos, not least the painter Polygnotus, the rhapsodist Stesimbrotos and the great athlete Theogones, who, according to Pausanias, won no fewer than 1,400 laurel crowns. For a short time Hippocrates of Kos also resided in Thasos, where, ever anxious to account scientifically for the causes of disease, he wrote a treatise on the island's climate and its seasonal and geographical variations. He is said to have been called to the island to deal with a virulent outbreak of mumps.

Retaining its prosperity throughout Roman and Byzantine times, Thasos was acquired by the Genoese Francesco Gattelusio prior to its conquest by the Turks in 1455. Some three centuries later it was given by Sultan Mahmud II to the family of the Egyptian ruler Mehmet Ali, but in 1770–74 the island was occupied by a Russian fleet intent on pillaging its rich timber resources. By this time the population of Thasos had gravitated to the inland villages as a protective measure against the ravages of corsairs. In 1912 the island was united with Greece.

Thasos town has an active night-life in summer, centred around a number of discothèques and numerous tavernas, some animated by off-duty Greek soldiers willing to display their dancing skills. The evening *volta* through streets closed to traffic is also enthusiastic and, perhaps more so than others in Greece, appears to be highly organized, the various directional flows taking care not to cause human bottlenecks. In July and August an added attraction is the occasional performance of classical Greek drama staged in the well-preserved ancient theatre, shrouded by aromatic pine trees. These plays form part of the annual Philippi and Thasos Festival sponsored by the National Tourist Organization of Greece.

Visitors should, however, make a point of exploring the remainder of the island by following the scenically attractive coastal road (a circuit of some eighty-five kilometres – $3\frac{1}{2}$ hours by bus), making forays into the interior wherever branch roads make this possible. Travelling south-eastwards from Thasos town, a two-kilometre drive leads to Makriammos (literally 'long sand'), whose hotels, bungalow complexes and beach installations illustrate the seriousness with which the island

is responding to tourism. This is the island's 'in-place' for holiday-makers, and its facilities include those for boating, fishing, skin-diving, tennis and volley-ball. As might be expected, prices are higher than the island norm, and if it is sea and sand only that the visitor needs, there are numerous coves and beaches that remain undeveloped.

Beyond Makriammos the circuit road makes one of its frequent short detours away from the coast to serve the delightful stone-roofed hill village of Panayia set on the eastern side of Mount Hyparion, amid forests and springs, the latter reputedly beneficial for kidney complaints. In such a setting its modern church appears incongruous, though it contains some interesting early Byzantine icons and relics. Back on the coast, the road leads to Christi Akri where fishing-boats put out for the night to the accompaniment of their hissing acetylene lamps. Here the local catch can be enjoyed in what appear to be makeshift tavernas – appendages to fishermen's cottages.

The south-eastern section of the island has old marble quarries, and at Archangelos cheerful nuns from the convent will dutifully indicate the spot where St Luke is said to have knelt in prayer, his knees having made hollows in the stone floor, though these impressions are the result of centuries of penitent kissing by Orthodox believers. The road now turns west, past other good beaches to Potos, where a branch road leads inland via a beautiful valley to the old mountain capital of Theologos, directly below the slopes of Mount Hyparion. Majestically situated, it has the ruins of a medieval castle and a house where Mehmet Ali is said to have spent part of his youth. This is as good a place as any to sample another type of Thasian honey, a sticky preserve made from whole figs or green walnuts. Its preparation seems to be the duty of the island's old ladies, who alone (perhaps) are the guardians of its traditional recipe.

Beyond Potos is Limenaria, the island's second largest settlement with seaside tavernas and a fishing fleet. Here the island's circular road begins its return journey to Thasos town, via the west coast. The scenery is less attractive, stretches of this area being marred by the dusty mining activities for cadmium and iron ore. Significantly, Limenaria once had offices occupied by the Krupp firm of the German Ruhr. Off the west coast are the oil-recovery operations which the Greeks hope will make this part of the Aegean a miniature North Sea. At Skala Prinou, near Kalives, is another port for the Kavala ferries.

The Mighty Ones of Samothrace

Lying off the Thracian coast, forty kilometres south of the seedy border town of Alexandroupolis, Samothrace rises out of the northern Aegean like some great religious shrine, mysterious, threatening, yet compulsively attractive. Oval in shape, the island consists of the deeply eroded slopes of Mount Saos or Fengari, whose summit, snow-capped for much of the year, reaches 1,600 metres.

Close to the entrance to the Dardanelles, on whose shores is ancient Troy, it was on this lofty eminence that Homer placed Poseidon to view the protracted struggle between the supporters of Agamemnon and the Trojan King Priam. A local guide is needed if the visitor wishes to experience something of what Poseidon saw. The climb is long and difficult, but the views are astonishing and must rank among some of the greatest scenes the Aegean can offer. To the north-west is the convexed green of Thasos with the coasts of Macedonia and Thrace beyond, southwards the irregular outline of Lemnos, west the peninsulas of Chalkidiki and the bold Mount Athos, whilst eastwards, beyond Imbros, are the hills of the Dardanelles, the Troad itself and, in the far distance, the peak of Bithynian Ida.

The great mass of Samothrace means that winds and currents render its approaches dangerous, a factor that has protected it from many of the historical traumas that have affected its Aegean neighbours. Today the island is approached from the west, where, at Karariotissa, near Cape Acrotiri, an open anchorage is protected by a stout breakwater. Chora (officially Samothrace), the island's principal settlement, lies some five kilometres to the north-east, an overgrown village, cradled in the mountainside, whose tiled-roofed houses, with precariously hanging balconies, are overlooked by the ruins of a Byzantine-Genoese castle. It is the centre of the island's relatively rich agriculture, the high slopes of Fengari assuring a plenti- ful supply of water as well as scrub and woodland for foraging goats. From Chora the ascent of the peak can be made in four or five hours, although there are other access points, some involving boat trips.

Chora, Samothrace's c
hillside capital

In antiquity there was a port on the north coast, its silted site being marked by a ruined medieval tower. The island owed its importance to the sanctuary of the Thracian Cabeiri, the Great Gods, associated with which were sacrificial rituals and mysteries not unlike, in their complexity, those of Eleusis on the Greek mainland. The extensive ruins are at Palaeopolis on the north coast, where there is also modest accommodation and some attractive beaches on which a small tourist industry is based. Other 'newcomers' to the island are Greek soldiers stationed in Chora.

Much dispute surrounds the interpretation of the Cabeiri cult. Excavations by the French and Austrians in the nineteenth century were followed by those of a French-Czech group between the two World Wars and the work of Americans after 1948. Collectively, these studies brought to light impressive remains of the sanctu- ary and many items of sculpture that now grace the museums of the world, the most famous being the Winged Victory in the Louvre. When it was found in 1863, it was shattered into over a hundred marble pieces. Painstakingly, it was fitted together to form the now familiar headless, windswept figure standing eight feet high with great wings outstretched. Yet despite the many artefacts and works of art, knowledge of the cult remains imperfect, partly on account of the secrecy its initiates maintained and partly because of the ravages that time has inflicted on the site.

It has been conjectured that the name Cabeiri is derived from the Phoenician 'Qabirim', meaning 'Mighty Ones', and there are few contradictions to the view that the original cult was pre-Hellenic. With the passage of time, however, other deities were added to the Samothrace pantheon, some having characteristics similar to those of the original gods, whereas others acquired compound attributes from the fusion of legends belonging to a variety of peoples. Yet all were fertility gods, and the phallus was their symbol. Among the pre-Greek deities was Axieros, the Great Mother whose cult was related to that of the Phrygian Cybele who was worshipped, along with her youthful lover Attis, in ecstatic rites and ceremonies of purification. The Cybele cult was common in Greece by the fifth century BC, when it became fused with that of Demeter, the object of ritualistic celebration at the Eleusian Mysteries, the latter concerned primarily with the spiritual rebirth of its initiates. For the Greeks, the attributes of Attis were represented in Adonis, himself a consort of the mother-goddess whose rites included a period of mourning followed by joyous resurrection. The role of the ithyphallic fertility god Kadmilos was given to Hermes,

whilst Hades and Persephone dubbed for the demons Dardanos and Aetion. Subsequently, through either assimilation or confusion, were added such immortals as Aphrodite, Harmonia, Kadmus and Artemis, whose darker side revealed the elements of sorcery inherited from Hecate, the primitive pre-Greek goddess of the underworld.

The classical writers provide only vague and frustratingly ambiguous comments on the nature and meaning of the rites and ceremonies at the Sanctuary of the Cabeiri. Was it the wrath of the implacable gods that its initiates feared, or were they sworn to secrecy as in some ancient equivalent of the Masonic Order, disclosure carrying with it the threat of social ostracism? Yet, unlike Freemasonry, initiation was open to both sexes, and neither age, nationality nor social class was a barrier to acceptability. According to Plutarch, there were a number of ceremonies held throughout the year, but the great festival was held at the end of July and the beginning of August, when dramatic performances were also staged. *Myesis*, the first degree of initiation, could be followed, without interval, by the second stage, *epoptia*, which involved some form of confession and absolution. The ceremonies took place by torchlight, and sacred banquets, libations and sacrifices were integral parts of the procedure.

The outcome of what was undoubtedly a lengthy series of ceremonies was the initiate's being issued with a certificate and his or her name entered in a register, proving *bona fide* membership of the Samothracian League. As such the new member was given promises of worldly salvation and good fortune, the latter probably being linked with the invocation of the deities against the perils of the sea. The Winged Victory was, in fact, a votive offering to the gods by Poliocretes in thanks for his naval victory at Salamis.

The sanctuary area was territorially independent of the adjacent city of Palaeopolis, which must have benefited commercially from the streams of pilgrims, dignitaries and foreign envoys who gravitated to Samothrace. Prosperity was further assured by the island remaining a neutral free state during the time of Greek internecine struggles. The Cabeiri cult appears to have reached its peak in Hellenistic times, when Philip of Macedon and his queen-to-be, Olympias, are said to have been initiates. The Romans were greatly attracted to Samothrace, for the island was associated with the ancestors of Aeneas, whom they regarded as the founder of Rome. They were largely responsible for re-establishing its fame following the sanctuary's sacking by corsairs and the great damage inflicted by an earthquake. The contemporary ruins form a large and complex site, and the main objective of the well-appointed museum is to explain to the novice visitor the arrangement and original character of the various buildings. Among its fascinating exhibits are lists of initiates and collections of religious and votive objects given either as tokens of faith in the power of the deities or as measures of gratitude for some spiritual transformation. It is of interest that such a practice has been transferred to the saints and holy relics of the Orthodox Church, where every revered icon and certain mortal remains are surrounded by siver, sometimes gold, *simulcura* – gifts, but also prompters to the Christian 'mighty ones' to answer petitions and prayers.

The spirit of the Cabeiri rests heavily on Samothrace, and the towering presence of Mount Fengari often cows rather than elevates the senses. Yet it is an island that pays getting lost in, for in few other Aegean domains is the wanderer so conscious of nature's all-pervasiveness. This feeling must have incensed the pilgrims of ancient times, whose greatest fault might well have been the organization of nature's mysteries into what was undoubtedly a commercialized cult.

SANCTUARY OF THE GREAT GODS (SAMOTHRACE)

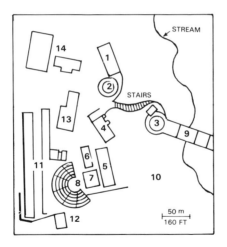

1. HOUSE OF THE MASTERS (GODS)
2. ROTUNDA CULT BUILDING
3. CIRCULAR BUILDING
4. SACRED HEART
5. SANCTUARY
6. HALL OF GIFTS AND OFFERINGS
7. ALTAR
8. THEATRE
9. CEREMONIAL ENTRANCE
10. NECROPOLIS
11. TERRACES
12. STOA
13. CEREMONIAL HALL
14. OTHER CULT BUILDINGS

Rhodes and the Dodecanese

The term 'Dodecanese' ('twelve islands'), applied to the south-east Aegean archipelago close to the coasts of Turkey, is a misnomer: the essential islands number fourteen in all. From north to south, they are Patmos, Lipsos, Leros, Kalymnos, Kos, Astypalaea, Nisyros, Simi, Tilos, Chalki, Rhodes, Karpathos, Kassos and Kastellorizzo (Megisti), the latter, 120 kilometres east of Rhodes, having the distinction of being Greece's most isolated island territory. In addition, the Dodecanese include at least forty islets, many of which are but uninhabited rocks and reefs. Collectively these insular territories have a surface area of 2,721 square kilometres, of which Rhodes accounts for over one half – 1,404 square kilometres – making it the fourth largest Greek island after Crete, Euboea and Lesbos.

The archipelago is sometimes known as the Sporades ('scattered') though, as previously noted, the name is prefixed by 'Southern' to distinguish the group from the Northern Sporades consisting of Skyros, Skiathos, Alonnisos and Skopelos etc. 'Scattered' is perhaps a more useful and meaningful term, especially when the irregular arrangement of the group is compared with the more compact and contiguous form of the Cyclades to their west.

With the Turkish occupation of the Aegean, the name 'Dodecanese' came to be popularly applied to those islands off the Asia Minor coast which had received administrative and commercial privileges from the Ottoman sultans, amounting almost to a charter of local automony. Neither Rhodes nor Kos, however, was fortunate in obtaining these favours, which were withdrawn in 1908. Between 1912 and 1945, when the Italians governed the archipelago, a variety of names became fashionable, including 'Tredeci Isole' ('Thirteen Islands') which was officially replaced by 'Rhodes and the Dodecanese' when the islands were finally united with Greece. Rhodes is the administrative capital of the group and is also the most important commercially, much of its economy now dependent on the tourist industry, a substantial part of its infrastructure having been developed by the Italians.

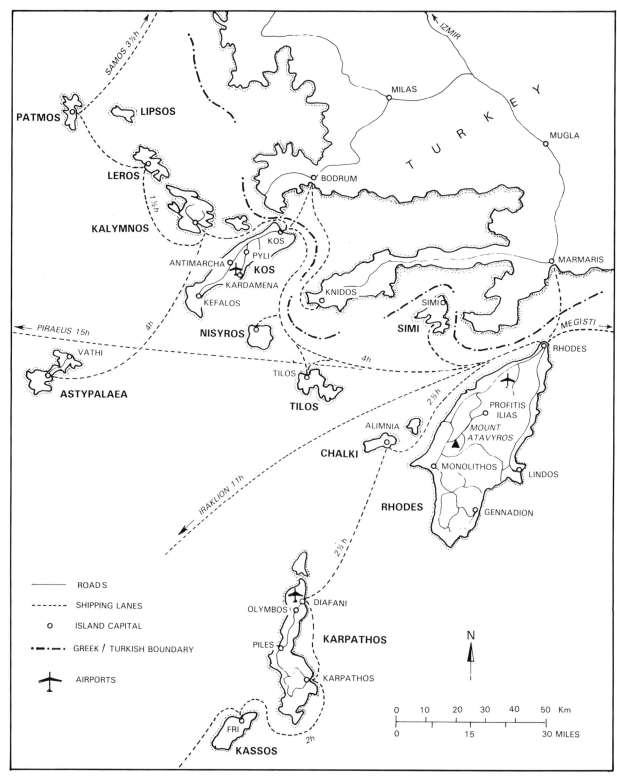

RHODES AND THE DODECANESE

Rhodes – the fortress island

There are many who would argue that Rhodes is the most beautiful island of the Dodecanese. Stretching from north-east to south-west over a total length of seventy-seven kilometres, and with a maximum width of thirty-five kilometres near the middle of the island, its terrain is both hilly and mountainous, though there are extensive coastal lowlands (richly farmed), numerous fertile valleys and also upland plateaux with large, compact village communities. The highest summit is Mount Atavyros (1,215m) in the centre of the island and to its south-west is Mount Acramytis, which reaches 925 metres. The latter extends to the west coast in the form of Cape Armenisti, complemented on the island's eastern side by the Marmari promontory on which the town of Lindos is perched overlooking the sea. Another conspicuous elevation is Profitis Ilias, which rises to 798 metres to the north-east of Mount Atavyros. The south-western tip of the island is formed by Cape Prassonissi, and the north-eastern extremity is occupied by the city of Rhodes and extensive suburban and tourism developments which now link it with the large villages along the north-east and north-west coasts.

The Rhodian story is long and eventful, as revealed by the island's great wealth of monuments, ancient, medieval and modern. Lindos, Cameiros and Ialysos were the main centres on the island prior to the foundation in 408 BC of Rhodes city, destined to become, particularly during the Hellenistic and Roman periods, one of the richest and most powerful centres in the eastern Mediterranean.

Of the complicated kaleidoscope of events and dramas that has collectively fashioned the city's (and, hence, the island's) history, the two that have most captured the imagination relate to famous sieges, separated in time by some eighteen centuries. The first, in 305 BC, was masterminded by Demetrius – subsequently labelled Poliocretes ('Besieger') – who was indirectly responsible for the erection of the famous Colossus (the shortest-lived of the ancient world's Seven Wonders). The equally momentous siege of Sultan Suleiman ('the Magnificent') led, in 1523, to the expulsion from the island and its Dodecanese dependencies of the Order of the Knights of St John of Jerusalem.

Demetrius was the son of Antigonus, the self-proclaimed ruler of the Syrian and Anatolian provinces of Alexander's once united empire (see page 39). Political trouble developed when Rhodes refused to co-operate with Antigonus, who was anxious for the island's support in his power-game with the Egyptian Ptolemy. The unwillingness of the Rhodians to take sides was understandable, for the island's lucrative trade with the great Asian and North African powers played too large a part in its economy to be placed in jeopardy. In particular, strong commercial links had been forged with Egypt, and Rhodes functioned as an influential depot

for the export of Alexandrian goods, not least spices. In retaliation for their non-co-operation, Demetrius, at the height of his military career, launched his attack on the Rhodians with an army specialized in assaults on heavily defended fortress cities. Rhodes was indeed a formidable challenge, for in addition to its eleven kilometres of walls – up to five metres in thickness, its five fortified harbours also made it one of the best equipped military ports in the Aegean. It was Rhodes that inspired Timosthenes' treatise *On Harbours* which then filled the place now held by *The Mediterranean Pilot*.

It is reported that the forces of Demetrius numbered 40,000 men, a figure which included strong cavalry, naval and engineering contingents, the latter necessary for servicing a wide range of sophisticated weaponry including giant catapults. But his most-dreaded weapon was the Helepolis, a nine-storey assault mechanism on wheels of oak that dwarfed the Rhodian walls. Replete with grappling-irons, catapults and drawbridges, it was capable of disgorging its infantry onto the parapets and, it was said, it took an operational force of some 3,000 men to propel it. The whole structure was given a tough outer skin of hides and plaited osiers, and the top tier was a nest for archers. There is some argument as to the size of the Helepolis: Diodorus claimed it was fifty metres high and twenty-five broad; Vitruvius calculated its weight at 125 tons.

Not surprisingly, the Helepolis caused extensive damage to the city's fortifications, but the Rhodian defenders, numbering barely half the total of the besiegers, showed little signs of weakening, and the enemy was repeatedly driven back. Lasting a year, the siege was abruptly terminated when Antigonus ordered Demetrius to conclude a truce with the Rhodians, the resultant treaty being particularly favourable to the island, which was guaranteed political freedom in exchange for an alliance with Antigonus against any enemy except Egypt. Either out of sheer necessity or as a mark of respect for the Rhodians, Demetrius left all his heavy battle equipment, including the Helepolis. According to tradition he requested that it should be sold and that from the proceeds the Rhodians should erect a statue to commemorate their valour. This was the Colossus of Rhodes, the massive effigy of Helios, the sun god.

Work on the monumental statue, undertaken by Chares of Lindos, a pupil of Lysippus, began in 302 BC and, it is said, it cost the sculptor twelve years of his life to cast and mould. Fashioned in bronze and measuring seventy cubits (something over thirty-five metres) in height, the precise site of the Colossus remains a mystery, as does the figure's pose, for no description of it remains. Yet it came to be regarded as the protector of Rhodes and served as a landmark for vessels arriving from all parts of the Mediterranean. However, the theory that it straddled the entrance to one of the city's harbours is a medieval confection, one that is still perpetrated by Rhodian guide-books and souvenirs. The spread of the legs in a figure of that height could hardly have been more than eight metres, and although ships were then small and masts could be lowered, such a passage would not have been feasible. A site at the back of Rhodes city, towards Monte Smith (where the ruins of the old acropolis exist), would seem more probable. Also, when the statue was overthrown, it appears that the great Helios fell on the land.

Placed in the catalogue of the ancient world's Seven Wonders, the Colossus stood for only sixty years, being destroyed by earthquake in 227 BC. For centuries it lay in ruins in the city it had adorned, legend relating that Helios was displeased with his likeness and that his oracle forbade restoration. It lay largely untouched, in fact, for nearly 900 years, until AD 635, when the remains were transported to the Levant by Saracen marauders who sold the metal to Jewish merchants. The 900 camels said to have been needed for the purpose is an obvious exaggeration, and an equally fanciful addendum to the saga of the Colossus is that Rhodes got its statue back in the form of cannonballs during the great Moslem sieges.

To pay but lip-service to the lengthy period when Rhodes was subject to Roman, Byzantine, Venetian and Genoese influence hardly gives the island the historical respect it deserves. Yet there is no doubt that its medieval centuries are remembered chiefly for Rhodes' role as the headquarters of the Knights of St John, one of a number of military orders that sprang out of the Crusades. Forced out of Palestine following their losses to the Arabs of Acre and Krak des Chevaliers, their possession of Rhodes

The Arms of the Grand
Masters of the Knights
St John

Arms of the Order

Foulques de Villaret
1310-1319

Hélion de Villeneuve
1319-1346

Dieudonné de Gozon
1346-1353

Pierre de Corneillan
1354-1355

Roger de Pins
1355-1365

Raymond Béranger
1365-1374

Robert de Juilly
1374-1377

Ferdinand d'Hérédia
1377-1396

Philibert de Naillac
1396-1421

Antoine Fluvian
1421-1437

Jean de Lastic
1437-1454

Jacques de Milly
1454-1461

Raymond Zacosta
1461-1467

G. B. degl'Orsini
1467-1476

Pierre d'Aubusson
1476-1505

Aimerie d'Amboise
1505-1512

Guy de Blanchefort
1512-1513

Fabrizio del Carretto
1513-1521

Ph.Villiers de l'Isle Adam
1521-1522

(subsequent to a brief sojourn of Cyprus) gave them full sovereignty of a recognized and defendable territory, their control also extending to the other Dodecanese islands. From manning a hospice originally founded to lodge and succour pilgrims to the Holy Land, the Hospitallers quickly transformed themselves into a powerful military force which gained papal approval in 1113. Their prime objective now became the defence of the Christian Church against the Moslem 'infidel', and recruits to the Order, most of them young members of influential European families, were required to make three fundamental vows of chastity, obedience and poverty, although the degree to which they adhered to such constricting precepts is a matter of speculation. The Knights were grouped according to their homelands, into *langues* ('tongues') – Provence, the Auvergne, France, Italy, Spain, England, Aragon and Germany, and each had its official headquarters and lodging place, known as an inn, which was under the command of a bailiff. Collectively the bailiffs constituted the Chapter of the Order, presided over by a Grand Master, elected to this position for life. During its time on Rhodes, the Order was served by a total of nineteen Grand Masters, the majority of whom were French.

Pre-occupied with their continual warfare against Islam and its followers, the Knights strengthened their position on Rhodes by establishing fortress bases on neighbouring islands as well as at Bodrum on the Anatolian mainland. Throughout Rhodes they erected, or restored, some thirty castles and strongpoints, but the main illustration of their scientific art of defence and military prowess comes from the old town of Rhodes itself, which still remains completely enclosed by its four-kilometre circuit of walls. With its succession of towers, bastions and barbicans, this enceinte is a magnificent example of thirteenth- to fifteenth-century military architecture and includes other integral elements such as great excavated ditches and highly defended gateways. During times of danger and siege, each section or post was allotted to a *langue* for defence, and the Knights further erected defence systems for the commercial and military harbours, each of which was protected by an independent fortress, of which the bulky St Nicholas Fort, which guards Mandraki, is a well-preserved example.

Within the fortified city a low internal wall separated the Knights' convent proper – the Collachium – from the merchant's town (*bourg*). The wall has gone, but the Collachium's main thoroughfare (popularly called 'the Street of the Knights') represents, thanks to discreet Italian restoration work, one of the most remarkable survivals of a medieval street in Europe. Linking the citadel with the port, via a defended gate, 'the Street of the Knights' contains the ornate, stone-built inns of most of the *langues*, together with the infirmary (now a museum) which was capable of accommodating one hundred patients and travellers and which symbolized the original mission of the Order. Then, as now, the Collachium and the entire walled city were presided over by the citadel and palace-residence of the Grand Masters. Now completely restored (another highly commendable piece of Italian work), it constituted a fortress within itself from which communication could be made with the ramparts. Further to withstand siege, it was designed with underground store-

rooms, though in peacetime the building acted as the Order's place of general assembly.

Many Moslem campaigns were launched against Rhodes, the greatest siege, lasting from 28 June to 22 December 1522 and ending in the Knights' defeat, being led by the Ottoman Sultan Suleiman II. For 177 days the city of Rhodes put up tremendous resistance, and Suleiman was considering a withdrawal when an informant – one of the Knights, so the story goes – got word to him that the Rhodian forces had greatly diminished, that the long-expected help from Christian Europe was not forthcoming and that supplies of food and ammunition were near exhaustion. A final Ottoman assault on the Post of Aragon took the city by sheer weight of numbers, forcing Grand Master Villiers de l'Isle Adam to surrender. Such was Suleiman's respect for the valiant Knights that the latter were awarded honourable terms, including a brief period in which to organize their departure. Escorted by some 4,000 islanders, who preferred exile to Ottoman rule, the Knights left Rhodes

e 'Street of the Knights'
he old Collachium
rter

on 1 January 1523. Their departure put an end to the sporadic proposals for further Crusades, for the loss of Rhodes and its dependencies now left the entire Aegean under Moslem sovereignty.

Most of the more detailed accounts of Rhodes under the Turks stem from visitors to the island during the nineteenth century, a time when the Ottoman Empire was rapidly disintegrating and Turkish administration, at best inefficient and corrupt, continued steadily to decline. Yet such indolence, inertia and unconcern were not characteristic of the island during the earlier years of Turkish rule, when a considerable amount of autonomy assured the continuance of some degree of commercial success. Inevitably, however, Rhodes town took on an oriental appearance as mosques, minarets, hammams, fountains, secluded courtyards and projecting wooden balconies were added to the urban fabric.

When the Italians acquired Rhodes (page 48), the old walled area, with its maze of narrow streets, alleyways and cul-de-sacs, was a curious mixture of medieval-Gothic and Turkish styles, and much of this character remains today. Orientation can be something of a problem, but visitors will find that the street-plan resolves itself in a number of principal thoroughfares and small squares. One of these main streets is Socrates, which, with its numerous shops, workrooms, tourist bazaars and cafés, retains the feel of the Orient, an atmosphere enhanced by its balconies, projecting upper storeys and, at its top, the imposing Mosque of Suleiman, reputed to be the only functioning mosque in Greece. In marked architectural contrast is the aforementioned Street of the Knights, an exceptionally well-restored medieval open museum. Exploration of the old town is an exercise in discovery, and the rewards are visual surprises at almost every turning. Its congestion and complex skyline are best appreciated from a walk along part of the battlements, the access point being close to the imposing mass of the Palace of the Grand Masters.

Rhodes' modern extensions are built on more spacious and regular lines. They originally date from the Turkish period when the Greeks working within the old town were not permitted to remain within its walls at night. The approach of curfew time could be watched on the large monumental clock close to the Mosque of Suleiman. Rapid development this century has united the earlier Greek suburbs into a pleasant, modern city whose commercial and administrative quarter occupies the area immediately west of the colourful Mandraki harbour. This is largely the product of Italian planning when public buildings lining the waterfront were designed in monumental styles. They include the town hall, the post office and the national theatre in sombre 'Mussolinian' block forms (typical of the Fascist era), but also the former Governor's Palace, now the prefecture, a most ornate Venetian-Gothic structure with marble decoration and an arcaded façade. Dominating the entrance

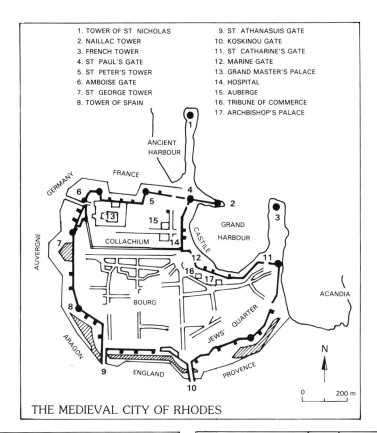

1. TOWER OF ST NICHOLAS
2. NAILLAC TOWER
3. FRENCH TOWER
4. ST PAUL'S GATE
5. ST PETER'S TOWER
6. AMBOISE GATE
7. ST GEORGE TOWER
8. TOWER OF SPAIN
9. ST ATHANASUIS GATE
10. KOSKINOU GATE
11. ST CATHARINE'S GATE
12. MARINE GATE
13. GRAND MASTER'S PALACE
14. HOSPITAL
15. AUBERGE
16. TRIBUNE OF COMMERCE
17. ARCHBISHOP'S PALACE

ANCIENT HARBOUR

GERMANY
FRANCE
AUVERGNE
COLLACHIUM
CASTILE
GRAND HARBOUR
ACANDIA
BOURG
JEWS' QUARTER
ARAGON
ENGLAND
PROVENCE

N

0   200 m

THE MEDIEVAL CITY OF RHODES

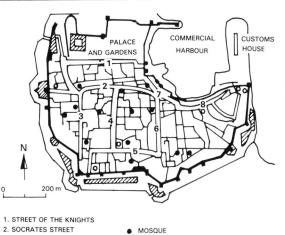

PALACE AND GARDENS
COMMERCIAL HARBOUR
CUSTOMS HOUSE

N

0   200 m

1. STREET OF THE KNIGHTS
2. SOCRATES STREET
3. HIPPODAMUS STREET
4. FANOURIOS STREET
5. OMIROU STREET
6. PYTHAGORAS STREET
7. ARISTOTELOS STREET
8. PINDAROU STREET

● MOSQUE
○ CHURCH

RHODES, THE OLD TOWN

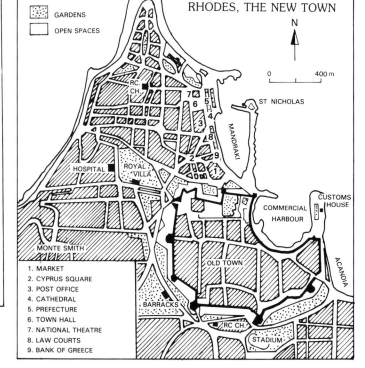

GARDENS
OPEN SPACES

RHODES, THE NEW TOWN

N

0   400 m

R.C. CH.
ST NICHOLAS
MANDRAKI
HOSPITAL
ROYAL VILLA
COMMERCIAL HARBOUR
CUSTOMS HOUSE
MONTE SMITH
OLD TOWN
ACANDIA
BARRACKS
R.C. CH.
STADIUM

1. MARKET
2. CYPRUS SQUARE
3. POST OFFICE
4. CATHEDRAL
5. PREFECTURE
6. TOWN HALL
7. NATIONAL THEATRE
8. LAW COURTS
9. BANK OF GREECE

to Mandraki is the Church of the Evangelist built in 1925 on the model of the Church of St John in the old town, which was destroyed in 1856. Fronting Mandraki the Italians also built a large polygonal market in a Turkish style, and this, together with the cafés and restaurants that surround it, acts as the modern focal point and social centre of the new town. Behind it, the streets that focus on Cyprus Square contain the main shops, banks and travel agencies, for this, together with the northern section of the town, with beaches to the north-east and north-west, is heavily dependent on the tourist industry, Rhodes having the greatest hotel capacity of any Greek town except Athens.

The Italians announced that they had come to Rhodes and the Dodecanese not as conquerors but as liberators. Not surprisingly, the Rhodians welcomed them as their emancipators from the Turkish yoke. The Italian platitudes were, however, quickly seen as hollow promises, and all dreams of freedom were shattered by brutal policies that suppressed the Orthodox Church, reorganized education along Fascist lines, expropriated agricultural land, made Italian the compulsory language of teaching and carefully controlled all movement between the islands and Greece. The Italians placed their cards firmly on the table in 1937 when the appointed governor, de'Vecchi, proclaimed that he had come 'to bring Fascist life and the Fascist spirit to the islands'.

Yet, in a material sense, Rhodes and the islands benefited, and still benefit today, from the works of their former Italian masters. Roads were constructed, villas were built, garden suburbs were laid out and many reclamation and irrigation works improved the efficiency of agriculture. In academic terms the Italians' interest was directed, primarily, to archaeology, and they excavated many ancient sites and restored numerous historical monuments, not least (as noted) the Palace of the Grand Masters, which proved to be their biggest project. Though much criticized, its exterior is a faithful reconstruction of the fourteenth-century building, but the interior was designed for modern occupation, the intention being to use it as a summer residence for Victor Emmanuel III and Mussolini. A special throne was brought from Italy, and electricity, central heating, lifts and other conveniences were installed.

Ironically, the preparations were barely completed when Italy was plunged into World War II and was forced to relinquish its colonial empires in Africa and the Aegean. The thirty-three-year occupation of Rhodes and the Dodecanese had cost the Italians much in terms of labour, money and emotional commitment. Their impact lives on, not least in the Rhodian parks and gardens which the islanders continue to tend and, where possible, add to the profusion of hibiscus, bougainvillea and other flowering plants. Rhodini, three kilometres south of the town on the island's eastern side, is a particularly well-landscaped municipal park with fountains and ponds, the scene in August and September of a popular wine festival.

The Rhodian countryside begs exploration, and this is made relatively easy by the eastern and western coastal routes that, together with a dense network of secondary roads, link the city with all the main villages and beauty spots. The island has a good bus service, though many schedules, as in most Greek island communities, operate for the convenience of the villagers rather than the tourists.

Lindos is the most frequently served centre and a tourist town in its own right, one that has been described as the Aegean's most picturesque settlement, though a large number of places most certainly compete for this title. Originating as one of the island's three ancient centres, it straggles the slopes of a precipitous rock (116 metres high) crowned by the impressive remains of the Temple of Athena and other monuments that formed part of its acropolis. The site was also chosen by the Byzantines and the Knights, the latter transforming it into a gigantic medieval castle, the entire complex preserving in a single site stone vestiges of the island's entire history. The coastal views are remarkable, as are those over the town – an irregular cluster of flat-roofed houses and belfried churches tortuously linked by narrow streets that follow the natural contours of the ground. As if this is not enough, Lindos also has a fine sandy beach which is now increasingly patronized by package-holiday visitors.

ew town of Rhodes is
f Greece's largest
entrations of holiday
nmodation

Unlike Lindos, Cameiros and Ialysos – the two other early Rhodian cities – survive today only as excavated museumpieces. The former, known as 'the Pompeii of Rhodes', is of exceptional interest, for the city's complete ground plan has been unearthed to reveal a complex of sanctuaries, stoas, streets and houses. It is situated thirty-six kilometres south-west of Rhodes city and occupies a natural bowl in the hillside close to, but largely hidden from, the coast. In contrast, the acropolis of Ialysos occupied the summit of Mount Philerimos (292 m) from which the city extended downslope towards the modern village of Trianda, some six kilometres from Rhodes city. Philerimos offers extensive views over the island's eroded hills and cultivated fields, and as well as the ancient ruins themselves the site contains a Byzantine church which adjoins a small Italian-restored monastery. A short walk from the summit leads to a well-preserved Doric fountain dating back to the fourth century BC.

A visit to Rhodes would not be complete without an excursion to some of its many agricultural villages – those of the south, less tainted by tourism, being the most traditional. Kattavia, Gennadion and Apolakia are large, compact lowland settlements; Embona, Apolona and Ayios Issidoros have mountain settings. The Rhodian mountains themselves offer many scenic attractions, though some are in danger of over-commercialization. Petaloudes ('butterflies'), for example, is a thickly wooded gorge usually crammed with people. Their objective is to see the countless 'butterflies' (actually they are moths) that settle on the trees, chiefly on their trunks and branches in June, July and August. A more peaceful spot is Mount Profitis Ilias, fifty kilometres south-west of Rhodes city. Covered with cedars, pines and cypress trees, this is a haunt of a variety of wild animals, including deer, the emblem of Rhodes, whose re-introduction to the island was another innovation of the Italians.

The Lesser-known Dodecanese (Chalki, Karpathos, Kassos and Kastellorizzo)
Rhodes is a convenient base for island-hopping. Daily sailings link it with Piraeus via the Cyclades or Dodecanese (a journey of up to twenty hours), and there are ferry connections to all the neighbouring islands and also western Crete. During summer hydrofoil services operate to Kos, Patmos and Samos, and for even speedier services there are air connections with Kos, Santorini and Karpathos, as well as regular daily flights to Athens. The boat for Karpathos calls at Chalki, which can also be reached by a daily service from Cameiros Skala on the west coast of Rhodes.

Chalki is a peaceful little island, hardly visited by tourists; hence it is short on accommodation, and its public transport is basic. Fortunately it is small enough to explore on foot, the poorly kept tracks from Chalki town leading to pebbly coves and a number of sandy beaches. The buildings of its port are grandiloquent (Italian inspired) for its small population – the entire island has less than 500 souls. Though it was once the centre of a copper-mining industry, most of the island's income now comes from fishing, which provides much of the fare of the local tavernas. The chief places of historical interest are the Castle of the Knights and the Stavros monastery, both of which provide good views over the island's somewhat bare landscape. Apart from the port the only other settlement is Chorio, an older and now semi-abandoned village.

Long, narrow and mountainous, Karpathos lies to the south-west of Rhodes and ranks as the third largest island in the Dodecanese, after Rhodes and Kos. Despite its sandy airstrip, it conveys a sense of unworldly isolation and retains many traditional customs. Its northern part is the most remote, and here the east coast settlements are more easily reached by boat from Pigadia (Karpathos town) to Diafani. From the island's capital, however, an astonishing mountain road, still in the process of making, snakes its way in a bold, precipitous attempt to link the northern villages. Aperion, Volada, Othos and Piles are majestically situated overlooking fertile valleys and shrouded by hillsides whose fruit trees give way, up-slope, to thick woodlands.

But in terms of its spectacular site and anachronistic lifestyle, the most fascinating village is Olymbos. Occupying a ridge descending to the sea on one side and a fertile valley on the other, this compact village, true to island form, focusses on a modest central square with some shops, cafés and a church. Its distinguishing feature is the traditional costume worn, by all but the young, as everyday dress. Visitors with a smattering of the modern Greek language might well perceive the singular local dialect, said to contain many ancient Doric words. Visitors to this northern part of Karpathos, or for that matter to other areas of the island, will certainly be unlucky not to witness, and become involved in, some local celebration, be it a wedding, a birth or a saint's day – events that seem to progress unabated for days. Invariably they are accompanied by the island's own special music – the fast and furious tones and rhythms of the three-stringed lyre, guitar and goatskin bagpipe known as *tsabouna*. In their verve and complexity the authentic island dances match in dexterity that of the local musicians.

Although in size little more than an overgrown village, Pigadia is a colourful and animated harbour capital with a surprisingly large number of comfortable hotels and good eating-places. It is the gateway to the island's fertile south, which is green with citrus plantations and vegetable gardens. Leading past the airport, a good road passes some attractive beaches, and at Ammopi a series of sandy coves are the cause of modest tourism development – in effect, an embryonic resort offering only scenic beauty, a few tavernas and modest accommodation. Other commercially developable beaches occupy the island's southern and south-western coasts, but

as yet the road is barely negotiable. However, the intrepid – those in search of tranquillity, bold mountainous settings and spectacular coastal scenery – will be richly rewarded.

One-fifth the size of Karpathos and lying between the latter and the east coast of Crete, Kassos is particularly remote and not the least geared to tourism, though visitors are warmly received. Most of the islanders live in and around the small port-village of Fri which, even by Karpathian standards, seems to indulge in an inordinately large number of religious feasts and other celebrations. Kassos is lacking in beaches but is ideally suited to the coastal walker (it has some fine caves) and to the explorer of rugged mountain scenery.

If the 'get-away-from-it-all' syndrome is the main attraction of visitors to the Greek islands, the ultimate in seclusion is Kastellorizzo. Although the smallest (9 sq km) of the Dodecanese, its alternative name is Megisti, signifying that it is the 'biggest' in an archipelago of otherwise barren islets. Mountainous, steeply cliffed and supporting few beaches, Kastellorizzo is rich in historical remains, a legacy of its position in the lee of southern Turkey at the very edge of the Moslem and Christian worlds. Many islanders remain largely on account of Greek government subsidies which have also attracted Greek émigrés from Australia and the United States. As a further attempt to keep this Greek enclave populated, the government is also actively promoting tourism, most development having taken place at the island capital (Megisti). Lying at the end of a narrow rocky inlet, this port is an attractive amalgam of traditional Dodecanesian architecture and Italianate buildings. Its many uninhabited homes, however, testify to a grander past.

North-west from Rhodes (Simi, Tilos, Nisyros and Astypalaea)

Northwards and westwards from Rhodes are the small and little-visited islands of Simi, Tilos and Nisyros, which act as Dodecanesian stepping-stones to the much larger island of Kos. Simi lies almost encircled by rugged Turkish peninsulas shaped like claws of a giant crab about to grasp for Asia Minor yet another of Greece's peripheral eastern territories. A mixture of mountains, rocky promontories and a number of fertile valleys, the island's main settlement, also called Simi, is a picturesque collection of houses and churches that rise in tiers above its waterfront. The whole pattern is presided over by the remains of a medieval castle built on the site of an ancient acropolis. A few tour-operators have 'discovered' Simi and its beaches, though, to date, development remains delightfully unsophisticated, and its limited accommodation is much sought after by the Greeks themselves. This means that it is not one of the best venues for island-hopping, unless 'sleeping rough' is of appeal. Those who prefer comfort should contemplate a day excursion to the island from Rhodes.

Tilos is another island where it is advisable to arrange accommodation in advance, preferably by someone who has full command of the Greek language. Its boat connections tend to be irregular, and this is no place to be forty-eight hours prior to a flight departure from Athens airport. But should the stranded visitor have time to spare, Tilos, with its fine beaches, offers a Shangri-La existence for those who expect little more than plain, wholesome local fare and basic sleeping-quarters. The island has one main road linking the two coastal settlements of Tilos and Livadi.

Nisyros is also isolated and mostly attracts those interested in its form and physical origin, for it is an extinct volcano whose large crater can be visited. As if to suggest that all is not yet quiet beneath its surface, there are sulphurous springs at Loutra, known since antiquity. The island's main village-port is Mandraki on the north-west coast where there is a castle of the Knights of St John and a subterranean church. Yali, the small island off its northern coast, has preserved many local customs including the wedding ceremony, performed on 1 May each year, and the main annual Panagiri on 15 August, when a free banquet is offered to all its inhabitants and visitors to the island.

Astypalaea is the most western of the Dodecanese and, as such, has many Cycladic

characteristics. It is an irregularly shaped island whose two rugged sections are linked by a narrow isthmus followed by the road from the main port, Astypalaea, to Vathi. The former is an attractive settlement which stands in the shadow of a Venetian castle, and good beaches are close at hand. The island was once known as 'Ichthyoessa' on account of the abundance of fish around its shores. Good catches still come from the many coves that festoon the island's complex coastline, and various fish dishes, some local specialities, can be sampled in unpretentious tavernas.

Being mid-way between the Cyclades and the Dodecanese, and with boat connections to Amorgos, Kos, Kalymnos and Rhodes, Astypalaea might well be on the brink of commercialized tourism. Already there is an unofficial nudist beach, which indicates its discovery by the summer sun-worshippers.

Kos – island of cures
Often described as a miniature Rhodes, Kos has the same Italian-style waterfront architecture, a large castle of the Knights of St John dominating its harbour, a number of old mosques and minarets and extensive areas of archaeological remains. Here, however, the similarities end, for Kos has its own distinctive scenery, human atmosphere and particular historical associations which, combined with superb beaches and a now active nightlife, make it the target of many European charter tours.

196

Fort of the Knights of
ohn guards the old
bour at Kos

This was not the situation some fifteen years ago, when its modest tourism earned it the title of 'the poor man's Rhodes'. Ironically it was the rapid increase in commercialization of the latter island that sent vacationers in search of less crowded venues, and the more casual life of Kos proved appealing. Such is the contagious nature of Greek island holiday development that Kos has now become extremely popular in summer, although it still offers a less hectic lifestyle without sacrificing the comforts now expected by many visitors to the Aegean.

Forty-three kilometres long and between two and eleven kilometres wide, the island stretches in a south-westerly direction from the Halicarnassos (Bodrum) peninsula of Turkey, from which it is separated by a channel barely four kilometres across. This eastern section of the island rises to 846 metres in Mount Dikaios Christos ('Christ the Just'), whose extension forms a lower central island ridge that separates the north-west and the south-east coasts. Many parts of the island have been deeply dissected by streams or other erosional forces, though there are many exceptionally fertile plains, particularly the area around Kos town, which has the appearance of a huge market garden ablaze with flowering plants.

The island's extensive antique remains are indicative of its early importance, for Kos developed a prosperous trade in luxury goods, not least Koan silk, which was worn by emperors, kings and princes throughout the eastern Mediterranean. Its reputation for luxury, together with its proximity to the Asia Minor coast, accounts for the island's periodic sackings, whose effect was often compounded by damaging earthquakes. Such was the fate in 412–411 BC of Astypalaea, the old city near Kefalos on the island's south coast, its destruction being one of the reasons for the founding in 366 BC, following the Rhodes example, of its new commercial and political centre of Kos on the wide bay at the island's opposite end.

Like Rhodes, Kos became an important Hellenistic and Roman city, and it was a favourite residence of the Ptolemies, who were patrons of a local school of pastoral poetry which nurtured the elegies of Philetas. It also attracted the Sicilian poet Theocritus, who has left a detailed description of the Koan countryside, in particular the island's agricultural richness:

> The rich, ripe season gratified the sense
> With summer's sweets, and autumn's redolence.
> Apples and pears lay strew'd in heaps around,
> And the plum's loaded branches kiss'd the ground.
> Wine flow'd abundant from capacious tuns,
> Matur'd divinely by four summers' suns.
> *Idyll* VII (trans. Francis Fawkes)

Following a severe earthquake in AD 142 the city was rebuilt on a magnificent scale, with agora, theatre, temples, gymnasia, several thermal establishments and large private houses with paintings and mosaics. But it, too, was destroyed by earthquake in AD 469, and the new dwellings, basilicas and baptistries that sprang up among the ruins belonged to the Byzantine era. Again the city was reduced to rubble in 554, and the result of this earthquake was the abandonment of the site, which appears to have suffered a complete eclipse for some eight centuries. Kos was subsequently acquired by the Knights of St John, who, between 1391 and 1396, erected a fortress and walls to protect a small, nameless settlement; additions to these defences continued until 1523, when the Knights were succeeded by the Turks, who raised mosques and built suburbs to the south and west. The Italians came in 1912 and built many grand public edifices, roads and harbours. As on Rhodes, they also planted gardens, excavated ancient sites and restored old monuments. But such was the fate of Kos that the town was again destroyed by earthquake on 23 April 1933. No new building was undertaken within the walled city, so that the ancient site could be systematically excavated. Only then was it realized that the ancient city extended so far.

Contemporary Kos occupies the site of the old Turkish quarter and the areas beyond. It surrounds what, on account of excavations, is a huge archaeological park containing a wealth of Archaic, Hellenistic and Roman remains, interspersed with Byzantine relics and surrounded by stretches of the ancient wall. Close to it is an intimate little square with an eighteenth-century mosque and an extremely old plane tree shored up, like some war-wounded soldier, with all manner of artificial aids, including pieces of ancient marble columns. This is the famous tree under which Hippocrates, the island's celebrated physician, is said to have taught his medical theory and practice. It is a nice story, and the gnarled tree, twelve metres in circumference, is certainly old, but hardly the age of 2,500 years. There is a further flaw in this tale, for the town of Kos was founded long after Hippocrates' death – though this in itself would hardly have prevented his using the site, which was close to the sanctuary of Asclepius.

Hippocrates was born at Astypalaea in 460 BC, by which time the cult of Asclepius, known from Homer as 'the blameless physician', was firmly established on the island. The origins of Asclepius are lost, but he seems to have been a form of, or a son of, Apollo, himself associated with healing. It was from Apollo that Asclepius inherited the skill to make miraculous cures, including the gift of restoring life. This aspect of his work naturally antagonized Hades, who saw his underworld being depopulated by the success of Asclepius' remarkable powers. On hearing Hades' complaints, Zeus struck Asclepius down with a thunderbolt (an act which meant deification) but not before the latter had passed the rudiments of his art to his daughters Panacaea and Hygeia, who also became the objects of healing cults. The Asclepion, six kilometres south-west of Kos, became (along with Epidaurus in the Argolid) the chief centre of the healing cult – a sort of ancient Lourdes where cures were sought for almost every illness and affliction that the flesh is heir to: paralysis, barrenness, pockmarks, gallstones, lameness, blindness, baldness (though Asclepius is always depicted with a hairless pate), dropsy, ulcers, gout, worms, migraine, lice, tumours, arthritis, gangrene and many more besides.

> And all who came Asclepius cured:
> Those whom some taint of nature had laid low,
> And those whose limbs were wounded by the blow
> of far-flung stone or bronzen-gleaming sword,
> Whom summer suns too fiercely smite
> And whom the freezing winters bite;
>
> Relieving each peculiar pain,
> And cleansing all from scar and blane.
> And one he healed with spells benign,
> And one with soothing anodyne.
> With simples too their flesh he bound,
> Or with the keen-edged knife restored the festering wound.
>
> Pindar, *The Third Pythian Ode*, (trans. C. J. Billson)

199

The strongly fortified entrance to the Castle of the Knights of St John at Lindos

Mosques and Turkish fountains greatly add the Oriental atmosphere the old town of Rhodes

Lunchtime at an island
taverna

Heavily-laden sponge
boats are still common
sights in the Dodecanese

The long period of Turkish rule is readily apparent in Kos

Twilight at Ayia Galini on Crete's spectacular southern coast

Initially excavated by R. Herzog in 1902 and further investigated by the Italians, the Asclepion (built on the site of a sacred wood of Apollo, in the vicinity of springs with iron properties) is a large sanctuary that occupies its sloping ground in a series of three terraces. The oldest of these, the middle one, dates between 350 and 270 BC and formed the religious-cult centre of the complex. Here is the site of the sacred altar and also the remains of an Ionic temple in which the treasures were kept. The lower terrace saw the addition of large stoas to accommodate the treatment rooms and living-quarters or wards. Sections of the colonnades that once surrounded it on three sides remain standing, though the Italians had no time to restore them completely. The upper terrace, close to the old sacred wood, had a Doric temple dedicated to Asclepius, and it too was surrounded by porticos on three sides. The ruins provide a fine vantage point over northern Kos, the straits of Halicarnassos and the shores of Asia. The whole Asclepion complex is an attractively landscaped site planted with cypresses and flowering shrubs.

The Asclepian cult relied largely on supernatural assistance for healing, and its priests would obviously have felt threatened by the rigorous scientific methods of Hippocrates, who separated medicine from superstition and made sound observations as to the causes of disease and death. That the Asclepion, as it remains today, was built after his death, indicates the strength of the old beliefs and their continuing reliance on ritualistic bathing, potions, spells and the efficacy (or otherwise) of sacred snakes etc. Whether Hippocrates challenged the 'priests of cures' on the actual site of the Asclepion is not known, but the father of medicine had many followers, and the wealth of medical treatise ascribed to him is indicative of his power to sweep away such legends as that man's fate was in the hands of the Olympian, and other, gods. He had closely observed and experimented on the workings of the human body, for he believed that detailed examination was the key to determining a patient's health. 'The examination of the body', he wrote, 'is a serious business, requiring good taste, good hearing, and a sense of smell and touch . . . and the power of reasoning.'

To Hippocrates the human body was a rational organism that obeyed rational laws, and his belief in the sanctity of life is fully revealed in his famous Oath, which has to be considered one of the greatest documents of Greek civilization. It records his ethical ideals, which are as pertinent to the medical profession today as they were in classical times:

I swear by Apollo the Healer, by Asclepius, by Health and all the power of healing . . . that I may keep this Oath and Promise to the best of my ability and judgement. To my master in the healing art I shall pay the same respect as to my parents. . . . I shall hand on precepts, lectures and all other learnings to my sons. . . . I shall use my power to help the sick to the best of my ability. . . . I will not give a fatal draught to anyone, even if it is demanded of me. . . . I will give no women the means of procuring an abortion . . . I will be chaste and holy in my life and actions. . . . I will not cut . . . but I will leave all cutting to the practitioners of the craft. . . . I will not indulge in sexual union with the bodies of women or men, whether free or slaves. . . . Whatever I see or hear, either in my profession or in private, I will not divulge. . . . If, therefore, I observe this Oath, may prosperity come to me and may I earn good repute among men through all the ages. If I break this Oath, may I receive the punishment given to all transgressors.

As with the city of Rhodes, the major phases of Koan history can be read in its urban skyline, which provides an intricate chronological and architectural document, best viewed when approaching the town from the sea. On the left of the main harbour is the low, bulky mass of the fortress of the Knights; ahead, behind the plane tree-fringed waterfront, is a medley of minarets, Byzantine domes, ornate Italian buildings and the modern, uninspiring, glass-and-concrete edifices of the large hotels. The fortress consists of an inner enceinte with rounded towers, leaning and showing earthquake cracks, surrounded by outer fortifications. It covers a bigger area than is apparent from its external features, and within it is a large collection of classical, Hellenistic and medieval sculptures. Much of the fortress was, in fact, built with the stones from the ancient and (when the Knights came) largely abandoned city. The landward approach across a narrow stone bridge, spanning a deep ditch, leads to a heavily defended gate, followed by a twisting path to the inner halls and enclosures. It is a quiet place (usually) to contemplate the complex art of medieval defence, though owls and other birds and a variety of lizard nest in its stonework.

The town's tree-lined and floral waterfront carries a large collection of cafés and tavernas which shield their customers under bright awnings. The latter can gaze at the fort, the collection of fishing-boats, yachts and caiques, or across to the shores of Turkey where, no doubt, there are similar clients gazing in the opposite direction at Kos. It is said that when this wind is in the right direction the Turkish call to prayer echoes towards the island's shores. Away from the waterfront the other main centre of Koan life is Plateia Eleftherios, a large tarmac area, colonized by café tables and bounded by the town's museum (Mussolinian in style), a well-kept mosque (Kos still preserves a small Turkish community) and other public buildings.

As throughout the Dodecanese, many of the Italian-built edifices, especially the Venetian-Gothic variety, have the appearance of impermanent stage sets, though such was the spate of building that the Italians also saw fit to hide the town's generator, across the harbour, behind an ornate whitewashed façade. Many of the most attractive residential areas are Italian-inspired, particularly the district served by

kish-style architecture
ue old quarter of Kos
n

Vassileos Georgiou Avenue with its old governor's house, metropolitan church and many large villas set in lush gardens. The large amount of Italian building is the result of the town's last damaging earthquake, for so much of the urban area had to be rebuilt. The humbler residential districts had been totally destroyed and were reconstructed on a regular, functional plan, their solid one-storey homes being further reinforced against earth tremors by strong spanning arches. Uniformity is now greatly relieved by brightly painted doors and shutters, and by the profusion of flowering plants and shrubs. The whole town is, in fact, one great floral display, conveying, as at Rhodes, an extremely attractive garden-city image.

The good roads enable easy exploration of the island's coasts and inland villages. Richly farmed areas, growing citrus fruits, vines, pomegranates, some bananas and all types of vegetables, alternate with rocky, barren, wastelands which, at best, support but the bare essentials for foraging goats. In the countryside the solid, square, flat-roofed dwelling is ubiquitous, and at Pyli and Antimachia they combine to form sizeable villages, the former having a fifteenth-century church with interesting frescos, and the latter a splendid ruined castle which was enlarged by the Knights. The island's other traditional livelihood has come from the sea, but a more recently found source of prosperity is tourism. Kardamena on the south coast is a fast-developing resort of hotels and tavernas, additions that as yet have not swamped its old fishing-village appeal. Its popularity is also based on a large stretch of sandy coastline, and from the village caiques regularly cross to the island of Nisyros. Other good beaches are found at Kamares (also called Ayios Stefanos) and at Kefalos.

Kos airport now receives international charter flights, and there are regular schedules to Athens and Rhodes. Its ferry services are also good and link the island with Piraeus, Rhodes and many Cycladic and Dodecanese islands. In summer a hydrofoil service operates to Rhodes, Patmos and Samos, and there are occasional excursions to Bodrum on the Turkish mainland.

Sponges, Hills and Pilgrims (Kalymnos, Leros and Patmos)
The rugged form of Kalymnos is clearly visible from the north-west coasts of Kos. Irregular in shape, largely mountainous and for the most part barren, much of its male population is still employed in the ancient profession of sponge-diving. Each year in late spring they depart to rummage the Mediterranean's sea bottom, much of this dangerous activity now taking place off the North African coast. The sponge fleet is absent for up to six months, and the last night before sailing is traditionally known as '*Ipnos tis Agapis*', 'the sleep of love'. The fleet's return, loaded with sponges, is a time of great celebration, though for some families it is a time of grief. The island's large number of women in black and the many males of all ages with missing limbs are a pertinent reminder of the spate of human injury and fatality.

The large port-town of Pothnia, Kalymnos

A sponge-fishing school is located in Pothnia, otherwise known as Kalymnos, the island capital. The school is often attended by the American sponge-divers of Tampa, Florida, many of whom are of Kalymnian descent. Emigration, on account of the island's meagre resources, has long been an economic safety-valve, and it is said that some 15,000 Kalymnians live in North America and an equal number in Australia. Many return on their retirement, and this accounts for the surprising number of islanders who speak English with a variety of accents.

A bustling port and commercial centre of some importance, Pothnia (10,000 inhabitants) is also a most picturesque town of brightly painted buildings set amphitheatrically within a mountainous backdrop. Its chief interest lies in its work-aday atmosphere and exuberant nightlife focussed on its waterfront cafés and tavernas. As might be expected, the town has numerous shops selling sponges of all shapes, sizes and colours. Most of the industrial varieties are exported. Excursions into the island's rugged interior are recommended, for there are many small, friendly villages and interesting excavated sites of Mycenaean and earlier times. The western shores of the island have attractive bays and good natural beaches, particularly at Myrties, Linaria and Platy Yalos.

The north-western peninsular extension of Kalymnos points to the southern shores of Leros, a few kilometres away. A hilly island, rising to 327 metres, its coasts are deeply indented by usually placid bays that have the impression of being land-

sponge-drying
ess

locked. Boats arrive at the little port of Lakki in the island's south-west from where a road leads to Ayia Marina, the main settlement, dominated by a Byzantine castle that was restored by the Knights and which is now used by the Greek military intent on surveying the Turkish coast. Beyond Ayia Marina the road continues to the village of Partheni, beautifully situated in the north-west of the island. In terms of entertainment and night-life, Leros is unsophisticated, but in this lies its great charm. Should visitors to this part of the Dodecanese require even more seclusion, Lipsos (north-west of Leros and east of Patmos) offers this and little else in great measure.

Once the haunt of pilgrims only, Patmos is currently becoming a busy tourist island and, as a result, its atmosphere has greatly changed, although it still retains a remarkable sense of piety. It was here in AD 95 that St John the Evangelist, banished from Ephesus by the Emperor Domitian, withdrew to the cave where, inspired by God – the Almighty's voice causing a triple rift in the cave's roof – he wrote his *Revelation* (the *Apocalypse*). The entrance to the holy grotto is marked by an impressively simple seventeenth-century church dwarfed, as indeed is the entire town of Patmos, by the great fortress-monastery up-slope, the latter's treasures (for it has never been pillaged) making it one of the richest ecclesiastical buildings in the Orthodox world.

This monastery, which carries the title of St John the Theologian, is the result of an eleventh-century hermit's powers of prophecy. When the blessed Christodoulos accurately foretold the ascent of Alexis Komnenos to the Byzantine throne, that emperor awarded him the island and the means to build a monastery, its construction beginning in 1088. The church contains many old frescos, valuable icons and the embalmed remains of Christodoulos, serenely at rest (despite the prying eyes of the devout) in a splendid silver shrine. Further icons grace the Treasury, which also houses the richest of Byzantine and Russian imperial gifts. In addition the monastery has a renowned library with a priceless collection of thousands of old manuscripts and illuminated gospels.

The ships arriving at Patmos dock at Skala. Here are most of the island's cafés and tavernas and, as if to prove its solid present-day image, it has one of the world's largest desalination plants, a necessity on this largely waterless island. Patmos town (Chora), reached either by road or by mule track, is a picturesque collection of whitewashed houses, churches and chapels. On the Thursday of Holy Week each year, an impressive religious pageant of the Last Supper is enacted. The leading role is taken by the abbot who, impersonating Jesus, washes the feet of twelve monks playing the part of the Disciples. For an authentic experience of Patmos there are several smaller monasteries on the island that offer accommodation to visitors. The expected payment is a donation to the Church funds.

arly 17th-century
of Saint George
rch of St George
rthiana, Patmos)

─── 10 ───

And So To Crete

Whole books have been devoted to Crete, and the greatest injustice that can be done to this island is to attempt to portray it within the space of a single chapter. Largest of the Greek islands and the fifth in size in the Mediterranean (after Cyprus, Sicily, Sardinia and Corsica), Crete is a world in itself, a place of unique fascination, differing in important aspects of history, character and culture from the rest of the Aegean islands. In view of its distinctiveness and complexities, one is reminded of the dilemma Shakespeare faced when writing *King Henry V* – the practical difficulties of conveying to his audience, within the restricted limits of the Elizabethan stage, the detail and scale of the battle scenes between England and France:

> Can this cockpit hold
> The vasty fields of France? or may we cram
> Within this wooden O the very casques
> That did affright the air at Agincourt?

Just as Shakespeare was forced to leave much of the drama unseen, so this chapter leaves much of it unwritten, commenting only on certain facets of an island that demands many visits and lengthy explorations off the tourist tracks if it is to be fully experienced and the authentic character of its people appreciated. As Homer wrote: 'In the middle of the wine-dark sea lies Crete. . . . There Greeks survive, there the great-minded Eteocretans live, there the Dorensians never out of war, the Cydons there, and there the singular Pelasgian people' (*Odyssey*, XIX,172).

'Singular' is an apt description of the Cretan character, which is the complex product of the island's troubled history, not least the 464 years under Venetian rule, which was anything but luxurious, and the ensuing centuries of Turkish domination marked by no fewer than ten major revolts. There is an intensity, even ferocity, about the Cretan character which, merged with friendliness and hospitability, has as lasting an impression on the visitor as the island's wild mountain

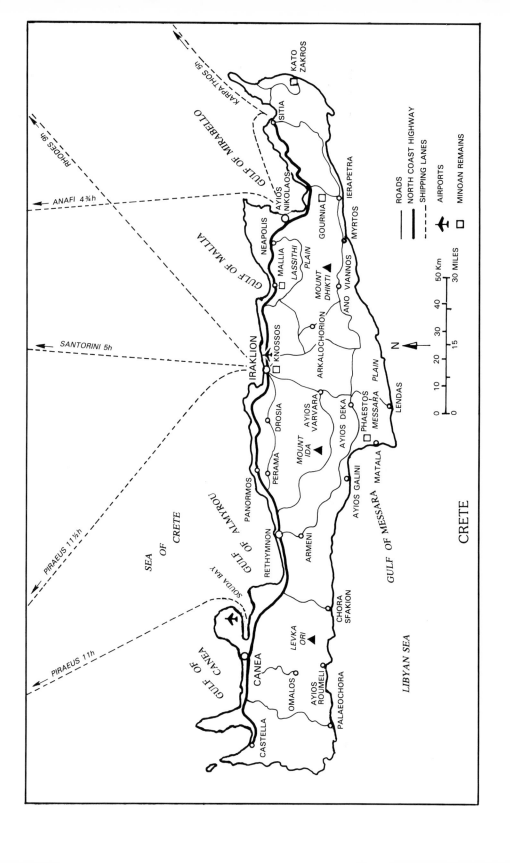

CRETE

scenery, rugged coasts and, away from the tourist developments, lonely beaches. The proud and fierce independence of the islanders was again demonstrated during World War II, when Crete fought long and bravely against the Germans, its mountains harbouring guerrilla bands and its villages, in consequence, suffering many cruel reprisals.

The island's past troubles are preserved in an extensive litany of folk-songs, and heroic stories of the last war abound to this day. The atmosphere lingers on, for in the mountain villages moustachioed men in their traditional garb of tasseled headdress, embroidered jacket, baggy trousers and sash also sport cartridge belts and have knives tucked into their high black boots. They have all the appearance of latterday partisans in search of some cause to support or some wrong to right. The forces that formed these men become clear from Nikos Kazantzakis' novel *Freedom and Death*, whilst his more popular *Zorba the Greek* authentically portrays the islanders' reckless and rugged individualism. Many contemporary Zorbas stalk the land, a few Madame Hortenses continue to reflect on halcyon days, family feuds are not things of the past, and strangers to remote villages, though courteously recieved, are still viewed with tinges of suspicion.

Proud of their island, the islanders regard themselves as Cretan first, then Greek – and this is a fair argument, for Crete was united with Greece only in 1913, eighty years after the official formation of the Greek state. The elderly will eagerly engage visitors with stories of the part they themselves played in the island's history, and it is this openness together with a large measure of inquisitiveness that forms the basis of the Cretan's proverbial friendliness. Yet it can be of the aggressive, masculine kind, handshakes and backslaps being as much a test of character as forms of greeting and farewell. Away from the towns and tourist centres the island is a chauvinist world where the sexes are sharply segregated. More so than in other island communities the *kafeneion* remains an exclusively male institution, the preserve of serious raki-drinkers, volatile backgammon-players, exuberant political activists and cautious marriage- and dowry-negotiators. It is here that the explosive temper of the Cretan is apt to emerge, one that frequently catches the visitor by surprise.

The ships that ply between Piraeus and Crete are some of the largest and best equipped of Greece's domestic fleet. Names such as *Knossos* and *Minos* immediately convey a sense of the past fused with the practical realities of the present and, in essence, this *is* Crete. Many of the ships leave Piraeus late in the evening to arrive in Iraklion or Canea some eight or nine hours later. The fact that they are sailing to what the Greeks refer to as 'the other continent' accounts for the honour and ceremony which Piraeus awards them. The deep, sonorous blasts of their sirens are respectfully acknowledged by an orchestra of sharper shrills from the lesser ships

A general view of Irakl
the Cretan capital

of the harbour and, as an added gesture, a loudspeaker bids '*kalo taxidi*' ('safe journey') in a variety of European languages. Even the humble deck passenger travelling to Crete feels important and that his destination is rather special.

On a clear night, invariably the case in summer, the great mountainous bastion of Crete, stretching across the southern Aegean for some 250 kilometres, announces itself hours before the big ships dock. *En route* for Iraklion it is the bold mass of Mount Ida or Psiloritis (2,456m) that elevates the island's profile against the star-festooned night sky, whilst approaching Canea the White Mountains (Lefka Ori, 2,452m) gain progressively in height. These mammoth limestone blocks are complemented in the east of the island by Mount Dhikti (2,148m) and the Tryptes range (1,610m). Effectively these divide the island into four rugged mountainous compartments, a pattern that permits a number of transverse routes, but few of them are exploited by modern roads. In the mountains, in fact, minor roads deteriorate into pot-holed tracks, which means that despite the relatively narrow width of the island – fifty kilometres in its centre, but decreasing to thirteen kilometres east of Ayios Nikolaos – journey times between north and south coasts are usually reckoned in terms of many hours.

212

The island's main artery extends along the north coast from Castella in the west to Sitia in the east, via Canea, Rethymnon, Iraklion and Ayios Nikolaos. These centres are the capitals of Crete's four administrative regions, whose boundaries are such that each contains one of the afore-mentioned mountain complexes. Collectively the island comprises an area of 8,259 square kilometres and supports a population of around 500,000, a quarter of whom live in and around Iraklion, which took over from Canea as the capital of Crete in 1971.

Whether by ship or by plane, most visitors enter Crete via Iraklion, which now ranks as Greece's fifth largest city and one that in recent years has grown uncontrollably. Congested, noisy, dusty and, in summer, unbearably hot, it offers first impressions that hardly raise the spirits, and many visitors vow to leave it once homage has been paid to its famous Archaeological Museum with its magnificent Minoan treasures. Approaching it by ship provides a curiously disappointing introduction to the island, for Iraklion seems to turn its back on the Aegean, though its extensive and busy dock area speaks of its function as a collecting centre for Cretan produce and distribution centre for all imported goods. Little can be seen of the city other than some housing, a few robust neo-Byzantine churches and harbour-side buildings. Only the solid structure of the old fort, commanding the entrance to what was once the Venetian harbour, and the partly demolished vaulted arsenals (now used as warehouses) hint at the presence of an historic city, the Candia of the Middle Ages, which held out for decades against the onslaughts of the Turks.

In truth, the city that lies largely hidden has much to offer the visitor, and although large sections of it are dilapidated and others given over to ugly redevelopment, Iraklion has a peculiarly infectious character, one that is unmistakably Cretan in spirit. The visitor has to accept that this pulsating city is a capital in every sense of the word, and while it does its best to accommodate newcomers, it also has a variety of other functions to perform – pandering to the special whims of tourists being low down on Iraklion's list. Total acceptance is the key to a successful stay in Iraklion, and its inhabitants expect visitors to adapt to their lifestyles, to jostle and argue with them by day and to relax with them and share their enjoyment at night. The city has many comfortable hotels and numerous eating-places – the tavernas in the old bazaar quarter being relatively cheap if rather unhygienic looking (Theodosaki Street is also called 'Dirty Alley'). An added advantage for visitors is Iraklion's role as the island's major communication centre – hence it is a good base for touring central Crete.

Unless one is interested in suburbs, the sight of which would make Hippodamus and other ancient Greek town-planners turn in their graves, everything of historical interest is contained within the massive Venetian circuit of walls which enclose the old town's landward sides for a total distance of five kilometres. First erected in the fifteenth century, these ramparts, greatly enlarged and strengthened in the sixteenth and seventeenth centuries, owe much of their layout and design to the skill and vision of Michele Sammichele of Verona, one of the leading European military engineers of the sixtenth century. In places up to twenty-nine metres in thickness and reinforced by the regular emplacement of powerful bastions, these walls were considered the strongest of their day in the Mediterranean world. An added defence was the outer perimeter moat – the *khandaq*, from which Candia derived its name – first dug by the Saracens in the ninth century and subsequently widened and deepened. Despite the momentous Turkish siege and centuries of neglect, the walls are well preserved, though large sections are put to inappropriate uses, as is the moat which in places acts as a rubbish dump and parking lot.

Faced by a heavy migration into the city from the Cretan countryside, the walls and moat have also been colonized by extensive shanty settlements. A walk along these ramparts, therefore, provides not only interesting views of the old city but also graphic pointers to some of the socio-economic problems affecting Iraklion and the island as a whole. Yet certain sections have been tidied up and are popular places for evening strolls, especially the Martinengo bastion which has the austere grave of Katzantzakis. Because of his somewhat unorthodox views and writing, he was denied a place in a Christian cemetery and was buried here without the full rites of the Orthodox Church. But his Cretan pride and staunch independence of spirit still shine through, for the inscription on his grave, taken from one of his novels, states: 'I hope for nothing. I fear nothing. I am free.'

Only three main access roads pierce the fortifications through the old and once heavily defended gates – the Gate of the Pantocrator (better known as Canea Gate), the Gate of Gesu (Jesus) or Kainouryia Gate, and the St George Gate or Porto del Lazzaretto. These funnel traffic into the heart of the city, a busy roundabout known as Nikephoros Phocas Square, named after the Byzantine general (later emperor) who freed Crete from the Arabs. Here a policeman, in summer shielded by a large umbrella, nonchalantly attempts to orchestrate the flow of traffic with theatrical hand movements and a whistle. His post is frequently abandoned to accommodate short breaks at the cafés in adjacent Venizelos Square, one of Iraklion's popular meeting points. It is more commonly known as 'Fountain Square' from the fountain erected in 1628 in honour of Francesco Morosini, the Venetian governor-general at the time and uncle of the famous defender of the city (with the same name) during the Turkish siege. It is decorated with marble lions (which are older) and *bas-reliefs* representing the spirits of the sea. Iraklion has several other Venetian (and Turkish) fountains, including the Bembo in Kornarou Square and the Priuli near the Histori-

cal Museum, but none is as charming as the Morosini.

Lined with shipping offices, banks, travel agencies, consulates and hotels, 25 August Street leads downhill to the port. It also contains a number of interesting historical buildings: the church of St Titos (first bishop of Crete) possesses a reliquary with his skull which was removed to Venice in 1669 and returned in 1965; the city hall is a restored version of the Venetian armoury and backs onto the reconstructed loggia; and the old Venetian basilica of St Mark, once converted into a mosque, now houses a collection of Cretan religious art and also functions as an auditorium. Also in 25 August Street is a small public garden, El Greco Park, containing one of the rarest sights in Greek urban centres –public lavatories.

Iraklion's popular district is situated to the south of Nikephoros Phocas Square. Here streets with lively food markets and artisans' workshops preserve much of the bazaar atmosphere of the Turkish period, and further reminders that the Orient is but little removed, either in time or in geographical distance, is the mingling aromas of ouzo and raki, *souvlakia*, coffee and spices emitted from a plethora of bars, cafés, small shops and tavernas.

Close to this neighbourhood, Ayia Ekaterini Square has an interesting collection of churches, including the city's cathedral, a large nineteenth-century neo-Byzantine edifice famed for its paintings rather than its architecture. Towards the end of the Venetian period, when the Turkish menace threatened, Cathoic rule

became more relaxed and Crete experienced a late renaissance in Byzantine art and letters, many of the venerated icons and frescos of the island's churches belonging to this period. Notable painters included Tzanfournares, Klotsas, Damaskinos and the famous El Greco (Domenico Theotokopoulos) whose major works were accomplished in Venice and Spain. Damaskinos also studied painting in Italy but returned to his native island, where fine examples of his work can be seen in the cathedral. The six icons, dating from about 1580, are considered his masterpieces and were brought to Iraklion from the monastery of Vrondisi on the southern slopes of Mount Ida.

Adjacent to the cathedral is the small church of Ayios Menas, which has fine wood carvings and icons by the Gastrophilakas brothers, who were also participants in the Cretan renaissance. A little to the north-east of the cathedral is the church of St Catherine, which functioned as a major centre of learning during the fifteenth and sixteenth centuries. This was really a monastery school founded by monks from

216

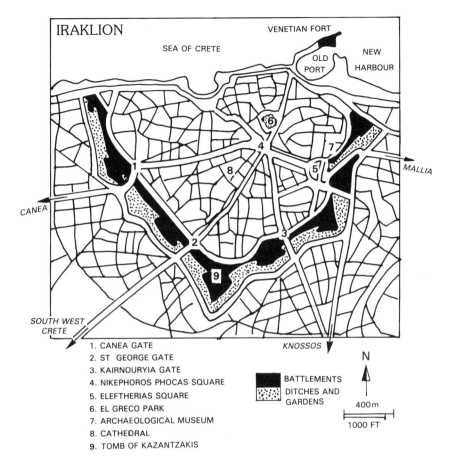

IRAKLION

SEA OF CRETE

VENETIAN FORT

OLD PORT

NEW HARBOUR

MALLIA

CANEA

SOUTH WEST CRETE

KNOSSOS

1. CANEA GATE
2. ST GEORGE GATE
3. KAIRNOURYIA GATE
4. NIKEPHOROS PHOCAS SQUARE
5. ELEFTHERIAS SQUARE
6. EL GRECO PARK
7. ARCHAEOLOGICAL MUSEUM
8. CATHEDRAL
9. TOMB OF KAZANTZAKIS

BATTLEMENTS
DITCHES AND GARDENS

N

400 m
1000 FT

Mount Sinai and was responsible for the training of many theologians, some of whom went on to become patriarchs. The church now houses an icon collection.

Iraklion's night-life is neither varied nor sophisticated. Certainly there are expensive bars and restaurants in the higher-grade hotels, and some have folk-dancing entertainment, but much of the evening's relaxation focuses on the large garden and pavement cafés of Eleftherias (Freedom) Square, located at the eastern end of King Constantine Avenue, which is lined with the city's better shops, cinemas, hotels and uninspiring government buildings. The square, shaded with eucalyptus trees and merging with ornamental gardens, stands above the eastern battlements and is the place to sit and watch the evening *volta*. Here a bust of Katzantzakis awards him more honour than does his grave on the battlements, and the terrace also has a life-size statue of Eleftherias Venizelos.

North of the square is the Archaeological Museum, whose earthquake-proof rooms, erected between 1937 and 1964, contain the largest and finest collection of Cretan antiquities from the earliest period up to Roman times – marvels that make it one of the world's great museums and certainly Iraklion's major tourist attraction. It demands more than one visit, preferably before and after excursions are made to the excavated sites – Knossos, Mallia, Phaestos, Ayia Triada, Gournia and Gortys etc – from which its rich and well-displayed artefacts have been acquired. These include splendid pottery, statuettes of gods, humans and animals, gold and silver jewellery, alabaster vases, jasper and mother-of-pearl goblets, inscribed seal-stones and delicately carved ivories. Then there are the magnificent frescos on the museum's upper floor, composites of pieces of the originals, with the missing detail

A pot decorated with an octopus – a favourite Minoan subject

filled in by imaginative restorers. Of them the most renowned are the bull-leapers and those that have been christened Prince of the Lilies and La Parisienne. Few artists in all the centuries have been able to surpass the Minoans in the naturalistic rendering of their subjects, especially flowers and animals. The same life they infused into their human figures.

Knossos, the largest and most famous of the Minoan palaces, lies five kilometres south-east of Iraklion. The site, an unimpressive mound known as Kefala and shut off from the sea by low hills, was discovered in 1878 by Minos (most appropriate) Kalokairinos. As at Troy and Mycenae, it was belief in the historical basis of Homer that brought the German archaeologist Heinrich Schliemann to the site in the hope of purchasing it from its Turkish owner, but the sum quoted was beyond his means.

It was only in 1899, after Crete became autonomous, that Arthur Evans was able to acquire the site and begin excavation, largely at his own expense.

The results of what proved to be thirty years of work were sensational, bringing Minoan culture out of the mists of legend and extending Crete's historical record back to at least 2000 BC. When Evans died in 1941, at the age of ninety, he had accomplished something no man had achieved before – he had discovered and written a new chapter in the history of the ancient world. Motivated by Schliemann's great discoveries, Evans had initially come to Crete for quite another reason; in the words of his sister Joan: 'in the hope of finding a seal impression and a clay tablet, and Time and Chance had led him to discover a civilization'.

The building complex unearthed by Evans was, in reality, several palaces jumbled together. The site itself had been inhabited at least from neolithic times but the distinctive Minoan culture belonged to the Cretan Copper and Bronze Ages, which are subdivided today into the more descriptive pre-palatial (2600-2000 BC), proto-palatial (2000-1700 BC) and the neo-palatial 1700-1400 BC) periods. Within this long time-span phases of great brilliance alternated with those of stagnation and periods of destruction. The first palace was probably built around 2000 BC and then, following an earthquake, was rebuilt on more luxurious lines after 1700 BC. Thus

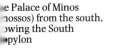

The Palace of Minos (Knossos) from the south, showing the South Propylon

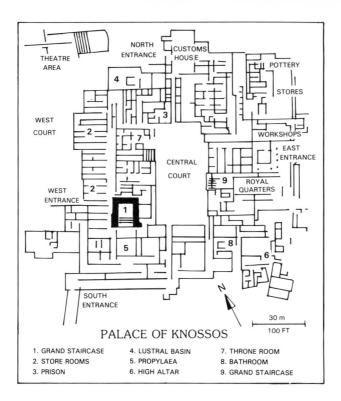

PALACE OF KNOSSOS

1. GRAND STAIRCASE	4. LUSTRAL BASIN	7. THRONE ROOM
2. STORE ROOMS	5. PROPYLAEA	8. BATHROOM
3. PRISON	6. HIGH ALTAR	9. GRAND STAIRCASE

most of the structures on view today belong to the new palace period which flourished until the civilization's decline around 1450-1400 BC (see page 34).

Over 1,300 rooms, arranged in five storeys, made up the palace complex, and rooms seem to have been added to others in a haphazard fashion. At its heart, however, was a great central court around which vast blocks of buildings were grouped. In addition to being the residence of the ruling household and their circle of attendant nobles and functionaries, the palace served as the centre of Minoan religion, for there were numerous shrines, small chapels and lustral baths for purification rites. The great complex also housed large magazines for oil jars, stores for equipment and foodstuffs, the commercial and manufacturing quarters, and their administrative adjuncts. The palace also had a drainage and sanitation system probably superior to any known in Europe until the nineteenth century, and certainly superior to that found in many a modern Greek town. The Queen's quarters had its own bathroom, complete with clay bathtub, and the lavatory at the end of the corridor had flush fittings as well as drains and sewers. An advanced plumbing system with separate lines for drinking, washing and waste water served other sections of the palace. Further examples of the skills of the Minoan builders can be seen in their liberal use throughout the complex of courtyards, breezeways and light-wells for ventilation and illumination. As noted, the Minoans combined their techni-

220

cal accomplishments with superb artistic refinements, and their civilization was one of great elegance, vigour, gaiety and well-being.

In order to present the various building levels and the general complexity of the palace, Evans undertook a considerable amount of reconstruction and restoration work, aided over the years by a qualified staff of archaeologists, architects and artists. Stairways, columns, window casements and walls were rendered in reinforced concrete incorporating, wherever possible, actual remains. Frescos were also copied and put up at the site, adding enormously to the dramatic effect of Knossos. Although these reconstructions make it easier for the ordinary visitor to comprehend the Minoan achievement in architecture, they have also been heavily criticized by those who maintain that Evans was over-imaginative in this aspect of his work. In many ways Knossos does have a theatrical air about it and is somewhat reminiscent of a vast, abandoned film set. For those with further interest in Minoan civilization therefore, it is instructive to visit at least one of the other palace complexes – Mallia, Phaestos or Kato Zakros – which have not been subjected to such treatment. The journey from Iraklion to Phaestos, near the south coast, is one of exceptional scenic and historical interest. Leaving the city by the Canea Gate, the road soon heads southwards, passing first through a well-tended agricultural landscape of tall vineyards and fruit trees surrounding large whitewashed villages which effectively occupy the undulating hillslopes of the Ida massif to the west. This is a long-settled countryside as the numerous ruins of Minoan villas, archaic temples and fortresses testify. After some twenty kilometres the road begins to climb steeply to the straggling village of Ayia Varvara, where a turning to the west leads to Kamares. Here mules and a guide can be hired for the strenuous ascent to the Kamares cave on the middle slopes of Mount Ida. This takes approximately four hours, the summit of Ida demanding another five hours climb and should not be attempted without a guide. Ayia Varvara is a watershed village beyond which the road navigates the impressive Askyphou pass to provide startling views of the vast Messara plain which has its broad exit halfway along Crete's southern coast on what is known as the Libyan Sea. Sandwiched between the inland ranges and the southerly Messara (Asterousia) mountains that parallel the coast, this lowland is watered by the perennial spring-fed Yeropotamos, and from earliest times it has served as the island's market garden, nowadays specializing in early season tomatoes together with bananas and oranges that supply the whole of Greece.

The road decends in hairpin bends to the village of Ayia Deka, named after the ten martyrs tortured and put to death in 260 AD. Close by are the excavated remains of the ancient city of Gortys, one of the most important settlements of Dorian Crete and in Roman times the capital of a province that united the island with Cyrenaica

across the Libyan Sea. The ruins are extensive and include an Odeum built in the second century AD under the Emperor Trajan and the remains of the church of St Titos, a disciple of the Apostle Paul and, as noted, the first bishop of Crete. It was in the Odeum that the inscribed plaques with the Code of Gortys were found, written in the Doric tongue and dating from about 500 BC. The Code dealt with matters of both civil and penal law such as inheritance rules, property rights, divorce and acts of violence and adultery.

From Gortys the road turns west through the Messara plain to Mires (a local centre with a colourful Saturday market), beyond which a minor road leads to Phaestos, whose raised situation provides magnificent views of Mount Ida to the north, the rich Messara plain all around and the Libyan Sea to the west. Though smaller than Knossos, the Phaestos palace appears to have been even more luxurious, its imposing entrance with an enormous monumental flight of steps being particularly impressive. It is traditionally associated with Rhadamanthys, the brother of Minos, but how closely it was linked with Knossos is a subject of dispute. Here again the excavation is mainly the achievement of one man, the Italian Frederic Halbherr, but there is no extensive reconstruction, merely the conservation of what remains. As at Knossos, the royal rooms and other quarters were grouped around a large central court, and the palace also had a series of huge storerooms. Among the finds from the site, now in Iraklion, is a round black disc, stamped in

hieroglyphics, which appears to have been of religious significance.

The Messara region was obviously favoured by the Minoans. Three kilometres from Phaestos, on the other side of the hill, is Ayia Triada, a prince's residence, the home of a wealthy vassal chieftain or, perhaps, a summer palace of the Phaestos kings. In Minoan times the sea came much closer to the villa's grounds, and its plan is in every respect a minor version of the larger palaces. Despite its destruction, it presents an uncommonly elegant appearance, one perfectly adapted to its residential requirements.

The great bay of Messara, enclosed on either side by rocky headlands, is now an important tourist area. From Phaestos the main road continues to the small town of Tymbaki, an authentic but dusty and untidy centre of market gardening. Close to it is Kokkinos Pyrgos, which attempts to combine its agricultural interests with those of tourism. The main holiday growth centre, however, is Ayia Galini (fourteen kilometres west of Tymbaki), which even ten years ago was little more than a fishing hamlet with a few modest *pensions*. Today it is a popular (in summer overcrowded) vacation centre with facilities for bathing, waterskiing and wind-surfing, and a large number of new hotels and a surfeit of tavernas which congest its small waterfront and main street. Ayia Galini has usurped the popularity of Matala on the opposite side of the bay of Messara. This was one of the first south-coast villages to be developed, largely because of its immense sandy beach flanked by

223

high cliffs pitted with caves. These were used for centuries as dwellings and shrines and still provide temporary homes for shoestring travellers, but the large hippy-type colonies that formerly gravitated to Matala are no longer welcomed by the authorities.

The majority of visitors in search of sun and sand frequent Crete's north-east coast which, well served by Iraklion airport, is the island's main package-tour reception area. The coastal highway from Iraklion traverses a heavily populated region where old villages, especially those located near sandy beaches, have witnessed a spate of hotel development. Heronissos, for example, has been transformed into a busy resort while Mallia (thirty-nine kilometres east of Iraklion) has also grown into a popular, if somewhat brash, holiday centre.

Close to such a modern setting, it is inevitable that the Mallia ruins – the remains of Crete's third largest Minoan palace and town – have an incongruous air, yet the fine state of preservation of the complex and its setting against the backdrop of the Dhikti mountains ensure its impressiveness. Associated with Sarpendon, another brother of Minos, the site was first discovered in 1914 and was partially excavated by Hadjidakis. Detailed work was, however, subsequently undertaken by the French School of Archaeology to reveal a palace complex of up to 300 rooms built on two and three levels with an extensive urban adjunct leading down to the sea. Unlike Knossos and Phaestos, the Mallia palace does not occupy an elevated site, though its general plan and the arrangement of its attendant town conform with those of its sister settlements. The finds from the excavations indicate that it was a centre of considerable commercial importance, and here, as at Phaestos, only minor and necessary reconstruction has been attempted, so that the ruins, for the most part, remain exactly as they were found.

Inland from the broad Gulf of Mallia is the upland plateau of Lasithi, bounded by coastal ranges and, further south, by the Dhikti mountains. Many roads and rural tracks lead to it but the most convenient means of access is the surfaced road, signposted Kastellion, which leaves the main highway some three kilometres before Heronissos. The approach is dramatic, for the road cuts through the girdle of mountains suddenly to reveal a vast intermontane plain (average elevation 850 metres) with hundreds of white-sailed wind-pumps drawing water for irrigation. This is made possible by a saturated subsoil fed by water from the encircling mountains. The Lasithi plain is a rich agricultural area. Too high for olives, vines and other Mediterranean crops, it specializes in apples, potatoes and other produce typical of more temperate climes. It is a long-settled region of Crete as its old villages, ancient ruins and Byzantine churches testify.

From Psychro in the Dhikti foothills, a long and arduous climb leads to a cave

complex that competes with a similar one on Mount Ida for the honour of being the birthplace of Zeus. There is evidence of its having been an important cult centre from Minoan to Roman times. The upper cave is easily visited, but the lower complex is subject to winter flooding, and at all seasons a local guide is needed.

A poorly signposted road leads north-eastwards out of the Lasithi plain to the small market town and administrative centre of Neapolis. Those who have continued along the northern highway from Mallia will have reached it via the magnificent gorge scenery of Selenari, one of Crete's many spectacular 'road-scapes'. At its summit a small church contains the icon of St George of Selenari, and all buses plying between Iraklion and eastern Crete make courtesy stops for passengers to pay homage – no doubt to thank the saint for a safe upward journey and to entreat his further protection on the equally vertiginous descent to Neapolis. This inland stretch from Mallia to Neapolis cuts across the prominent headland (ending in the rugged Cape St John) that separates the Gulf of Mallia from the Gulf of Mirabello. On the latter's western shore is the modern village of Elounda (linked by road to Neapolis),which faces the island of Spinalonga. Here in 1579 the Venetians built a large fortress whose impressive ruins stand testimony to the fact that it held off the Turks until 1715. Five kilometres to the west is the site of ancient Dreros, with the remains of walls, an agora and temple of Apollo famous for the discovery of the oldest Greek hammered-bronze statue.

225

Ayios Nikolaos, the capital of the *nomos* of Lasithi and Crete's premier holiday resort, lies fifteen kilometres east of Neapolis (sixty-four from Iraklion) on the south-western shore of the Gulf of Mirabello. Its resident population of around 5,000 inhabitants almost doubles during the summer months, when the attractive whitewashed and pastel-painted town is transformed into a cosmopolitan centre catering for tourists from all parts of Europe and elsewhere. Part of the town surrounds a deep lake – Voulismeni, which links with the picturesque fishing harbour teeming with bars, tavernas and a quota of lively discothèques. Safe sandy beaches lie close at hand and are now overlooked by modern hotels and bungalow complexes. Those fortunate to find accommodation can use the town as a base for exploring the eastern segment of Crete, and archaeology enthusiasts will head for Gournia (19 km), the only completely excavated Minoan town. Its palace occupies a hill overlooking the Gulf of Mirabello, whilst below it the visitor can wander through streets, alleys, houses, storerooms and workshops that make it, for many, the most fascinating of the Minoan sites.

Close to Gournia a road leads south, crossing Crete's narrowest part, to Ierapetra, the most southerly town in Greece and the nearest to the shores of North Africa (370 km). Founded by the Dorians, its position made it a prosperous Hellenistic and Roman centre, and here the Venetians built a fortress whose impressive remains stand on an adjoining promontory. Though having much of the atmosphere of a frontier town, Ierapetra is now a popular winter resort, with new hotels overlooking a fine beach shaded with tamarisks. Its small museum contains interesting local finds, including some from nearby Myrtos where the British School of Archaeology has excavated an early Minoan settlement above which tower the steep slopes of the Dhikti mountains. From Myrtos an interesting route runs via Ano Viannos, Arkalochorion and Knossos to Iraklion, the distance from Ierapetra to the Cretan capital being approximately a hundred kilometres.

East from Ierapetra another coastal road skirts the Tryptes mountains and then heads northwards to Sitia, more easily reached by the coastal highway from Ayios Nikolaos. This small port-town (with boat connections to Piraeus, via Ayios Nikolaos, and Rhodes, via Karpathos) rises amphitheatrically from an attractive harbour to the scant remains of a Venetian fort. La Sitia had originally been planned as another of the north coast's great fortified cities, but such a vision never came off, and the Venetians themselves dismantled much of the fort, carrying off its armaments to Iraklion and the cities of western Crete. The town's greatest claim to fame is as the birthplace of Vicenzo Cornaros, a leading figure of the Cretan renaissance of the seventeenth century and author of the romantic epic *Erotocritos*. Today it is the centre of a sultana-producing region and each August a lively Sultana Festival is held, a colourful event with national costumes and traditional songs and dances.

An efficient round-the-region bus service operates from Sitia. Fourteen kilometres to the east is the isolated and magnificently situated monastery of Toplou, at one time reputed to be the richest in Greece. Its name derives from the Turkish word for 'cannon', the monastery having played an active role in Cretan insurrection and resistance. To its north, almost at the tip of the rugged Cape Sideros, are the Hellenistic and Roman ruins of Itanos, built on the site of an early Minoan settlement. Close to it on the peninsula's eastern coast is Vai with its palm-fringed beaches – Europe's only natural date-palm groves. Further south, near the modern village of Palaeokastro, are the remains of a Minoan settlement set high in olive groves above the sea. But the main Minoan ruins in this part of Crete are at Kato Zakros situated midway along the island's east coast. Remains of a luxurious palace were discovered in 1961, and the entire town seems to have functioned as an important naval base of the Minoan maritime empire. Its finds (for example, bronze ingots from Cyprus and ivory from Syria) indicate that it had far-reaching trade connections with other lands.

With much of Crete's tourism development in the island's eastern half, fewer visitors make for western Crete unless on some organized excursion from Iraklion or the coastal resorts of the north-east coast. As a result the towns and villages

to the west of Iraklion have managed to preserve a greater degree of authenticity, which, together with a plentiful supply of majestic coastal and inland scenery, makes them fascinating places to visit. Whereas the east tends to be dominated by the impressive remains of Minoan and the subsequent archaic civilizations, the west is more fully representative of Crete's Venetian and Turkish periods, with numerous memories of the part the island played in the Cretan–Turkish struggle.

The coastal road from Iraklion to Rethymnon first hugs an irregular shore of wild capes and coves. A few kilometres after Marathos a by-road leads to the small village of Fodele, birthplace of El Greco. Its villagers anticipate the reason for the visitor's detour and helpfully point in the direction of a ruined building believed to have been his family home. This area is laced with a maze of country lanes which serve picturesque valleys overshadowed by the ominous slopes of Mount Ida. Hidden in the pine-clustered landscape is Axos, with its classical ruins, while close to the large village of Perama is Melidoni, famous for its cave where some 370 Cretans lost their lives in 1824 when the Turks choked them to death by filling the cavern with smoke.

Back on the coastal road, Panormos has the ruins of the Venetian fortress of Milopotamo and an impressive fifth-century basilica. Panormos is situated on the eastern edge of the vast bay of Almyrou at the centre of which stands Rethymnon, Crete's third largest town. Seven kilometres from it a side road to the south-east leads to the historic monastery of Arkladi where in 1866, during one of the many Cretan insurrections against the Turks, the abbot blew up one of its wings, killing over 800 assailants and defenders. This fortified monastery has a fine renaissance façade, and close to it is a tourist pavilion which caters for visitors to what is one of Crete's national shrines.

With a long sandy beach and an attractive inner harbour, both of which buzz with café and taverna life, Rethymnon is a pleasant town with a number of Venetian buildings and many wooden Turkish balconies, the latter conveying the impression of picturesque, old-world charm. During the Venetian period it was a flourishing seaport from where the famous sweet Malvasia wines were shipped to Europe. Following its pillage by Turkish corsairs, the Venetians built the huge ramparts and fortress that dominate the town, the latter finally falling to the Turks in 1645. Through the walls encircling a hill that was once occupied by an ancient acropolis, an impressive gateway leads into the fort, from where there are fine views of the town and the bay of Almyrou. In the centre of the largely overgrown plateau contained by the walls is a well-preserved mosque with attendant palm tree – as oriental a scene as the visitor will ever find in Crete. Among the town's other interesting buildings are the Venetian loggia – the old exchange house for merchants and now a museum, the church of San Francesco and the elegant Arimondi fountain built in 1623.

·vesting the Cretan
s

A number of interesting excursions to the south coast are possible from Rethymnon, including a visit to the monastery of St John the Theologian (there are older monastic ruins close by) which overlooks the Libyan Sea. Approached via the magnificent gorge of Kourtaliatiko and the village of Assomati, the monastery played a vital part during the German occupation of Crete, hiding Allied soldiers within its walls until they could be safely smuggled out in submarines. After Preveli the road continues to Plakias, a resort fast in the making, whose sandy beach is one of the finest on the island. From Rethymnon Ayia Galini (see page 223) can also be conveniently reached. Another scenically inspiring journey is that which heads south-eastwards through the Amara valley, a narrow defile sandwiched between the Mount Ida range and Mount Kedros. Beyond the village of Amarion the road hugs the slopes of Ida, passing through Kamares and Zaros to reach the Iraklion–Phaestos road at Ayia Varvara.

West of Rethymnon, the road to Canea (71 km) skirts the rest of Almyrou Bay before crossing the base of the rugged Drapanon peninsula, the southern guardian arm of the extensive natural harbour of Souda Bay. Part of it serves ships on the Piraeus-Canea route, although its fame is that of a naval base that has intermittently functioned as a harbour for NATO fleets. First impressions of Canea, the old Cretan

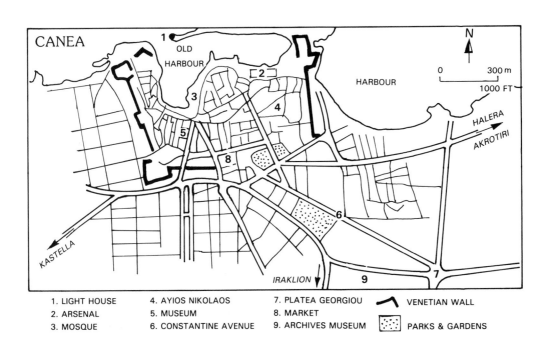

1. LIGHT HOUSE	4. AYIOS NIKOLAOS	7. PLATEA GEORGIOU
2. ARSENAL	5. MUSEUM	8. MARKET
3. MOSQUE	6. CONSTANTINE AVENUE	9. ARCHIVES MUSEUM

VENETIAN WALL

PARKS & GARDENS

capital, are hardly more impressive than those of Iraklion. Its suburbs are remarkably ugly, its modern business centre sports a graceless array of concrete offices
and apartments, and its old town, with its faded mansions, crumbling fortifications
and dilapidated buildings, leaves the visitor questioning as to whether it is in the
process of being built or pulled down. The answer is redevelopment, for the city
was badly damaged during World War II, the target being Souda Bay. Renewal
and conservation are important, for Canea, like Rethymnon, is a city most
reminiscent of Crete's Venetian period, and its old mansions, ramparts and arsenals
are listed buildings, their tardy rehabilitation being a factor of finance rather than
lack of interest. Not having the cleanliness and urban order of Rethymnon, visitors
to Canea should direct their thoughts to what this powerful city must once have
looked like, or will look like when the mammoth task of restoration and improve-
ment is completed.

In detail the old town has many picturesque corners and districts, its warren
of narrow streets and side lanes providing a wealth of harmonious vistas of great
appeal to the photographer and student of townscape. Like other Cretan cities it
has an 'eastern' atmosphere about it, one that is enhanced by a few remaining,
if battered, minarets and many wooden balconies dating from the Turkish occupation. Yet Canea certainly will not appeal to everyone, especially those expecting
a resort town, for it has largely escaped the onslaught of tourism, and its entertainments are modest and few.

The city's most attractive parts lie around its old harbours. The earlier Venetian
port still has the original stone breakwater, and among the interesting buildings
is the sixteenth-century arsenal with its seven vaulted loggias. Close by are sections
of the Venetian walls and the Sabbionara Bastion (built in 1549) together with
the church of Ayios Nikolaos, a former Dominican convent that became a Turkish
mosque. The newer, outer harbour – now also idle due largely to Souda Bay competition – is dominated by a graceful Venetian lighthouse, though its otherwise attractive waterfront of old Venetian mansions is marred by a cement-rendered tourist
office whose curious shape indicates its former function as the Mosque of the Janis-
saries. Busy at all times of the day, this waterfront is most attractive during the evening,
when the entire town seems to promenade its pavements or visits its numerous
cafés and tavernas. This is the place to sample the good local red (kokkino) wine
and Canea cheese, while most of the tavernas offer excellent, if not cheap, fish dishes.

Canea has a small archaeological museum housed in what was once the Latin
church of St Francis. It contains finds from the various sites in western Crete, but
for those interested in Venetian and Turkish history, the historical museum and
archives have one of the largest collection of manuscripts outside Athens. The huge

cruciform-shaped market might be said to mark the centre of Canea. From here Constantine Avenue leads to Platea Georgiou where the Government House is situated, a memorial to the time when autonomous Crete (1898-1913) had Prince George of Greece as its High Commissioner. Beyond is Halepa, a pleasant suburb of large nineteenth-century residences and fashionable apartments which includes the former house of Venizelos. From Halepa a road leads to Akrotiri, a limestone peninsula that protects Souda Bay. Here on the hill of Profitis Ilias are the tombs of Venizelos and his son. Impressive views are afforded of the bay itself, Canea and, to the south, the Lefka Ori.

One of the great attractions of western Crete, which brings many Greek and foreign visitors to Canea, is the Samaria Gorge, the longest (18 km) and deepest ravine in Europe – its vertical walls rise to a height of over 300 metres and, at places, are only a few metres apart. Walking its entire course is an expedition that requires some seven to eight hours, though mules and guides can be hired at Ayia Roumeli at its southern, seaward end, or at the village of Omalos (1,050m) on the high plateau, where the small stream, aided by run-off, begins its incision through the limestone strata of Lefka Ori. Omalos is connected with Canea (39 km) by road, but Ayia Roumeli is entirely cut off from the rest of western Crete by the towering slopes of Lefka Ori whose highest peak, Mount Pachnes (2,453m), dominates the village. Boats link Ayia Roumeli with Chora Sfakion to the east where buses return the intrepid to Canea (or Rethymnon). It is, of course, possible to accomplish the Samaria excursion in the opposite direction, but this involves some strenuous uphill hiking along the last half of the trail.

Despite the large number of visitors who traverse the gorge every year, Samaria has managed to retain its spectacular natural beauty and is home to many species of wild flowers and shrubs that cling to its sheer rock walls. Some might be lucky enough to glimpse the nimble agrimi – the Cretan wild mountain goat, Samaria being one of its few remaining natural habitats. The gorge is closed to visitors from October to May, when the stream is in spate and re-continues its centuries-old task of erosion. The Canea Forest Service, entrusted with the preservation of this natural wonder, forbids smoking, hunting, cutting and uprooting of plants, camping and singing!

This south-western coast of Crete is the most isolated and unspoilt of the island. In history the region was famous for the fighting qualities of its inhabitants, who maintained their independence throughout the Turkish period, and it also acted as a strong centre of resistance against the German occupation. As well as Chora Sfakion and Ayia Roumeli, there are other coastal-mountain villages – Frango-castello, Loutro, Palaeochora and Sougia – where vast sandy beaches and intimate coves provide the ultimate in escapist environments. For the most part the available accommodation is spartan, for this is Crete at its most traditional and primitive level, and also at its most mysterious. The locals graphically relate the tale of the 650 Cretans who were massacred by the Turks at Frangocastello in 1828 and, according to what is regarded as one of Greece's most persistent ghost stories, the Cretan dead rise up on 17 May, the anniversary of the slaughter, and silently march into the sea. Many villagers are convinced they have witnessed such a sight.

— 11 —

Corfu and the Ionian Islands

The Ionian islands take their name from the sea in which they are situated – that section of the eastern Mediterranean basin lying south of the Strait of Otranto and bounded by the foot of Italy and the Greek mainland. Strung along the western littoral of Greece, these islands have traditionally acted as cultural intermediaries between the Italian peninsula and the Greek world in general, sharing in the civilizations of both regions and providing a bridge over which armies and ideas have moved. This factor of geography has given them their peculiar 'Ionian stamp', and many have regarded them as western ante-rooms to Greece proper, providing fascinating introductions to the country's landscape and way of life, although possessing atmospheres which ardent Philhellenes regard as an amalgam of western European and Levantine characteristics.

In the physical sense, especially to visitors approaching Greece from the Italian ports of Venice, Ancona and Brindisi, the Ionian islands convey a delusive impression of the country's fertility, for they receive some of the highest rainfall totals of all Greek lands, and consequently, even in summer, their vegetation cover is luxuriant. On the human level, however, critics of the non-Hellenic character of this Ionian world have really failed to understand the islands for, in spite of their remnants and undertones of foreign influence, they are, and always have been, undeniably Greek.

In the course of a long and colourful history the Ionian Islands have had many masters and witnessed wars, revolutions, sieges and naval battles, treacheries and power politics, yet out of this complicated background they have succeeded in establishing their own identity, not only as a group but also individually. The Greek language has remained the common tongue throughout the centuries, and the

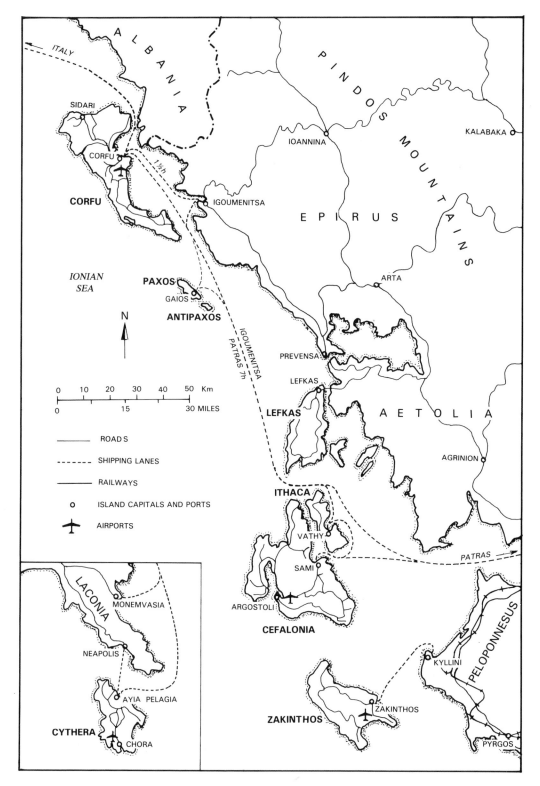

THE IONIAN ISLANDS

Orthodox church, the other great cultural bastion of Greek life, has provided further continuity.

In the conventional use of the term, the Ionian islands include the larger entities of Corfu, Paxos, Lefkas, Ithaca, Cefalonia (Kefallinia), Zakinthos (Zante) and Cythera (Kithira), and are also known as the Heptanesus – the 'Seven Islands'. Cythera, although belonging historically to the group, is situated in a southerly position off the eastern peninsula of the Peloponnesus and has consequently shared the fate and fortune of this part of Greece. In addition to the seven main islands there are numerous smaller territories, some attractive and fertile like Antipaxos, others no more than uninhabited rocks. The entire archipelago forms one of Greece's nine administrative provinces with its capital at Corfu; it is further divided into departments based on Lefkas, Cefalonia, Zakinthos and Corfu. Interestingly, the title 'Ionian Islands' is a conception of nineteenth-century politics and was first used in 1800 by the Russian Admiral Ousakov in a proclamation to the inhabitants of what the Venetians had called the 'Isole di Levante'.

Corfu – the 'cultivated' island

Of the Ionian islands Corfu is not only the most famous but also the most visited. In addition to its Olympic Airways domestic service, international scheduled and

Vlachernai Monastery
Mouse Island viewed
Kanoni – Corfu's
ous beauty spot

charter flights serve the island, whilst its port has up to eight ferry crossings a day to Igoumenitsa on the Epirus coast, the journey taking about two hours. This mainland port has bus links with Athens (nine or ten hours distant) via Ioannina, Arta, the Rion-Antirion ferry and Corinth. Corfu is also served by ferries from Patras and a daily link with Brindisi in southern Italy. Ships from other Adriatic ports call at Corfu *en route* to Piraeus, and its harbour is also used by cruise liners.

Corfu's history – largely that of the Ionian islands as a whole – vividly illustrates the conditioning influence of its geographical position at the entrance to the Adriatic Sea. It is the nearest Greek territory to Italy (74 km away), whilst its northern cape, Varvara, is less than three kilometres from the south coast of Albania, from which it is separated by the Corfu Channel.

The island has been the battleground of contending cultures and of conflicting political and commercial interests, for strategists and statesmen of both East and West regarded it as a possession of great value. In antiquity Corinthians, Athenians, Spartans, Syracusans, Illyrians and Romans represented some of the rival powers bent on securing the island, and throughout the medieval centuries it was the political pawn in the ideological game between western Europe and the Byzantine Empire. Corfu's significance as a naval and commercial base was emphasized by its subsequent control by Venice, a domination which lasted from 1387 to 1797. Consequently, the island and its Ionian neighbours were saved from the fate of mainland Greece and the Aegean by remaining free of Ottoman rule.

The waves of the invading Turks lapped around Corfu and on two occasions tried to engulf it, but the island resisted and formed a boundary stone in the history of the Ottoman conquest. Writing in 1596, Fynes Morison regarded it as 'one of the Chief Keys of Christendom', occupying a similar role to Rhodes in the east, held, as noted, by the Knights of St John. Hence, when other Greek lands were subject to the regime of the Ottomans, Corfu grew rich as a centre of east-west trade, protected by the banner of St Mark, militant symbol of the Christian West. It helped to guard the vital trade routes to Crete and Cyprus, and it further enabled the Venetians to control the entire Adriatic. A text to the Senate (17 March 1550) called Corfu 'the heart of the Venetian state', and large sums of money were invested in its defences.

With the declining political and commercial prestige of the Venetian Republic, the strategic value of Corfu and the Ionian islands assumed increasing importance. By the end of the eighteenth century France, the Ottoman Empire, Russia and Britain all cast envious eyes on the islands, Bonaparte seeing them as springboards to the East, and Britain regarding their possession as a major factor in the 'Eastern Question'. The islands were occupied by the French on two occasions, their political

presence being separated by a brief period when Corfu became the capital of the
Septinsular Republic, the first independent Greek state of modern times. Britain succeeded in dislodging the French from their Ionian possessions in 1814, and a year
later established a British protectorate under the title of the United States of the
Ionian Islands, a political entity that lasted until 1864.

Under British rule the Ionian islands prospered materially, socially and economically, yet the period represents a curious episode in their history – often amusing,
often bizarre – when the standards and attitudes of Georgian and Victorian Britain
were applied to – or, more appropriately, forced on – an insular Mediterranean community. Many British expatriates found difficulty in adjusting to what appeared to
them as extremely foreign conditions, and this led to the emergence of a small and
closed 'ruling' society which mixed very little with the islanders. Edward Lear, the
father of English nonsense rhymes, found Corfu a 'very very very small tittle tattle
place', and the British habits and way of life on the island 'monotonous'. Along
with the adminstrative officials, clergymen, army and naval officers came
gentlemen, governesses and nannies. The ladies set a pattern of social etiquette

and decorum, and the nannies and governesses demonstrated the principles of strict upbringing for children. Paper-chases on horseback became popular, much to the chagrin of the local native farmers across whose fields these 'wild romps' were organized, and various clubs, a racecourse and, above all, promenading provided other sporting and leisurely activities.

Little of this British 'culture' permeated the rural classes, but in the town the islanders learned to drink tea and ginger-beer, to eat beefsteak, plum cake and apple chutney, and to play cricket. At which stage of the protectorate the game became popular cannot be determined, but it has remained on Corfu as a vital sporting interest. Many terms related to cricket (though twisted out of phonological recognition) have slipped into the Corfiote Greek language, and many of the islanders speak excellent English, as well as Italian. A further measure of the British impact is the fact that it is only relatively recently that the island has adopted the metric system.

Under the British the Ionian islands were governed from Corfu by a succession of Lord High Commissioners, all of them colourful figures, a number autocratic – not least Sir Thomas Maitland – and a few more than a little eccentric, Sir Frederick Adam falling into the last category.

The former High Commissioner's Palace, and subsequently that of the Greek royal family (before their move to Mon Repos to the south of Corfu town), is the most impressive monument to British rule in Corfu. It stands on the northern side of the Esplanade, the Venetian Spianda which was the old parade-ground separating the Old Fort from the town proper. This large Regency, neo-classical building is constructed of white Maltese stone and has an elegant Doric portico which projects on either side to form a curving screen pierced with triumphal arches and terminating in balanced pavilions. Dedicated to St Michael and St George, and built between 1818 and 1823, the palace is the oldest official building in Greece and, as many would argue, the finest non-ecclesiastical building to be erected since antiquity. During the protectorate it was the scene of British colonial pomp and ceremony, for it also acted as the headquarters of the Order of SS Michael and George, instituted by the Prince Regent in 1818 to reward services in Malta and the Ionian islands. In 1954 a private trust was established for its renovation by Sir Charles Peake (then British Ambassador in Athens), for during the Greek Civil War it had housed a constant stream of refugees. The state rooms have been restored to their original splendour and now house archaeological items and *objects d'art* bequeathed by private donors.

Unlike most Greek towns, Corfu was unaffected by the destruction resulting from the War of Independence. Considerable architectural damage was, however,

The impressive Bull Portico of the Palace of Minos, Knossos

The attractive wooded coast near Benitses, Corfu

incurred during World War II, when the Italian-German conflict was compounded
by Anglo-American bombardments. Yet the town contains buildings relating to each
major phase of its history, up to and including the mushrooming growth of modern
suburbs and tourist complexes. 'This town', according to J. Forte, 'is Venice, Naples,
a snatch of France and a dash of England, mellowed and mulled, like all good wines,
until it achieves its own unique and in this case fascinating bouquet.' It is this strange
rapprochement of different architectural styles and urban atmospheres that makes
the Corfiote townscape unique.

Early maps and sketches depict the town as contained within the walls of the
old citadel which lies to the east of the Esplanade and is separated from it by a
moat. Its massive fortifications enclose a rocky promontory which now forms a picturesque amalgam of masonry, buildings and trees. Pietro Casola's description of
it is as apt now as it was in 1494: 'All the town is built on a rock. . . . The houses
are numerous and so crammed that their roofs touch one another and the sun is
not bothersome.' Unfortunately for the visitor, access to the old citadel is restricted,
yet the character of this Venetian fortified town can be appreciated from the
Esplanade. By the sixteenth century population expansion necessitated the relaxa-

241

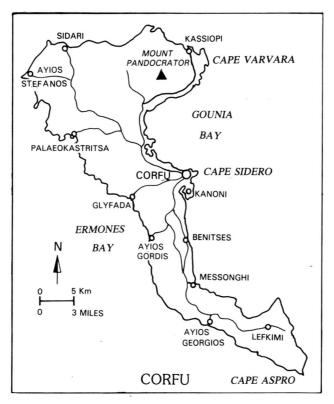

SIDARI
KASSIOPI
MOUNT PANDOCRATOR
CAPE VARVARA
AYIOS STEFANOS
GOUNIA BAY
PALAEOKASTRITSA
CORFU
CAPE SIDERO
KANONI
GLYFADA
ERMONES BAY
N
AYIOS GORDIS
BENITSES
0   5 Km
0   3 MILES
MESSONGHI
AYIOS GEORGIOS
LEFKIMI
CORFU
CAPE ASPRO

tion of this strict defence consideration, and a small undefended settlement developed outside the fortress gates but beyond the open space, originally termed El Bazaro, which formed the drill-ground.

Disaster awaited the unfortified town in the form of the Turkish siege of 1537, and this awakened Venice to the need for new defences. Within a few decades a massive bastioned wall and a new fortress, now dominating the modern port, were constructed, a military work that provided not only security but room for urban expansion. Building restrictions, however, produced a town that was compacted, with high, narrow buildings separated by alleys – a townscape that survives today.

Defence considerations were particularly important in dictating the form of the town in the area of the Esplanade, where narrow streets leading off at right angles allowed cannon-fire from the old citadel to penetrate the heart of the town – a major advantage if the latter was taken by invaders. But the regularity of this part of Corfu was also related to social factors, the frontage area of residences having no more than two windows, a restriction, it is reported, that was devised to reduce the number of 'privileged ones'. Such a residential pattern was partly obscured by the French, whose major architectural achievement is the celebrated arcaded buildings bordering the northern part of the Esplanade. The two handsome rows of houses became known as 'the Liston', from the 'list' of families entitled to walk and sit under its arcades. The style resembles that of the Rue de Rivoli in Paris and must have provided a nostalgic reminder of the delights of the French capital. The horse-drawn landaus, used throughout the town, add further to Corfu's partly Europeanized atmosphere. Today the Liston, with its cafés, is the social centre of Corfiote life, and the tables that extend to the edge of the Esplanade are especially crowded when a spring or summer cricket match is in progress.

Corfu's oldest and most picturesque quarter is the Campiello district, a maze of tall buildings, stepped streets (*skalinades*) and twisting alleys (*kantounia*) located between the old port, N. Theotoki Street and the Old Palace. During the nineteenth century it was cramped and insanitary, though the British introduced a series of regulations to improve and clean up the district. Few homes in the Campiello possessed sanitary conveniences; hence those in other parts of the town with WCs and adequate water supplies earned the title 'English fashion' and were much sought after. If still lacking in certain basic amenities, the Campiello district today is a clean and interesting quarter through which to wander and witness the form of an old Italianate townscape. Its tall tenement buildings (often six to eight storeys) are separated by narrow lanes and alleys that are hives of local life. Fortunately vehicles are unable to penetrate much of the district, where washing hangs on poles and lines over the streets in Neapolitan tradition.

In addition to its fortifications, a number of other Venetian monuments survive, including the elegantly decorated well of Kremasti (built in 1699) hidden among the alleys of Campiello. But by far the most impressively ornate Venetian building is the present town hall, originally built in the sixteenth century as a loggia. In 1720 it was converted into a theatre, and it continued as a centre of art and drama until the early years of this century. Following war damage it was reconstructed on a slightly different plan, when an upper floor was added giving the building its present appearance. The bust and relief on the external eastern wall commemorates Francesco Morosini and his successful battles against the Turks. Another worthy reconstruction of a Venetian building is the Cavalieri Hotel at the southern end of the Esplanade. Formerly a dilapidated town house, it has since been renovated to form a tastefully designed building preserving much of its original structure and character. Throughout the old town there are many Venetian porticoed residences, whilst arches and colonnades run down many of the principal streets, above which peeling colour-washed buildings have seasoned wooden shutters and decorative plaster features. The traditional roofing material of the old town is red tile.

The influence of Italy is most marked in church architecture, which on Corfu

The Well of Kremasti in
Corfu's Campiello district

and the other islands has been termed 'Ionian Baroque' – much of it dating from
the seventeenth and eighteenth centuries. The town's most celebrated church is
that of St Spiridon, which houses the mummified remains of the island's patron
saint. Building began on the site of an earlier foundation, and although the exterior
appears dull and uninteresting (except for its towering *campanile*), this is compensated for by the splendour (perhaps a little overdone) of its interior. Its chief features
include an impressive stone screen, a gilt-scrolled and painted panelled ceiling and
the body – rather grotesque – of the wonder-working saint, whose withered feet,
clad in embroidered slippers, protrude from vents at the bottom of the glass-topped
sarcophagus. The adjacent screen is littered with a profusion of lamps and votive
offerings which the faithful have placed either in thanks or to prompt his
intercessions.

It has been said that in St Spiridon the Corfiotes have a non-appointed director
of all their affairs, for by his miraculous intervention he is believed to have saved
the town once from famine, twice from major epidemics of the plague, and was
also instrumental in the defeat of the besieging Turks. Significantly, as far as the
islanders are concerned, in 1944, when Germans and Italians fought for the possession of Corfu, though widespread shell-damage resulted, the church and those who
sheltered in it remained unharmed. For the sceptic, there is a booklet on sale that
lists more minor miracles – a policeman cured of epilepsy, the evil eye averted, an

old man cured of the 'distressing' gift of tongues, and there is further record of his dealings against croup, diphtheria and lice!

In Greece there seems to be no peace for the saintly, for four times a year the body of St Spiridon is paraded through the streets of Corfu, the processions preceded by bands and followed by town and church officials, contingents of the armed services, boy scouts and girl guides and schoolchildren in their Sunday best. His palanquin is borne under an old canopy of crimson and gold, supported by silver poles and accompanied by priests – there is a touch of the macabre, for the conveyance is a type of sedan chair. The St Spiridon feasts (*panagiria*) are some of the most impressive and animated in the Greek islands.

Of the many visitors to Corfu, few actually stay in the island's capital, contenting themselves with excursions to visit its gift-shops and places of interest. They miss a great experience, yet they can be forgiven, for the Corfiote countryside and coastal locations offer as many delights, and it would be equally unthinkable if the vacationary resident of the capital failed to visit some of the scenic and historic interests offered by the roads that fan in all directions from the town.

The Corfiote landscape is green and lush, and first impressions convey delusions of a countryside abandoned to its natural state. Large areas are, in fact, overgrown with semi-natural woodlands and areas of scrub festooned (especially in spring) with flowers and aromatic herbs, but this deceptively shields from view the small pockets of cultivated land, the terraces of grapes and vegetables and the groves of twisted olive trees. Closer inspection will reveal the olive as being, in the words of Laurence Durrell, 'dominant in a landscape of richer greens', its green-grey foliage, exploding from gnarled, hollow trunks, often reaching great heights to appear collectively as inpenetrable forests. In fact, most of the trees have been carefully planted in serried ranks to form extensive orchards, a pattern that dates back to antiquity, although the predominance of the tree is a legacy of the Middle Ages when its cultivation was encouraged by the Venetians and land values were, and often still are, computed on the basis of the size of the olive grove.

Immediately south of the town the coastal promenade leads to the suburb of Anemomilos where, overlooking a small bay, though shielded by trees, is the royal palace of Mon Repos. Its grounds contain the remains of Palaeopolis (the ancient Corcyra) which occupied the Kanoni peninsula, today the scene of extensive hotel and villa development. At the peninsula's termination is Corfu's most celebrated beauty spot, though photographs take pains not to feature the steady stream, especially in summer, of approaching and departing aircraft. A magnificent view of the Chalikiopoulos lagoon and the island's south-east coast is afforded from the high vantage point, fully colonized by cafés. In the foreground, and linked to the mainland

A procession in honour
St Spiridon – Corfu's
patron-protector

by a causeway, is a tiny islet which is the site of the Vlachernai monastery, and to its rear (reached by boat) is Pontikonisi (Mouse Island) with its large clump of trees and chapel. This is claimed to be the Phaecean ship used to transport Odysseus back from Scheria to Ithaca, though Poseidon intervened and turned it to stone.

Since antiquity Corfu has been equated with Scheria, the kingdom of Homer's Alcinous and the land of the Phaeceans where Odysseus was romantically entertained by Nausicaa. According to Homer, Alcinous' noble city stood on a headland between two harbours, and a number of island sites, including Kanoni, have contended for the situation of the palace with its 'bronze walls and golden doors hung on posts of silver'. Gradually archaeologists – such as Victor Berard and Dorpfeld – turned their attentions to the island's northern and western coasts, scanning the headlands, creeks and cliffs for physical details that fitted Homer's description of the site and situation of the Phaecean capital. Many believe that Palaeokastritsa, on the north-west coast, twenty-three kilometres from Corfu town, corresponds most closely to Homer's details. Be that as it may, this areas of the island needs no legendary associations to boost its appeal, for the trefoil-shaped harbour, separated by rocky promontories and fringed by sandy bays, is of outstanding beauty. Not surprisingly, it is one of the island's major hotel resorts and forms the western extension of Corfu's rugged northern territory, which reaches its greatest height in Mount Pantocrator, a barren summit to the east (914m high), providing magnificent views over the island and the coastal regions of Albania (2.4km away). Other spectacularly attractive coastal resorts are found in the north, not least Kassiopi, where Nero is said to have fiddled to the dubious delight of his audience.

Between the north-eastern capes of Varvara and Sidero is the wide Gounia Bay, now lined with an endless string of hotels, holiday camps, cafés, souvenir shops and tavernas. Such development is repeated to the south of Corfu town, *en route* to Benitses and beyond. Here villa development is prominent, and Benitses itself now tends to specialize in taverna holidays – noisy, sleepless affairs in view of the nocturnal habits of the Greeks. It is hard to envisage that little over a century ago this coast was selected, on account of its beauty and peacefulness, as the site for the summer retreat of Elizabeth of Austria, the restless wife of Franz Josef. Her Achilleion Palace (now a casino) is situated in the hills – a grandiose, slightly vulgar building which has been described as 'the late nineteenth century's idea of the Italian Renaissance's idea of Greek classicism'. Following her assassination in Geneva in 1898, the Achilleion (so-named from its garden statue of the 'Dying Achilles') was purchased by Kaiser Wilhelm II, who transformed the interior, much of which remains, into a weird and wonderful Teutonic residence, commissioning the sculpture of another Achilles – colossal, prefabricated and warlike – which still carries

CORFU

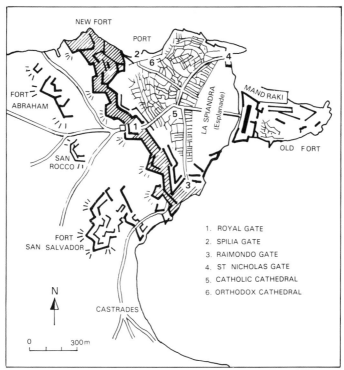

1. ROYAL GATE
2. SPILIA GATE
3. RAIMONDO GATE
4. ST NICHOLAS GATE
5. CATHOLIC CATHEDRAL
6. ORTHODOX CATHEDRAL

THE LATER VENETIAN TOWN AND DEFENCES

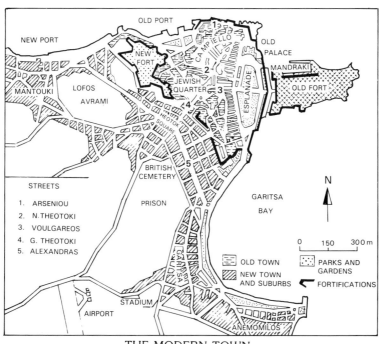

STREETS

1. ARSENIOU
2. N. THEOTOKI
3. VOULGAREOS
4. G. THEOTOKI
5. ALEXANDRAS

OLD TOWN
NEW TOWN AND SUBURBS
PARKS AND GARDENS
FORTIFICATIONS

THE MODERN TOWN

The bays and headlands of Palaeokastritsa on Corfu's north-west coast

the original inscription: 'From the greatest German to the greatest Greek.'

Further resorts are now developing all the way to the southern tip of the island, and on the whole they tend to blend with the landscape of verdant rolling hills and attractive villages, inland and coastal. The best of Corfu's beaches are, however, located along the west coast, where fashionable holiday complexes, such as Glyfada, Ayios Gordis, Ermones and Mirtiotissa, are epitomes of commercialization in idyllic settings – this forming much of the character of contemporary Corfu.

Olive-clad Paxos

Ferries link Paxos, the smallest (18 sq km) of the designated Heptanesus, with Corfu, the journey time to Gaios being some three hours. The route closely skirts Corfu's south-eastern coast and also offers grandstand views of the rugged Epirot ranges. From Parga, the picturesque town midway along the coast of Epirus, a caique service, weather permitting, operates to Gaios, which is also linked to Patras via Cefalonia. Paxos has no airport, for the island's inhabitants number fewer than 2,250 (of whom 750 or so are in Gaios) and, as yet, its level of tourism fails to warrant air links. Consequently, it is less easily reached than the other main Ionian islands, this factor of relative isolation preserving its unspoiled, tranquil atmosphere. Increasingly, however, Paxos is being discovered, to the extent that accommodation during the summer months is often difficult to find. Yet it still remains essentially an escapist's island, for there are no organized entertainments, and visitors who

249

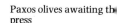
Paxos olives awaiting the press

come expecting little in the way of commercialization will not be disappointed.

What Paxos does offer is natural beauty in the form of fine beaches, spectacular cliffs and sea caves, small villages with modest, yet attractive churches and acres of well-tended olive groves. The island's agriculture is based almost entirely on the latter and, as on Corfu, the gnarled, twisted and immense size of the olive trees are testimony to their great age. Olive-oil presses scatter the island, nets hang under branches to catch the fruit at harvest time, country lanes are olive-blackened, and the smell of Paxos is the smell of olive dross – curiously addictive.

Gaios, the island's main port and miniaturized capital is a one-square town – around which the main cafés and tavernas are grouped – with a busy waterfront protected by the off-shore islet of Ayios Nikolaos and its fourteenth-century-founded fortress. There is another islet beyond – Panagia – that suddenly bursts to life on 15 August, the Feast of the Assumption. When evening comes, small boats transfer the revellers back to Gaios, where the celebrations continue long into the night and are often concluded the following day. Of the town's buildings, the only one that exudes pretension is that of the former British residency, its official functions now devoted to port activities. The bus station at the back of the town marks the termination (or beginning) of the island's main road, a bifurcation in the uncomplicated system linking Gaios with the coastal villages of Lakka and Logos. Paxos is, however, really small enough for the energetic to explore it on foot, and should the weary fail to find a convenient refreshment station, the locals will deem it an honour to proffer some cooling water in exchange for friendly conversation. The island's east offers a landscape of gentle hills and shallow, sandy bays, whereas, and as if to prove that small need not be monotonous, the coasts of the west consist of dramatic cliffs that drop steeply into the indigo-deep Ionian.

Barely inhabited, Antipaxos lies some two kilometres to the south, its handful of energetic farmers being responsible for the production of some most palatable red and white wine. Structurally and landscape-wise, it is a continuation of its northern neighbour, having the same bold contrasts in its eastern and western coasts. The golden sandy beaches that lie to the north and south of Ormos Agrapidias – the small harbour settlement – are among the most beautiful in the Ionian islands. Its southern shores, protected by a lighthouse, are rugged, beyond which are the smaller insular tracts of Bourdoubou and Daskalia. The south-west of Antipaxos has wild cliff scenery, the haunt of numerous species of sea birds.

Lefkas – a mainland appendage

A shallow canal, some twenty-three metres wide, first constructed by Corinthian colonizers and re-cut in 1925, is all that separates Lefkas – the Venetian Santa Maura – from the mainland coast of Acarnania, whose low-lying, lagoonal tracts, sultry in summer and windswept in winter, have an atmosphere all their own. A somewhat primitive-looking chain-driven raft makes the short crossing to what is a disappointingly dilapidated village capital – Lefkas or Lefkada – a sight relieved only by the limestone range that rises beyond, to reach over 1,000 metres in the summits of Elati, Stavrotas and Meganoros. The capital, devastated by earthquake in 1948 (which repeated the destruction of 1867), is an uninspiring advertisement for what is, in general, a most attractive island of pine and scrub-covered hills, cultivated plains, currant vineyards and a number of pretty coastal villages.

Buses from Athens and Patras use the chain ferry, and Lefkas is also linked with Ithaka, Cefalonia and a number of mainland ports, including Patras. A circular road, along which the local buses ply, follows much of the island's coast, linking all the villages, whose handicraft specialities include woven fabrics, lace and delicate embroidery work. The island's south terminates in a bare, rocky headland with sheer cliffs, the highest point (72m) known as Sappho's Leap (see page 152). It was here in ancient times that those wishing to prove their innocence, or be cured of the pangs of lost love, would leap into the Ionian. Many were killed in their attempts, which at least put an end to their feelings of heartbreak!

Elsewhere, small sandy beaches dot the island's coastline, and Nidri is fast developing as a fashionable holiday resort, not least with the yachting fraternity. Across its bay are the wooded islets of Madouri, Sparti, Scorpio and Scorpios, the latter

Women of Lefkas laying the warp

the heavily guarded private preserve of the famous Onassis family. Most of the island's accommodation is in or close to the capital, and an interesting time to visit Lefkas is during its August Prose and Arts Festival, with its concerts, theatrical performances, academic lectures and folk music.

Homeric Ithaca

Ithaca is separated from the much larger Cefalonia by a channel two kilometres wide. Many visitors are drawn to it on account of its Homeric association, for this was the island kingdom (which seems also to have included Cefalonia and Zakinthos) of Odysseus, the 'precipitous isle' of the *Odyssey* which Homer further describes as having 'no meadow lands . . . no broad riding-grounds . . . but an island of goat-pastures . . . rising rock-like from the sea'. The description remains apt, for Ithaca (94 sq km) is an irregular, elongated and rugged island consisting of a northern and a southern part linked by an isthmus only 600 metres wide. It supports little more than some vineyards, olive groves and a few small pockets of cornfields, the most common farming sights being its herds and flocks of goats and sheep.

Little wonder that Odysseus and his compatriots took to their ships as adventurers and were absent from the island for long periods, a tradition that has remained part of Ithacan life. Such were its meagre resources that it remained largely unin-habited after classical times until the Venetians recolonized it in the sixteenth cen-tury with settlers from their other Ionian possessions. By the nineteenth century, many islanders were again setting their sights on far-away lands, Australia and South Africa in particular. As is common throughout Greece and its islands, some of this century's migrants have returned to the island of their birth, and visitors will soon be aware of the curious Greek and colonial-English language mix – often incomprehensible, despite the fact that these friendly expatriates pride themselves on the acquired skills of bilingualism.

A number of weekly ferries from Patras, with connections with Cefalonia, and Corfu, run to Vathy, Ithaca's exceptionally attractive capital. As noted elsewhere, 'Vathy' ('deep') is a common island place-name and, perhaps more than other similarly designated ports, this one fully lives up to its description, for the town is beautifully situated in horseshoe fashion around the shores of a long, mountain-shrouded natural harbour. Its lengthy waterfront is the town's commercial and social centre, where, true to island form, the tavernas and cafés charge inflated prices compared with those in the intimate backstreets. But here, as indeed in water-front settings throughout the Greek islands, many find that the sensually scenic views and atmosphere are fair recompense for the higher tariffs.

It was at Vathy (the ancient Phorcys) that the Phaeceans landed Odysseus from Corfu, and a short but strenuous walk leads to the Cave of the Nymphs, where Odysseus, wily to the end, is said to have hidden his homecoming treasures. At the southern end of the island are other sites with Homeric connections, disappoint-ing in themselves, though providing the reasons for visiting some breathtakingly beautiful inland and coastal scenery. The spring of Perapigadi is identified with Homer's Fountain of Arethusa, where the swine of Eumaios were watered, and the neighbouring cliff is known to the locals as Korax (Raven Rock). At the island's southern tip is the bay of Ayios Andreas, where Odysseus landed on his return from Pylos to escape the ambush laid for him by the suitors of Penelope, his faithful, though at times disenchanted wife.

As on Corfu, scholars from the time of Heinrich Schliemann onwards have sought to discover the island's places described by Homer. The remains of the buildings found by Schliemann on the 669-metre-high hill of Aetos, commanding the island's isthmus, was wrongly identified as the Homeric capital, though locals refer to it as 'the Castle of Odysseus'. It is, in fact, what is left of the post-Mycenaean settlement of Alalkomenai, which dates from *c.*700 BC, its impressive walls offering magnificent views. A better contender for the hero's palace and city are the discoveries made in 1932 by the British School on Pelikata hill near the northern village of Stavros. Mycenaean walls and pottery are of the right date, and the main artefacts from the excavations are in the museums at Vathy and Stavros, the latter building, the villagers are convinced, marking the site of the wanderer's palace. The museum contains an eighth-century BC shard bearing the name Odysseus, and a later Attic *lekythos* (narrow-necked oil flask) depicting the goddess Athena, Odysseus and his son, Telemachus.

But it is in the Ithacan landscape with its rugged hillsides, deserted olive groves, turquoise-coloured seascapes and distant views of the mist-shrouded form of Cefalonia, that the senses and emotions are conditioned into accepting the island as Odysseus' kingdom. From Stavros, well endowed with cafés and tavernas, there are many scenically enjoyable walks and other excursions. The attractive bay of Polis recalls the nearby presence of an ancient city, while to the north and east of Stavros are the beautifully situated coastal villages of Frikes and Kioni. No visitor to Ithaca should miss the Katharon monastery, for the drive up to it, especially from Stavros, is through Ithacan ruggedness at its best, the final reward being magnificent views of the complex sea entrance that ends in Vathy bay.

Fertile Cefalonia

Separated from Ithaca by a narrow channel, Cefalonia (781 sq km) is the largest of the Ionian islands and one that has some of the archipelago's most dramatic scenery. It is an island where fertile plains are abruptly separated by barren mountain ranges (Mount Ainos reaches 1,619 metres), and dark green fir forests merge with the lighter hues of olive groves and vineyards that abut onto sandy beaches interrupted by long stretches of rocky coastline, particularly in the west. The island's irregular shape is the result of three large bays that cut deeply inland, the largest being Linadi in the west where, on a subsidiary inlet, the island capital, Argostoli, stands. But, except for those arriving by air (there are daily connections with Athens), the majority of visitors land at Sami on the east coast, a dusty, utilitarian-built port that partially occupies the site of Cefalonia's ancient capital. The remains of the latter, including sections of cyclopean and polygonal walling, are found on the two hills above the town, and other traces of the island's antique past, not least numerous domed and vaulted Mycenaean tombs, suggest that Cefalonia had a prominent place in Odysseus' kingdom.

From the thirteenth century BC onwards, the Cafalonians proved themselves to be astute seafarers and the naval and commercial rivals of Mycenae, Thebes and Athens. Allied with Corinth against the colony of Corcyra (Corfu), the Cefalonians subsequently supported Athens in the Peloponnesian War but, when the Greek states lost their independence, the island became a pirates' nest. It continued as such until it was conquered by the Norman leader Robert Guiscard, who died on the island in 1085 and is remembered in the name of the little port in the island's north – Fiscardo. Cefalonia was later ruled by two Italian families, the Orsini and Tocchi, and then by the Venetians from 1500 to 1797. Thereafter its history is broadly similar to that of the other Ionian islands.

An attractive coastal road leads along the island's northern promontory from Sami to Fiscardo and first traverses an area of great speliological interest, particularly in the environs of Melissani, where the roof of a large cave has collapsed to reveal

Cefalonian olive grove

an underground lake with remarkable colouring. Beyond the small coastal village of Ayia Evfimia the road crosses to the western side of the peninsular to reach Assos, an attractive re-built village where a Venetian castle stands on a rocky headland commanding two anchorages. Fiscardo is situated seventeen kilometres to the north and is one the few settlements that escaped the disastrous earthquake of 1953. Consequently it has an architecture typical of Cefalonia before the widespread destruction, and such is its attractiveness that it is fast developing as a tourist centre.

The other main road from Sami leads south-westwards through the island's widest part to the capital, Argostoli, passing first the monastery of Ayios Gerasimos, the island's patron saint, though much of the building and many of its treasures were damaged in the earthquake. Argostoli itself was almost completely destroyed, and the re-built capital has an inevitable utilitarian concrete appearance, visually relieved somewhat by its wide, tree-planted streets. It is a busy town and the centre of the island's bus services. It is also well endowed with hotels and eating-places, and there are some good beaches close at hand. A ferry crosses the gulf to Lixouri, the island's second largest settlement, from which attractive walking excursions can be made in this western peninsular extension of the island. Argostoli has an interesting archaeological museum (though many of its former exhibits were lost in the earthquake damage) and also a cultural-historical museum. The latter, like similar provincial ones found throughout Greece, is a crowded collection of antiques, curios and general bric-à-brac, the most interesting exhibits being the collection of photographs portraying the effects of the earthquake and the architectural character of Argostoli prior to its destruction.

Six kilometres to the west of the capital is Castro, the old Venetian administrative centre known as San Giorgio. It had already been destroyed by earthquake in 1636 and was finally abandoned in favour of Argostoli in 1757. Its ruins include the shells of numerous churches and the remains of barracks and fortifications of various conquerors and governors of the island. South of Argostoli the main road passes the airport and then skirts the southern coast to the small coastal port village of Poros. Northwards the landscape is dominated by Mount Ainos, the magnificent views from its summit offering full recompense for what is a long and exhausting climb.

Zakinthos – Flower of the Levant

The third largest in size of the Ionian islands (177 sq km), Zakinthos lies off the coast of the Peloponnesian *nomes* of Achaea and Elis. It is easily reached by a hydrofoil service from Patras and the busy ferry from Kyllini, both ports being linked to Athens by trains of the north coastal branch of the Peloponnesian railway, and

Many traditional rural homes survived the Cefalonian earthquake

The tranquillity of the Zakinthos countryside

waterfront at
inthos

untry church near
s, Corfu

by a regular bus service; many of the buses, in fact, accompany their passengers on the Kyllini ferry. Zakinthos also has daily flights to and from Athens, and during the summer months its airport now receives an increasing number of charter flights from European cities, their passengers heading mainly for the new hotel and bungalow complexes at Alykes, Argassi, Planos and Laganas, though only the latter can be considered as a real beach centre. The island rivals Corfu in terms of natural beauty and the quality of its beaches, yet to date tourism is but modestly developed and the island's capital, Zakinthos town, is in no way braced for what could be, if the speculators and developers have their way, a big upsurge in the number of visitors.

The Venetians called the island Zante and, on account of its profuse natural vegetation and soils that supported a rich agriculture, christened it 'flower of the Levant', expressing this sentiment as a jingle – 'Zante, fior di Levante'. Like Corfu, it was and still is, intensively farmed, though marked differences occur between the mountainous and more barren west (reaching 721 metres in Mount Yeris) and the fertile east, whose highest point is Mount Skopos (482 metres). Currants, wine grapes and olives have long dominated the island's economy, which has seen periods of great prosperity alternating with those of general agricultural decline. Land has passed in and out of cultivation as economic conditions have dictated, but the landscapes of the island's east are the products of centuries of tending and management which have effectively reduced much of the natural woodlands referred to by Homer, Pliny and Strabo. Many of the island's past difficulties (and this applies to the whole Ionian group) have been the result of devastating earthquakes, one of the most powerful having occurred in 1820. Less severe tremors followed in 1840 and 1873, but that of 1953 wrecked the entire island, as it did Cefalonia.

Prior to its destruction, Zakinthos town had been a smaller version of Corfu with tall Venetian mansions, Ionian-Baroque churches and arcaded streets. It had also been a cultural centre of considerable repute, and in the literary field it is best remembered for the poetry of Andreas Kalvos, who died in 1867, and Dionysios Solomos (1798-1857), the great Greek national poet and champion of the demotic language, raising its status to that of an influentially expressive medium. The island's cultural past is represented in the town's two museums, the one in St Mark's Square being built above the mausoleum of the two poets, the remains of Kalvos having been returned to his native island in 1960 from Lincolnshire, where he had lived with his English wife. The museum also exhibits the works of another island poet, Ugo Foskolo, together with the legacies of a number of noble Zantiote families. The Museum of Art in Solomos Square, where the poet's statue proudly stands, contains displays of Ionian art, icons and elaborately carved altar screens, saved from the

The monument to the poet Solomos in the town of Zakinthos

island's earthquake-torn churches.

Many of the town's rebuilt churches are noteworthy, particularly the Panagia Faneromeni and Ayios Dionysios, both of which have tall, elegant Italianate *campanili*. The latter church houses the remains, surrounded by gold and silver

259

votive offerings, of the island's patron saint. They were returned to Zakinthos in 1716 from a strongly fortified monastery on the larger of the Strophades islands some forty five kilometres to the south. Ayios Dionysios also has frescos by Cozzari, a student of Tiepolo.

As for the rest of the town, such was the totality of its destruction that it was quickly rebuilt in a style that has attempted to recapture something of the old Venetian townscape. The result is, however, monotonous, for even the once charmingly arcaded streets, so beneficial against the summer sun and winter rain, are of rectangular uniformity. Yet this bland, functional architecture is greatly softened by the friendliness, humour and hospitality of the townspeople, human characteristics common to the entire island. Much of the evening activity is concentrated along its waterfronts and around Solomos Square, the latter having restaurants and pastry shops whose tables partly colonize the formal gardens. Here visitors can sample the locally produced red and white wines and other island specialities, including *mandalato*, a white nougat with nuts, and *pasteli*, a biscuit-like confection with sesame seeds.

Unstable-looking hills with earthquake scars surround the town's landward sides. On one of them stand the remains of a fifteenth-century *castro* whose site has been used as a fortress since ancient times. It is reached via the suburban village of Bohali, its old walls providing fine views over the town, the island and parts of the adjacent Peloponnesus. The coasts and interior of the island also deserve to be visited, and a lot can be accomplished by the local buses that link the town with all the principal villages and popular beaches. Marine caves are a particular feature of the island's rocky coastal stretches, especially in the vicinity of Cape Skinari in the north-east. Leisurely exploration of the interior is recommended, for it is laced with tracks and winding lanes, shielded by verdant hedgerows and leading to friendly farmsteads and villages. In the north a number of old monasteries offer splendid coastal and interior views, as does the summit of Skopos in the south, the prominent mountain that dominates the scene from Zakinthos' waterfront. It can be climbed in three or four hours and provides expansive vistas of the island's two southerly peninsulas that bound the Gulf of Lagana, and also across the corrugated north of the island beyond which the sombre peak of Ainos in Cefalonia is usually visible.

Anomalous Cythera (Kithira)

Despite its Aegean situation, albeit peripheral, and Cycladic landscape – brown and rocky with whitewashed villages – a significant part of the history of Cythera has linked it with that of the Ionian islands, to which it was annexed by Venice in 1717, and known to the Republic as Cerigo. Even today its administration is anomalous,

for rather than being tributary to the Peloponnesian *nomos* of Laconia – it lies fourteen kilometres south of the Mani peninsula – it falls under the jurisdiction of Piraeus, from which it is served by two ferries a week and a more regular hydrofoil service during the summer months. Good ferry connections exist with a number of small Laconian ports, for example Neapolis and Gythion, and there are also regular scheduled flights to and from Athens, a service that has greatly relieved the former isolation of this curious island and which undoubtedly accounts for the recent spate of affluent villa development along parts of its rocky but beach-fringed coasts.

Rugged and dry, though not particularly mountainous, Cythera has suffered acutely from the debilitating effects of migration, and today a large proportion of its visitors are former natives or their descendants, returning for a nostalgic holiday

261

A Cytheran ornamenta
pot

from their new homes abroad. It is estimated that many thousands of Greeks with Cytheran connections live in Australia, the island's economy being more dependent on remittances from the Antipodes than on aid or decision-making emanating from Athens. For the ordinary tourist the island presents problems, for there is hardly any hotel accommodation, and the local bus service is at best erratic and follows a daily schedule known only to the driver. Visitors should be aware of the strong possibility of being stranded, and though rooms to rent are available in most of the small villages, the accommodation tends to be spartan and will offer no appeal to the luxury-seekers. A small hotel exists at Ayia Pelagia, where the ferries call before proceeding to Chora (Cythera) in the south of the island, and communal board is usually available at some of the monasteries, where the accent is again on experience rather than on comfort.

Much of the island remains uncultivated, though there are small pockets of richer land devoted to grain crops, vines and olives, and the local honey is much esteemed. If Cythera can be regarded as having a main settlement, then this is Chora, which stands on a rugged ridge that terminates at its south-eastern end in a precipitous rock crowned by a medieval castle. It is an attractive but poor village, lacking in all but the most basic facilities, disadvantages more than compensated for by the gracious manners and friendliness of it citizens. Among the places to visit on Cythera are Avlemonas, where in 2000 BC the Minoans had a trading settlement, the monastery of Panagia Mirtidion with its gold-framed icons, Palaeocastra (believed to be the site of the ancient city mentioned by Homer), the busy market village of Potamos and the spectacular cave of Milopotamo, which is said to have some of the best stalactites and stalagmites in Greece.

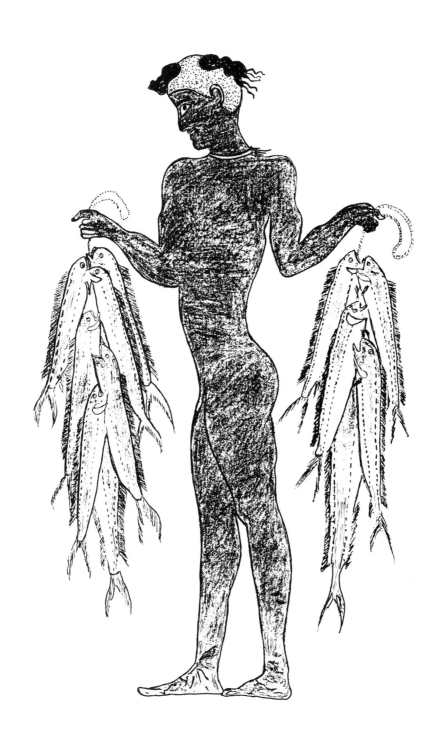

—————— 12 ——————

Advice and Information for
Visitors

This final chapter groups together commentaries and items of information which, it is hoped, will help visitors gain more from their stay in the Greek islands. For the armchair traveller these pages will amplify those aspects of island lifestyles lightly glossed over in earlier chapters. The topics do not pretend to be exhaustive, and those who have visited the islands will already have gained their own impressions and experiences, many emanating from contact with the islanders themselves. As much of the Greek island experience comes from its people, it is appropriate to begin with some comment, however mundane, on those aspects of Greek temperament and personality that collectively produce what may loosely be termed 'national characteristics'.

Xenios Zeus

'It is impossible in any manner', wrote Colonel Leake over 150 years ago, 'to avoid inconsistency.' His comment was directed to the problem of transliterating Greek place-names into the Roman alphabet, but he might well have been expressing the difficulty in summarizing the Greek character. The purist would argue that such a task is an impossibility, for no nation can be characterized without resort to gross generalization. As throughout the Greek mainland, the attitudes and temperaments of the islanders greatly vary, and some visitors – especially those on highly organized party travel – might well remain oblivious to Ionian, Cretan, Dodecanesian and Cycladic (etc) differences. Nor without fully mixing with the islanders, will they detect the personality dichotomies between farming communities and those whose livelihoods have traditionally come from the sea. There are other profound contrasts between urban islanders and the country people, and nowadays between tourism-tainted communities and those that still warmly and graciously receive strangers with no thought of recompense. The latter communities still pay more than lip-

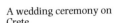
A wedding ceremony on Crete

service to Xenios Zeus, the patron god of hospitality, and their welcome of visitors can be vigorous and often overwhelming, recalling Nestor's orders to his servants when Telemachus was departing: 'After him and force him to come back!' In many of the Greek islands the goodwill to welcome the visitor and to render a service or help is a matter of pride and personal honour. Yet there are some areas where the visitor is treated with suspicion and avoided, and others where the mass influx of tourists has inevitably broken down the intimate contact that once existed between *xenos* (plural *xenoi*) and local. The former word has the traditional meaning of both 'stranger' and 'visitor', though in many islands it is rapidly being replaced by the less attractive term *touristas*.

During the centuries when the Greeks were subjected to a variety of foreign rules, the two pillars of their cultural unity were the Orthodox Church and the Greek language. It was inevitable, however, that this crossroads country – geographically and culturally – would inherit the attitudes, manners and values of both the Occident and the Orient. To the traveller from Western Europe this Balkan terminus presents many of the attributes and experiences of the East, yet it was here that Western civilization was born, and visitors reaching Greece from Turkey or other parts of the eastern Mediterranean are left in no doubt that they have crossed a major

266

Greek dancers in traditional *fustanella* dress

cultural divide. The interplay between East and West is recognizable and felt at all levels, though the casual visitor might notice only the pungent aroma of oriental tobacco, or the *souvlakia* stalls with their sizzling meat and the smell of spices and herbs, or the sound of the timorous *bouzouki* and the clinking of *komboli* (worry beads) in the hands of old men as they pass the time in cafés. In reality Eastern attitudes penetrate much deeper, and it is in the countryside, in spite of many economic and social changes, that the face of the Orient is most prominent. Here the women continue to work long hours in the fields; here the menfolk adorn the village squares playing *tavli* and sipping Turkish-style coffee; here at evening the youth of both sexes still stroll separately, and it remains common that a young man cannot be seen alone with his betrothed until their marriage has been fully arranged and the dowry negotiated. It is in the countryside, too, that the men continue to perform variations of strange and soulful dances, and the elaborate local festivals, under the guise of Christianity, preserve many superstitious beliefs, a fair proportion of which emanated from Asia.

Many have argued that the complex character of the Greeks has developed out of what has been a cultural identity crisis, the most striking outward signs of this being a people who are vibrant, volatile and passionate, with a predilection for

267

crowds, conversation and, it might appear, noise. In this, of course, they display a number of characteristics commonly associated with the Mediterranean temperament in general, and adjectives particularly apt in describing their personality are 'frank', 'generous', 'curious', 'proud', 'honour-bound' and 'hospitable'. The Greeks see themselves as those who touch the stars with one hand and the mud or dust with the other. Though a typical Greek exaggeration, it is not without truth, and the Western philhellenes who still cling to the view that the modern Greek is the direct descendant of his classical forebears and the inheritor of their ideals should, perhaps, be reminded that there was a Sparta as well as an Athens, whose contradictory philosophies are borne out in the modern Greek character.

Perhaps the national trait that strikes the visitor most forcibly is that of innate curiosity and inquisitiveness which, for the uninitiated, can reach embarrassing proportions. This is a facet of the Greek personality that has certainly not changed from ancient times, and the interrogation of Athena by Odysseus' son Telemachus in the opening pages of the *Odyssey* could well be the script for a first meeting between contemporary Greek and visitor: 'Do tell me who you are and where you come from. What is your native town? Who are your people? And since you certainly cannot have come on foot, what vessel brought you here? How did the crew land you in Ithaca, and who did they claim to be? Then there is another thing I would like to know. Is this your first visit to Ithaca, or have my people received you before . . .?' (Translated by E.V. Rieu). In a modern situation this verbal attack would quickly approach an even more personal line of questioning as to age, occupation, salary, marital status, family matters and political inclinations. The visitor should guard against indulging too deeply into the latter and, at all costs, refrain from thoughtless criticisms of conditions in Greece, as this might well be interpreted as a slight to a Greek's personal honour or self-esteem. The Greek is well aware of his country's many problems and would rather not be reminded of them by the visitor.

The concept of Greek honour – *philotimo* – is a complex one and is the basis of an individual's status within the family, village or district, and above all the basis of nationalism. It rests on inviolability and freedom, and in many ways Greek behaviour is constrained by the fear of appearing ridiculous or losing face. As a consequence the Greeks have little respect for society drop-outs, and as far as tourists are concerned they dislike seeing the unwashed, barefoot and shabby youth who have, on occasion, descended in large numbers on small island communities.

A Modicum of Manners

There are certain conventions and customs that, in the cause of politeness, should be adhered to when meeting and sharing the company of Greeks. At all introductions, subsequent meetings and temporary and final partings the handshake, more especially between men, is *de rigueur*. Visitors should also master at least a few of the Greek greetings, for especially in country districts it is customary to acknowledge strangers on the road. The question of language is dealt with elsewhere in this chapter, but here it might be noted that there are many good phrase-books on the market that provide the basic language acceptable in most situations.

The Greeks are not the world's best time-keepers, and for them the 'afternoon' means any time between the end of the mandatory siesta period (from the conclusion of lunch to *c.*5.30-6.00 p.m.) to dusk and sometimes later. It is considered impolite to call at a Greek house (or even telephone) during the siesta period, for most Greeks need the rest, having indulged in a late night followed by an early start to their working day. Nocturnalism is, however, more a habit of the towns and tourist areas, rural communities tending to retire earlier to meet the demands of their farming schedules.

What is often a cause of embarrassment to the visitor is the Greek's insistence on paying for a meal or a round of drinks. It is considered bad manners to offer to share a bill, unless the acquaintanceship is of long-standing, and even then it is more prudent for the visitor to play host the next time. Café and taverna bills are often settled over the head of the visitor being entertained, and the latter should adopt a similar 'clandestine' attitude when the compliment is being returned. On the question of food and drink, it is not considered good manners to over-fill a wine glass, nor for the drinker to drain its contents completely. The visitor will find that the attentive Greek host will keep it 'topped up', each replenishment being the cause for yet another toast to health, prosperity, friendship and also the wine itself.

In a Greek household the Anglo-Saxon equivalent of a welcoming cup of tea, or the offer of a drink, is a procedure that is both more formal and complicated. The usual sign of hospitality is for the visitor to be offered preserves, usually on a spoon, along with coffee and water. To conform with custom the water should be drunk first, the preserves eaten and the spoon placed in the glass; the coffee is enjoyed at leisure.

Polite as the Greeks tend to be in most personal relationships, their attitude in the street and in public places can, ironically, appear ill-mannered to those with a strict Anglo-Saxon upbringing. It all hinges on the concept of the great British queue, the latter being a form of organization alien to the Greek, as indeed it is to many Continental peoples. Boarding buses and boats, entering cinemas and other places of entertainment, and getting served in banks, post offices, travel agencies and even shops, is a free-for-all challenge. The Germans, Italians and French play the game by a similar set of rules, and their bulldozing techniques, allied with the Greek mastery of the martial arts of pushing, nudging and dextrous body manœuvres, increasingly isolates the less persistent from the original object of their endeavours. The cardinal rule is to give way to no one, not even persuasive grannies who have had decades of experience in getting there first.

The Three Seasons

All the Greek islands may be said to experience variations of the southern Mediterranean climatic regime, with its warm winters, wet from a progression of low-pressure systems which pass from west to east through the Mediterranean basin, and hot and dry summers. Summer is, in fact, a protracted period and merges rapidly in late October/early November with the rainy season, whose intermittent showers and occasional storms continue into March, the month that heralds a glorious, if short, spring. Rainfall in the southern and eastern Aegean is low, averaging about 400 millimetres in the year, thus resembling the southern Greek mainland, although winters are milder and summers less scorching on account of sea breezes. Frosts seldom occur, and snow, common on high peaks (notably in Crete), is rarely seen at sea-level. One of the main climatic differences between the Aegean and the Ionian islands is annual rainfall, which is considerably higher in the latter, averaging on Corfu, for example, 700 millimetres.

The majority of the holiday pilgrims to the Greek islands tend to favour June, July and August, thus making many destinations exceptionally crowded, for this is also the main vacationing period for the Greeks themselves. In the more popular islands the combined result is a heavy demand on all available accommodation, as well as crowded beaches, boats, cafés and restaurants. This is also the hottest time of the year, and whereas high temperatures may well appeal to the languishing sun-worshippers, such conditions can prove extremely exhausting for those more intent on exploring the wealth of scenic and historical attractions the islands have to offer.

On many islands drought conditions and heavy summer demand bring water shortages, and even some of the better hotels (see below) are forced to ration supplies. The highest temperatures are experienced in parts of Crete, the Cyclades and the Dodecanese, where they average around 26.5°C (79°F) but have been known on Crete to reach 45.7°C (113°F). It is certainly the case that only 'mad dogs' and 'tourists' venture forth when the indigenous islanders siesta. Such foreign forays are largely counter-productive, for most places, including many archaeological sites,

The flat roofs of Naxos baking under a hot sun

are closed for the siesta period, and the camera buff is also poorly rewarded with stark, shadowless pictures. As noted elsewhere, the summer months, especially in the southern Aegean, can also be irritatingly windy, whereas the Ionian area can experience hot and humid conditions that prove equally debilitating.

For many visitors, therefore, late spring and early summer are an idyllic time to visit the islands, for the sun shines, temperatures are more moderate and the landscape retains its freshness from the winter rains. At the other end of the season, late September, October and even November are good months for sightseeing, but it should be noted that as winter approaches, harsher conditions increase from south to north in the Aegean. Even so, when other parts of Europe are suffering from deep winter chills, it is still possible in the southern Aegean to enjoy periods of mild, sunny weather. Some islands are, in fact, now actively promoting their winter holiday image; it is a question of paying your money and taking a chance.

In the Steps of Hermes

If not exactly equipped with wide-brimmed hat, travelling staff and winged feet, the modern visitor to Greece, by using the country's dense network of domestic air services, can zoom the length of the mainland and its island appendages almost as efficiently as did Hermes, the ancient patron of all wayfarers and travellers. Operating from the separate Olympic Airways terminal at Athens airport, regular daily flights serve the larger and also many of the more tourism-conscious islands. This air travel is usually quick and efficient, though timetables cannot always be implicitly relied on, which means that the visitor should make advance checks that a particular flight is operating at the time stated. The islands with scheduled connections with Athens are Rhodes, Crete (Iraklion and Canea), Kos, Mykonos, Skiathos, Santorini, Lemnos, Chios, Lesbos, Samos, Corfu, Karpathos, Cythera, Cefalonia, Zakinthos and Milos. In addition there are a number of useful inter-island flights, such as the Rhodes-Iraklion connection, and a number of island links from Salonica. The mainland airports at Kavala and Alexandroupolis can be used for visiting Thasos and Samothrace.

Getting to the majority of the Aegean islands from the Athens area presents no real problems, for Piraeus, as already noted, is the focal point of the country's sea transport. Travel from the Greek capital to the Ionian islands, however, demands more effort and stamina from visitors not intent on flying. There are shipping lines that operate from Piraeus, via the Corinth Canal, to Patras and then through the Ionian archipelago to Corfu and on to the Italian ports of Brindisi, Ancona and Venice. These usually large ships provide a leisurely cruise through fascinating waters, although quicker access to Greece's western coasts can be affected by road

otilla of small boats
nsport tourists from
konos to Delos

or the northern branch of the Peloponnesian Railway via Corinth and Patras. The port with a number of important Ionian ferry connections, Patras is linked to Athens by a fast national highway, but visitors heading for Corfu might wish to také the Rion-Antirion ferry (a few kilometres east of Patras) which lands vehicles on the northern shore of the Gulf of Corinth – that is, the southern shore of mainland Greece proper. From here a lengthy journey through the heart of Aetolia (via Agrinion) and Epirus (via Ioannina) eventually terminates at Igoumenitsa, where there are regular sea connections with Corfu.

The Athens-Igoumenitsa journey can be undertaken by long-distance buses, the Greek mainland being covered by a dense network of services. The major bus organizations are the OSE (operated by the State Railways, which, incidentally, have more bus that train routes) and KTEL (a consortium of private bus companies). The former usually ply from the vicinity of railway stations, and the latter from bus stations which in many Greek towns are little more than dusty parking lots. Relatively inexpensive compared with other modes of transport, bus travel is extremely popular, and tickets for most journeys need to be purchased in advance – hence guaranteeing (at least in theory) a seat.

Inter-town and inter-regional buses operate on the larger Greek islands, the remainder being dependent on the local 'market' bus, which is an entirely different

273

experience. Invariably unpunctual and always overcrowded, the one thing that can be said in favour of these 'bone-shakers' is that only rarely do they fail to arrive and reach their destination. Despite delay and discomfort this form of travel is a colourful and (for those with a sense of humour) often hilarious means of travel, providing further insights into the island way of life. The philosophy is the same as that for boarding boats – everyone for themselves. In addition to the ubiquitous contingent of elderly, who seem to materialize like traditionally clad extras for some film set, the other common human element is the large number of vociferous children attached to parcel-laden mothers. If anything, the children come off best, for they are enormously indulged and are usually given seats whilst the weary adults of all ages stand wedged between packages and large wicker baskets whose contents are discreetly hidden by a cloth-sewn top. The rural bus is also a mail-carrier and delivery van, and it further functions as a mobile forum in which news is exchanged and gossip diffused to the accompaniment of the driver's blaring radio. The driving area is highly personalized with small plastic bouquets, family pictures and religious bric-à-brac. For the tourist these latter items, together with the frequency with which the passengers cross themselves when passing wayside shrines and at precipitous bends, are comforting concomitants to a journey often made hair-raising by the nonchalance, bravado and unpredictable road sense of the driver.

Cars can be hired on all the larger islands, particularly on Crete, Rhodes, Corfu, Kos and Euboea. Although extremely useful in getting entirely off the beaten track, they are expensive, and the more adventurous might well opt for a moped or, for shorter distances, a bicycle.

The preceding pages have also stressed the rewards of walking excursions along the lanes and tracks that lace the majority of the islands. Lengthy forays should be well-planned and thought should be given to the provisions that might be needed. The Greek country code is much the same as that applying in Britain and farmers, for the most part amiable, take a poor view of those who walk over their crops, clamber over walls and fences, and camp on their lands without permission. In mountain areas the visitor might well encounter a ruthless breed of sheep dog, guardians, *par excellence*, of flocks and herds. These large, powerful mastiffs, heavy jowled and incredibly bad-tempered, answer to no-one but their masters, and they take sadistic pleasure in terrorizing unsuspecting strangers venturing near their domains. Visitors should tread warily of these formidable creatures, for even in villages they can prove a problem.

Finally, it might be noted that, in this still largely chauvinist country, women travelling (and certainly walking) alone are often the cause of annoying curiosity and, at times, total mistrust.

It's Greek to Me

Visitors with little knowledge of modern Greek will have few language difficulties in the tourist resorts of the islands where English and other major European languages are widely understood. However, in the lesser-visited and non-commercialized parts of the Aegean and Ionian the monoglot traveller will certainly encounter some initial confusion. The ability to speak a smattering of the Greek language, no matter how faulty in grammar and pronunciation, will add immensely to the visitor's profit and experience, for attempts at the native tongue are warmly appreciated by the Greeks, and in many areas a few Greek words and phrases can lead to invitations for a coffee or ouzo, fishing trips and, sometimes, overnight accommodation in a villager's home.

All intending travellers should be familiar at least with the twenty-four letters of the Greek alphabet and their sounds. Such knowledge is indispensible in reading street and bus signs and, once mastered, the number of Greek words that have almost direct English equivalents (English, of course, being the borrower) will be fully appreciated. There is a great sense of attainment and satisfaction in deciphering ΤΕΛΕ-ΦΟΝΟ (*teléfono*) as telephone, ΠΑΤΑΤΕΣ (*patátes*) as potatoes, ΛΕΜΟΝΙ (*lemóni*) as lemon, ΣΑΛΑΤΑ (*saláta*) as salad and ΣΟΥΠΑ (*soúpa*) as soup. These examples are, however, written in the upper case and, as the practioner develops in expertise, familiarity with the lower case will prove even more beneficial. This script is quite different, but each word carries a stress mark – τελέφονο, πατάτες, λεμόνι, σαλάτα, σούπα – which is needed for authentic pronunciation.

A modest ability to count in Greek is also of great advantage when parting with coins and notes. The unit of Greek currency is the *drachma* (pl. *drachmes*) which is abbreviated to *dr* or *drs*. There are coins for 1 dr, 2 dr, 5 dr, 10 dr, 20 dr and, more rarely, 50 dr, Greek notes being in denominations of 50 dr, 100 dr, 500 dr and 1,000 dr. Technically the drachma is subdivided into 100 *lepta*, but such is the small monetary value of the drachma that there are now coins only for 50 lepta (0.5 drachma). Visitors to Greece not so long ago will certainly remember accumulating the thin aluminium lepta coins with their characteristic central holes.

No one can pretend that the Greek language is easy to master, though the modern tongue is decidedly less complicated than its ancient predecessor. One of the main problems confronting the contemporary learner is the existence of two main Greek forms – *demotiki* (demotic or popular Greek) and *katharevousa* (the purer, more official and, in certain cases, the literary language) – which differ in grammar, vocabulary and pronunciation. In addition there are a large number of local dialects which are particularly at variance throughout the islands.

Demotic Greek is the product of a long process of organic development. The ancient language knew a number of dialects and, although they stemmed from a variety of geographical environments and variations in customs and political organization, they rarely showed any tendency to develop into separate tongues. The classical dialects, such as Attic, Ionic, Doric and Aeolic, were subsequently standardized by the Hellenistic grammarians and, as a general instrument of communication, this language spread throughout the empire of Alexander and the kingdoms that succeeded it. By the first century BC *koine*, common Greek, had become a *lingua franca*, and the Romans made little attempt to displace it. In fact, with the addition of Latin words and idioms, *koine* become the second language of the Roman Empire, then the first in the thousand-year-long Byzantine Empire. Over the centuries, however, through the rise and fall of Constantinople's influence, a gap developed between the language of the masses, particularly the peasants and serfs of Greece, and the more refined tongue of the lettered and the Church. The complex history of mainland Greece and the islands meant that the 'vulgar' tongue (*demotiki*) absorbed a wealth of foreign words and expressions, and the once universal Greek speech reverted to a series of localized dialects.

By the end of the eighteenth century such variation in speech had reached its widest span, and with the establishment of Greek independence a movement to

impose a unified and purified language gained support from many educated people, particularly in the Ionian islands where *katharevousa* formed an essential part of what was an all-embracing Greek cultural revival. Unfortunately it was never thoroughly understood on the lower social levels, and towards the end of the nineteenth century a new 'school' arose, consisting essentialy of poets and writers, who upheld the merits of the demotic tongue. Thus the question of language, like most things in Greece, became a political issue. Some sort of academic compromise was reached in *kathomiloumeni*, which combined elements of both extremes. This was, however, rejected by both the political right and left, and Greece remains a country where the language issue, affecting every aspect of national life, is still capable of overthrowing govenments. Most Greeks now realize the difficulties of two language systems and, as a result of major improvements in education, people tend to avoid both the use of the more 'common' expressions and the old forms of ancient and foreign derivation. But a gulf still exists and is well illustrated in some newspapers that print political views in the 'official' language and the more popular items in the demotic tongue.

As mentioned at the beginning of this book, there is much confusion with the spelling of Greek place-names, part of the problem being that many of them have both a demotic and *katharevousa* form, for example Athína and Athíne, respectively, for Athens. Further difficulties result from the grammatical declining of Greek place-names which, like other nouns, can appear in nominative, accusative and genitive forms, with corresponding differences in spelling and stress. To complicate matters further, many names, particularly of rivers, mountains, villages and certain islands, have two totally different forms, one purely local (and often of Slavic, Albanian, Frankish or Turkish origin) and the other an official style which is usually a reversion to its ancient nomenclature. In order to make names on signposts and maps comprehensible to tourists of all nations, Greek officialdom has transliterated them in accordance with the phonetic system codified by the Permanent Committee on Geographical Names. Most English-speaking visitors will have little difficulty in recognizing Ródhos for Rhodes, Piréefs for Piraeus, Míkonos for Mykonos and Límnos for Lemnos – yet there are many more testing ones: for example, Kérkira (Corfu), Ídhra (Hydra) and Khaniá (Canea). The problem is that English got many of its Greek names through the Latin, the very name 'Greece' being a corruption of the Latin *Graecia*, a term not used in the Greek language, where the country is known as Hellas (ΕΛΛΑΣ). Archaeologists and classical scholars have been partly responsible for giving ancient names English forms, though now their journals have reverted to using the international phonetic system. However, many anglicized Greek names are part and parcel of the English language, and it would be pedantic and presumptuous to replace, for example, Athens by Athína, Crete by Kríti and Corfu by Kérkira etc. Yet the traveller to Greece should be aware of the place-name problem and should be familiar with the transliterated versions that come as near as possible to the original Greek pronunciation. The list below provides the accepted English, the Greek (upper case) and the transliterated Greek equivalent of the names to the main islands, regions, towns and cities covered in this book.

In Greece street-names in most urban centres are indicated in both alphabets, though visitors should beware that the renaming of a street (*ódos*), avenue (*leofóros*) and square (*platía*) etc is something of a national pastime, and these are liable to alter with a major change in government or when some other national (and international) event seems worthy of honour. Further complications arise with the Greek habit of displaying street-names only in the possessive or genitive, omitting, in particular, the word *ódos*. To take but three examples, Venizélou in Piraeus (and in many other Greek towns and cities) stands for Venizelos Street, which honours the famous Greek statesman; Vasíleos Konstantínou in Iraklion for King Constantine Avenue; and Sokrátou in Rhodes for Socrates Street. When in doubt the visitor should ask – preferably in Greek!

Recognized English version	Greek version (upper case)	Transliteration of Greek pronunciation with stress
Aegina	ΑΙΓΙΝΑ	Aíyina
Agrinion	ΑΓΡΙΝΙΟΝ	Agrínion
Alexandroupolis	ΑΛΕΞΑΝΔΡΟΥΠΟΛΙΣ	Alexandhróupolis
Alonnisos	ΑΛΟΝΝΙΣΟΣ	Alónnisos
Amorgos	ΑΜΟΡΓΟΣ	Amorghós
Anafi	ΑΝΑΦΗ	Anáfi
Andros	ΑΝΔΡΟΣ	Ándhros
Argolid	ΑΡΓΟΛΙΣ	Argolís
Argo-Saronic Islands	ΝΗΣΟΙ ΑΡΓΟΣΑΡΩΝΙΚΟΥ	Nísi Argosaronikoú
Astypalaea	ΑΣΤΥΠΑΛΑΙΑ	Astipálaia
Athens	ΑΘΗΝΑΙ	Athínai
Athos/Ayion Oros	ΑΘΩΣ/ΑΓΙΟΝ ΟΡΟΣ	Áthos/Áyion Óros
Attica	ΑΤΤΙΚΗ	Attikí
Ayia Triada	ΑΓΙΑ ΤΡΙΑΔΑ	Ayía Triáda
Ayios Efstratios	ΑΓΙΟΣ ΕΥΣΤΡΑΤΙΟΣ	Áyios Efstrátios
Ayios Nikolaos	ΑΓΙΟΣ ΝΙΚΟΛΑΟΣ	Áyios Nikólaos
Boeotia	ΒΟΙΩΤΙΑ	Viotía
Chalcidice	ΞΑΛΚΙΔΙΚΗ	Khalkidikí
Chios	ΞΙΟΣ	Khíos
Corfu	ΚΕΡΚΥΡΑ	Kérkira
Corinth	ΚΟΡΙΝΘΟΣ	Kórinthos
Crete	ΚΡΗΤΗ	Kríti
Cyclades	ΚΥΚΛΑΔΕΣ	Kikládhes
Delos	ΔΗΛΟΣ	Dhílos
Delphi	ΔΕΛΦΟΙ	Dhelfí
Dodecanese	ΔΩΔΕΚΑΝΗΣΑ	Dhodhekanísa
Eleusis	ΕΛΕΥΣΙΣ	Elefsís
Epidauros	ΕΠΙΔΑΥΡΟΣ	Epídhavros
Epirus	ΗΠΕΙΡΟΣ	Ípiros
Euboea	ΕΥΒΟΙΑ	Évvia
Folegandros	ΦΟΛΕΓΑΝΔΡΟΣ	Folégandhros
Gortys	ΓΟΡΤΥΣ	Górtis
Gournia	ΓΟΥΡΝΙΑ	Gurniá
Hydra	ΥΔΡΑ	Ídhra

Ierapetra	ΙΕΡΑΠΕΤΡΑ	Ierápetra
Igoumenitsa	ΗΓΟΥΜΕΝΙΤΣΑ	Igumenítsa
Ikaria	ΙΚΑΡΙΑ	Ikaría
Ioannina	ΙΩΑΝΝΙΝΑ	Ioánnina
Ionian Islands	ΙΟΝΙΟΙ ΝΗΣΟΙ	Iónii Nísi
Ios	ΙΟΣ	Íos
Iráklion	ΗΡΑΚΛΙΟΝ	Iráklion
Ithaca	ΙΘΑΚΗ	Itháki
Kalymnos	ΚΑΛΥΜΝΟΣ	Kálimnos
Karpathos	ΚΑΡΠΑΘΟΣ	Kárpathos
Kasos	ΚΑΣΟΣ	Kásos
Kavala	ΚΑΒΑΛΑ	Kavála
Kea	ΚΕΑ	Kéa
Kefallinia (Cefalonia)	ΚΕΦΑΛΛΗΝΙΑ	Kefallinía
Khania (Canea)	ΞΑΝΙΑ	Khaniá
Kimolos	ΚΙΜΩΛΟΣ	Kímolos
Knossos	ΚΝΩΣΟΣ	Knosós
Kos	ΚΩΣ	Kós
Kythira (Cythera)	ΚΥΘΗΡΑ	Kíthira
Kythnos	ΚΥΘΝΟΣ	Kíthnos
Lefkas	ΛΕΥΚΑΣ	Lefkás
Lemnos	ΛΗΜΝΟΣ	Límnos
Leros	ΛΕΡΟΣ	Léros
Lesbos	ΛΕΣΒΟΣ	Lésvos
Lindos	ΛΙΝΔΟΣ	Líndhos
Macedonia	ΜΑΚΕΔΟΝΙΑ	Makedhonía
Melos (Milos)	ΜΗΛΟΣ	Mílos
Mycenae	ΜΥΚΗΝΑΙ	Mikínai
Mykonos (Myconos)	ΜΥΚΟΝΟΣ	Míkonos
Nauplia (Nauplion)	ΝΑΥΠΛΙΟΝ	Náfplion
Naxos	ΝΑΞΟΣ	Náxos
Nisyros	ΝΙΣΥΡΟΣ	Nísiros
Olympus	ΟΛΥΜΠΟΣ	Ólimbos
Paros	ΠΑΡΟΣ	Páros
Patmos	ΠΑΤΜΟΣ	Pátmos
Patras	ΠΑΤΡΑΙ	Pátrai
Paxos	ΠΑΞΟΙ	Paxí
Peloponnesus	ΠΕΛΟΠΟΝΝΗΣΟΣ	Pelopónnisos

Phaistos	ΦΑΙΣΤΟΣ	Festós
Piraeus	ΠΕΙΡΑΙΕΥΣ	Pireéfs
Poros	ΠΟΡΟΣ	Póros
Rethymnon	ΡΕΘΥΜΝΟΝ	Réthimnon
Rhodes	ΡΟΔΟΣ	Ródhos
Salamis	ΣΑΛΑΜΙΣ	Salamís
Salonica	ΘΕΣΣΑΛΟΝΙΚΗ	Thessaloníki
Samaria	ΣΑΜΑΡΙΑΣ	Samariás
Samos	ΣΑΜΟΣ	Sámos
Samothrace	ΣΑΜΟΘΡΑΚΗ	Samothráki
Santorini (Thera)	ΣΑΝΤΟΡΙΝΗ (ΘΗΡΑ)	Santoríni (Thira)
Saronic Gulf	ΣΑΡΩΝΙΚΟΣ ΚΟΛΠΟΣ	Saronikós Kólpos
Serifos	ΣΕΡΙΦΟΣ	Sérifos
Sifnos	ΣΙΦΝΟΣ	Sífnos
Sikinos	ΣΙΚΙΝΟΣ	Síkinos
Skiathos	ΣΚΙΑΘΟΣ	Skiáthos
Skopelos	ΣΚΟΠΕΛΟΣ	Skópelos
Skyros	ΣΚΥΡΟΣ	Skíros
Spetses (Spetsai)	ΣΠΕΤΣΕΣ (ΣΠΕΤΣΑΙ)	Spétses (Spétsai)
Sporades	ΣΠΟΡΑΔΕΣ	Sporádhes
Simi (Symi)	ΣΥΜΗ	Sími
Syros	ΣΥΡΟΣ	Síros
Thasos	ΘΑΣΟΣ	Thásos
Thessaly	ΘΕΣΣΑΛΙΑ	Thessalía
Thrace	ΘΡΑΚΙΑ	Thrakía
Tilos	ΤΗΛΟΣ	Tílos
Tinos	ΤΗΝΟΣ	Tínos
Troizen	ΤΡΟΙΖΗΝΑ	Trizína
Volos	ΒΟΛΟΣ	Vólos
Zakinthos	ΖΑΚΥΝΘΟΣ	Zákinthos

Rooms with Views

In addition to writing great histories, Xenophon, a pupil of Socrates, was a prolific writer of treatises, one of which subscribes to the state's establishment of *xenodochia*, literally translated 'receptacles for strangers'. The Greeks still call their hotels by the same word, and over the last few decades various governments have actively sponsored programmes of hotel-building and modernization. Among these new additions are a group called the *xenias*, government-built establishments (some now privately managed) whose initial concept was to ensure the availability of reasonably high standard accommodation at important tourist sites. But unlike the *paradors* of Spain and the *posadas* of Portugal – luxuriously occupying old mansions, castles and even convents – the Greek *xenias* are atmospherically less memorable. Being, for the most part, uniformly modern, they vary in standards, although they do belong to the upper categories into which all Greek hotels are officially classified.

Both on the mainland and throughout the islands the country's hotels are rated from A to E, in addition to which is a small L (Luxury) category which is very expensive. In their charges the A, B, C and D varieties correspond with the description of expensive, moderately priced, inexpensive and cheap, whereas the E-class establishments are more difficult to generalize, some being suprisingly comfortable for their modest tarrifs, others being extremely seedy and providing fewer facilities than those available by sleeping rough on a beach. The majority of E-class 'hotels', it should be noted, are far less desirable than a *pension* or a room in an islander's home.

Up until 1981 maximum prices were legally set for accommodation in each category, but now official control tends to work more in favour of the hotelier than the guest, for it is the minimum price that is fixed. The system that currently operates is complex, and charges vary wildly and as unpredictably as in any unregulated system. Different rates, particularly in the lower categories, operate according to such criteria as the number of bathrooms, the presence of facilities (such as air-conditioning or telephones) room furniture, location and views from the balcony (should one exist). Proprietors are entitled to charge ten per cent extra for stays of less than three nights and twenty per cent extra in high season (1 June–15 September). Some might demand that the visitor takes breakfast, or may squeeze an extra bed (or two) into an already small room, whereas showers in the lower categories are often charged for separately. The problem is that in high season it is a seller's market, and in some letting establishments the visitor, when bargaining for a room, should insist that the proprietor (unless one agrees) will not let any of the other beds in the room, so that it is the room itself, and not the bed only, that is being let. With a language barrier this might be difficult to negotiate and some prepared written guarantee in Greek, which the proprietor can be asked to sign, is useful in overcoming misunderstandings and potential problems. It should be remembered that the Tourist Police, with offices in all the main resorts, are (technically) there to help the visitor, especially if the latter feels that the accommodation offered is unreasonably expensive, or proprietors have not kept strictly to an initial agreement. The Tourist Police are usually more helpful than the local information officers, though both tend to take lengthy siestas.

Italian-style tenements in
Corfu town

Greece is a relative newcomer to the Mediterranean tourism scene, and ensuring the complete comfort of the visitor is often a theoretical rather than a practical concept. The quality of service varies greatly, and even in the luxury and large 'chain' hotels it can err towards indifference. In part this relates to the shortage of trained personnel (managers, cooks, waiters and housekeepers), and visitors will learn to tolerate dripping taps, broken light switches and temperamental plumbing. Had Xenophon been alive, he might well have been moved to pen a treatise on the scientific wonders of the Greek WC, shower unit and bathtub. One of the most valuable of all holiday accoutrements is a sink plug, for invariably it is missing, the theory being that this is a precaution against flooding should the tap be left on; waste pipes in most establishments are totally incapable of dealing with the problems of drainage. At the risk of injuring sensibilities, the difficulties of waste disposal from WCs is even more acute and the cause of many a period of anxiety. Certainly there are warnings to the effect that 'papers' should be placed in the plastic bin and not where most visitors would automatically deposit them, but this demands considerable 'cultural' adjustment on the part of most Western European guests. Less frustrating, though still a source of annoyance, is the lack of coat-hangers, and travellers are advised to come well provided with a pack of the light plastic variety.

It might well be that visitors to the Greek islands on package deals will be shielded from some of the petty annoyances encountered by the traveller 'on spec'. Many of the organized holidays are, in fact, good value, and more recently the form of accommodation has expanded to include tavernas and villas, especially in the Ionian islands. Small *pensions* are also available throughout the islands, and there are a large number of rooms to let, many of them government approved. These are the cheapest places to stay, and should the plumbing and other facilities prove deficient, the visitor can at least gain some consolation from the knowledge that his hosts also share the same inconveniences.

Islands à la Carte

One of the features of the Greek islands that greatly appeals to many visitors is the general absence of organized entertainment. Certainly Mykonos, Skiathos, Corfu, Rhodes and the main holiday centres on Crete have their late bars, clubs and discothèques, but this aspect of island night-life is but a pale reflection of that common in the commercialized resorts of the Spanish *costas* and the Italian 'rivieras'. Essentially it is a reflection of the Greek's own views on entertainment, for in this respect they have undemanding tastes and seem content with life's simpler pleasures, which can be more than adequately satisfied by a taverna meal or an extended visit to a café in the company of family, friends, and new acquaintances. As noted, the nocturnal habit is a major national characteristic, the evening *peripato* or *volta*, particularly during the summer months, being followed by lengthy relaxation in open-air eating and drinking establishments, the conversation and general enjoyment continuing through to the early morning hours. As visitors will quickly find themselves following the Greek habit, it seems pertinent to make some general comment on the fares that these establishments offer.

The broad distinction between the *kafeneion* (coffee house) and the *zakharoplasteion*, (café-pastry-shop) has already been referred to. The former specializes in Greek (Turkish) coffee, which is an acquired taste. There are three main variations – *gliko* (sweet), *metrios* (made with less sugar – but still sweet for many palates), and *sketos* (made without sugar). The *zakharoplasteia* specialize in expresso coffee and the ubiquitous Nescafé, a term used by Greeks for all instant varieties. The latter is usually uncermoniously served as a cup of hot (rarely boiling) water and a sachet of coffee, the test being to mix the two without summer winds scattering the fine powder in all directions other than into a cup. Few Greeks, or visitors for that matter, can resist a snack with their coffee, a yoghurt, perhaps, or an ice-cream or a cinnamon-covered rice pudding. Then there are the wide range of highly calorific pastries (some of the islands having their own specialities), most *zakharoplasteia* offering *baklava* (honey and nuts between layers of thin *filo* pastry), *kataifi* (a nut-filled and sticky shredded wheat), *galakoboureko* (custard-filled *filo* pastry) and *mandolato* (honey and almond paste). These, largely of Turkish origin, tend to be tastier than the more colourful, creamy pastries which often turn out to be bland.

The Greeks usually visit the *zakharoplasteion* after a taverna meal, this typically Greek eating-house (see page 62) rarely serving coffee, though a waiter will often oblige by procuring one from a nearby café. The atmosphere of the taverna is often incomparably better than the quality of its food, which is usually limited in range and tends to be savoury rather than subtle, with little thought given to temperature and presentation. It is somewhat ironic that the high standard of Greek home cooking is rarely maintained in restaurants, though this is not to say that quality meals are unobtainable, and the visitor will quickly discover the better eating-places by noting the extent to which they are patronized by the Greeks themselves. Whereas there are hints of British and French *cuisine* in the Ionian Islands, the predominant influence on Aegean cooking is Turkish, the exception being the larger hotels which offer an 'international' style of fare in response to their cosmopolitan clientele. Here attempts to combine the 'delicacy' of some continental *cuisines* with the 'succulence' of the Orient sometimes come off.

The fact of the matter is that certain standard dishes are common throughout Greece, and they regularly appear on taverna menus, resulting in a somewhat

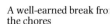

monotonous choice, especially for visitors on lengthy stays in the islands. Within the space of a week they are likely to have sampled *souvlakia* (pieces of veal, lamb or pork grilled on a skewer), *moussaka* (baked aubergines and mincemeat pie), *keftedes* (savoury meat balls), *dolmades yemitses* (tomatoes stuffed with meat and rice – there is also a stuffed pepper equivalent) and *dolmades* (stuffed vine or cabbage leaves). Other common denominators are spaghetti and macaroni dishes, chicken prepared to a variety of recipes, lamb-mutton presentations and a selection of soups which, with bread and a side salad, can be filling meals. The typical Greek salad (*horiatiki*), in fact, is usually a substantial plate of tomatoes, onions, cucumber, peppers, olives and *feta* (goat's cheese). In many parts of the islands fish are more of a rarity than one would expect, and dishes are often expensive. Typical sea-foods include octopus, red mullet, whitebait, squid, tuna, crawfish and lobster, the latter sold by the kilo, as are some other varieties of sea-food. The Greeks go in for collective eating, ordering a number of different dishes, including a variety of vegetables which they can share. The meal is usually concluded with a fruit course – melon, grapes, figs, watermelon or apples and pears (depending on season).

Constant companions at outdoor tavernas are the battalions of semi-wild Greek cats who, under the command of a large battle-scarred male, function as 'feline gangs' within their defended territories. They have the uncanny ability of singling out the tourist, experience telling them that titbits, especially the heads and tails of fish, will be thrown to them – much to the incredulity of the Greeks.

Dionysian Rites

The disorderly escapades of Dionysos, usually in the wild company of satyrs and maenads, are illustrated in various forms of Greek art. His orgiastic career on earth centred on the discovery of wine, the enjoyment of which he readily promoted, though the many myths that surround this god (who appears to have spent more time on earth than on Mount Olympus) make constant reference to the often devastating effects of strong wine. It is arguable whether the contemporary Greeks take these ancient warnings to heart. Drunkenness is certainly not a common sight, but the oft-quoted assertion that the Greeks are moderate drinkers is regarded by Kenneth Young (*The Greek Passion*) as 'a myth, floated by Methodists on tour'. The numerous religious festivals, anniversaries, birthdays and national holidays (not to mention the wine festivals held during the summer, many as part of the country's tourism programmes) are all marked by the liberal consumption of wine, and slight inebriation is considered a necessary part of enjoyment. The Greek wine glass, it should be remembered, is really a small tumbler and, as noted, etiquette demands that it is constantly replenished.

The claim that most Greeks are abstemious citizens is also coloured by their passion for other liquids, coffee in particular, but also soft drinks and water. The latter is considered one of the greatest delicacies, and Greeks who claim to distinguish between different qualities of water according to the spring from which it was drawn are not boasting. The water jug is an integral part of every meal, and a glass is

287

always served as an accompaniment to coffee, ice-cream, and pastries etc.

Greece has many wine-producing regions, and many of them are on the islands. The main distinction is between the resinated and unresinated varieties, the former, the retsinas, being a Greek invention and an acquired taste. An ancient practice was the storing of wine in goatskins sealed with resin, and some wines also had resin added as a means of strengthening the quality of those that were sourish and difficult to keep. The practice has survived the centuries, and the sharp, distinctive aroma and flavour of the retsinas prove an excellent foil to the oily character of Greek food. Yet many visitors would tend to agree with the comment of the twelfth-century Metropolitan of Athens who, wishing to give a friend some idea of the taste of retsina, wrote that it 'seems to be pressed from the juice of the pine rather from that of the grape'.

The country produces many non-resinated red, white and *rosé* wines, some of which, often the most palatable vintages, are only available locally. The EEC has now made its mark on the country's wine industry in that some varieties carry labels to indicate that they comply with Common Market directives. The Ionian islands produce some good red and white wines – for example, the *Ropa* of Corfu, *Verdea* of Zakinthos and *Santa Maura* of Lefkas; some of the better-known Cretan brands are *Malvasia*, *Romeiko*, *Creta* and *Gortys*; Rhodes produces *Malvasia* (Malmsey) and *Lindos*, and Santorini, *Thira*, *Santorini* and *Vinsanto*. Samos is, of course, famous for its sweet *Muscat* (*Samos*), and another wine well known outside Greece is the *Mavrodaphne* of Cefalonia. Thasos, Lemnos, Andros, Paros, Naxos, Icaria, Amorgos, Ios and Kos are all wine-producing islands, some of their varieties not found outside their places of origin.

The production of good-quality lager beer dates from the time of Greece's independence, when the country's first king, Otho of Bavaria, brought with him brewers to serve the royal Court and Greece's newly acquired officialdom. Interestingly, beer is still considered a slightly up-market drink among many urban Greeks, and *Hellas-Fix* (a corruption of Fuchs) is a national institution, though one currently suffering from financial problems. There are several other continental-style beers, particularly Dutch and German, that are brewed in Greece under licence, and in the larger towns and tourist centres the cafés and bars offer a variety of imported brands.

The spirit of the country is ouzo, a colourless aniseed-flavoured schnapps usually drunk as an aperitif with the addition of water that miraculously turns it a cloudy white. Ouzo is traditionally served with a plate of *mezes*, appetizers that can vary from small pieces of cheese, bread and tomato to a splendid array of grilled octopus, sausage, peppers, shell fish and salad items. Unfortunately this is one Greek tradition that is rapidly disappearing, especially in the tourist venues, where *mezes* need to be ordered (and paid for) separately. Some of the best *mezes* still come from the unpretentious back-street establishments where, incidentally, the price of an ouzo is usually a fraction of its cost at a crowded harbour-front café. There are numerous national brands of ouzo and also locally produced varieties which, like the Cretan *raki*, tend to be coarser and stronger. Greece also produces vermouths and a variety of sweet, sticky liqueurs, many of them local specialities. Perhaps the most famous of the Greek brandies is the rather fruity *Metaxa*, available in three-, five- and seven-star quality.

The Faith of the Present

In its attempt to displace the ancient gods and heroes, Christianity has been only partly successful, for the rich body of folklore and contemporary superstitions, especially in country districts, is firmly embedded in the myths and legends of earlier times. In the manner in which the Olympian deities were transmuted as Roman equivalents, many of the old gods and goddesses became Christian patrons, protectors and even saints. Most boats and ships, for example, carry their icon of St Nicholas, and a church or monastery to this patron of sailors often stands on, or close to, the site of an earlier temple of Poseidon. The sun god, Helios, later identified with Apollo, has been succeeded by the Prophet Elias (Profitis Ilias), whose chapels crown almost every prominent eminence in Greece. In addition some of the attributes of Athena have been passed to the Virgin, who, in times of difficulty, is seen as the protectress of the Greeks; St Dionysios has dethroned Dionysos; Demeter has become the Christian St Dimitria, and the story of St George and the dragon is really a late version of Theseus and the Minotaur. In short, worship in some parts of Greece is often a sort of primitive Orthodoxy allied to folklore, each village and each seasonal activity being associated with saints whose attributes and powers emanate from those of the gods and demi-gods of antiquity.

The Christian Orthodox religion, it should be stressed, is a vital force in Greece and has been a powerful factor in preserving a deep national awareness, acting, along with the Greek language, as a major unifying factor, particularly when the Greeks were the subjects of Catholic and Moslem ruling powers. The Greek Church is a branch of Eastern Orthodoxy, a loose federation of four independent partiarchs (Constantinople (Istanbul), Jerusalem, Antioch and Alexandria) and fourteen self-governing bodies located in various countries. After 1833 the Greek Church became autonomous, and since 1850 it has been recognized by the Oecumenical Patriarchate of Constantinople as autocephalous – that is, governed by its own synod and having the power to appoint its own patriarch. Since 1864 it has been the estab-

A cloistered life, but worldly-wise

lished State Church, its supreme head being the Archbishop of Athens. Only the monastic republic of Mount Athos and, on account of their late unification with Greece, the Dodecanese, remain subject to Constantinople, while Crete occupies a special position as a semi-autonomous province of the Church. Greece is the world's only officially Orthodox country, and some ninety-four per cent of its population is registered with the Church. The remaining six per cent are mainly Mohammedans, Jews, Protestants and Roman Catholics, the latter found chiefly in the Cyclades and a legacy of the Middle Ages.

When pagan worship was gradually eclipsed with the strengthening of Christianity, some of the old temples were converted into churches. The traditional style of a Byzantine church, however, follows the cross-in-square plan which evolved from that of the fourth-century Christian basilicas. Similar in function to the *cella* of the Greek temple, the square plan of the main body of the church (*naos*) allows for central and lateral aisles (the 'cross' structure) which helps to support the central dome and often several small cupolas.

GREEK CHURCH

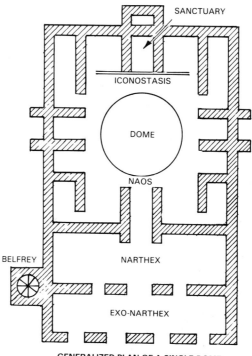

GENERALIZED PLAN OF A SINGLE-DOME
CROSS-IN-SQUARE GREEK CHURCH.

Symbolically, the cross and the dome mark the union of Heaven and Earth, or the two natures of the incarnate Christ. Typical additions to this essential church plan include inner and outer porches (the *narthex* and *exonarthex*, respectively), a belfrey and various wings and side chapels which take their form from internal walls. Although there are many architectural variations on this traditional structure, the cross-in-square plan continues to influence the neo-Byzantine-style churches of modern Greece.

Interior church design also follows strict rules. The *naos* is separated from the altar by a tall screen (the *iconostasis*) of ornately carved wood or sculptured marble. Beyond this only the priest is normally allowed to enter and, symbolically, this separation of sanctuary from congregation represents the division between the divine and the human, or the spiritual and 'sensible' worlds. Yet the iconostasis also unites the two, for it is adorned with icons (Christ, the Virgin and saints) that portray this double function – that is, they represent the world of imagination that stands midway between the worshipper and deity. Icons are also placed around the entire body of the church, and often the whole interior wall surface is decorated with frescos, richer churches having mosaic panels, many of them (like the frescos) centuries old.

The veneration of holy images and objects is a central aspect of the Orthodox faith, for they are regarded as testimonies of the process of transfiguration, and in them is felt to be present something of the deified reality of the prototypes. Many are covered with small siver votives, the intention being to put a prayer into visual form. In time these *simulacra* are melted down to add more silver (and often gold) adornment to their respective icons. Another visual feature, usually filling the central dome, is the image of Christ, a stern, often fierce, representation of the Saviour on the Day of Judgement.

In its architecture and decoration, therefore, the Greek church is a visible projection of the spiritual world. The Greeks are fervent believers in divine-human co-operation and in the former's intervention. All faculties – physical and mental – are used in worship; hence the need for icons, incense, candles, colours and chanting.

Feasts and Festivals

Religious feastdays and festivals are an important part of the Orthodox calendar, and hardly a day passes in the Greek island world without some town or village church paying homage to its patron saint in what is known as a *panagiri*, a glorious mixture of piety and merriment. Many of the local saints are names without pedigree, and the mystery surrounding their lives, entangled in legend and frag-

Religious mosaics (St Stephen) and silver-clad icons (the Holy Mother) play major roles in Greek Orthodox worship

ments of history, is known only to the celebrating community. Religious ritual incorporates much that is of 'grass-roots' origin, and in rural areas, in particular, it is interwoven with superstitious and other dubious beliefs but lightly glossed by the precepts of Christianity. These remain all-pervading forces in many a local community where belief in the evil eye and in the prophetic power of dreams is widespread. Deeply held 'unorthodox' views surround, for example, pregnancy and childbirth, although many country practices, tried and tested through time, prove to be efficacious, whilst local remedies reveal shrewd medical knowledge.

All *panagiria* are occasions for religious worship, but a visit to the local church, especially decorated for the occasion, is accompanied by music and dancing, an abundance of wine, hawkers peddling trinkets, and the inevitable lamb roasting on a spit. As noted in the previous pages, many festivals last well into the night and are often continued throughout the next day, and sometimes for periods much longer. 'The little saint of local fame', it has been said, 'keeps the broad current of Greek life flowing in the right direction.' As far as visitors are concerned (and they are usually welcomed), the *panagiri* provides the opportunity to witness one

293

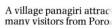

A village panagiri attrac[...]
many visitors from Poro[...]

of the least-changing scenarios in contemporary Greek life.

In addition to the great wealth of local *panagiria*, the Greek Church celebrates a number of major festivals. The most important in terms of pomp, dignity and fervour are those that surround Lent and Easter. There seems little doubt that some of the rituals are the Christianized version of the ancient Lesser Eleusinia – the return of Persephone from the underworld and the general awakening of nature after the winter months. It is a period of red eggs and roasted lamb and is ushered in by forty days of fasting (little adhered to nowadays), the two Sundays before Lent being known, respectively, as Meat Sunday and Cheese Sunday. The week between them is usually celebrated by carnivals and masquerades, reminiscent of the Old Cronia festivals of antiquity. Lent, many scholars suggest, commemorates Demeter's long abstinence from food during her search for her lost daughter, Persephone.

The Greek Orthodox Easter is calculated in a complicated manner, and its date, still based on the Julian-style calendar, can occur up to a month later than in Western Christendom. Easter involves as much preparation in the kitchen as Christmas does in Western Europe, and work starts at least ten days before the events. On Maundy Thursday the paschal lamb is killed and hung until Saturday, when Easter soup is prepared from its offal. Friday is a day of universal mourning, and most churches have their evening *Epitaphios* procession when the flower-covered symbolic bier of Christ is followed by the clergy, church dignitaries and the general population.

John Forte describes something of the atmosphere of Easter celebrations on Corfu:
'. . . at midnight when the bishop, standing on a raised dais in the centre of the
multitude, reads his solemn benediction, all the lights of the town and on ships
at sea become illuminated. . . . The great Venetian fort, until now a dark and forbidding mass on the skyline, shines forth with the words '*Christos Anesti*' – 'Christ
is Risen'. The tiny bobbing, weaving candles, which are in fact people, now hurry
home, taking good care that the precious flame will not die before they reach their
destination'. (*Corfu, Venus of the Isles.*) Easter Sunday is usually spent in eating,
drinking and dancing, and authentic celebrations are still found throughout island
towns and villages, where lamb, basted with lemon juice and olive oil, is cooked
slowly over an open spit and then eaten with copious quantities of wine and spirits.

Easter is, of course, but one of the Orthodox Church's numerous official celebrations, an especially important day being 15 August, the Dormition of the Virgin
Mary, which is equivalent to the Assumption of the Virgin in other lands. As saints'
days are more important than birthdays in Greece, even for young children, 15
August is an important name day for the country's countless Marys. A large proportion of Greek first names are derived from the saints, and a name day is celebrated
with family reunions. Saints Constantine and Helen are celebrated on 21 May, and
traditionally this marks the beginning of summer, when indoor cinemas and
theatres close and outdoor life begins.

Of Greece's non-religious festivals the two most important are those of 25 March and 28 October. The former, Independence Day, remembers the country's long struggle against the Turks, and the latter, 'Ochi Day', celebrates the anniversary of the rejection of Mussolini's ultimatum to Greece during World War II. Both are now national holidays.

Greeks Bearing Gifts

One of the more obvious character traits the Greeks have inherited from the Orient is their skill in pressurizing visitors to enter their shops and boutiques, the first and major step to what they see as an ultimate purchase, provided the hard-sell technique is maintained. Greece is predominantly a country of the small shop-owner, each dealing in a fixed number of items and sometimes in only one type of a product line. This largely accounts for their untiring vigilance and persuasive tactics, no matter how often a potential client has successfully resisted or, for that matter, has

Tempting the tourist (Socrates Street, Rhodes)

already entered and made substantial purchases. Although the country is not bargaining territory, in all other seller-purchaser aspects Greece more readily resembles Turkey and such North African countries as Morocco and Tunisia.

Nowadays the most common shops in many of the islands are those devoted to tourist souvenirs, and the large influx of visitors has inevitably brought mass-produced products, the wares of the Piraeus pavement bazaars being almost identical to those found on Rhodes, Crete, Mykonos, Hydra etc. Yet there are still some Aegean and Ionian craftsmen turning out authentic handmade items whose extra cost make them worthwhile purchases compared with locally hand-painted plates that originated (in their undecorated form) in the potteries of Stoke-on-Trent.

As noted in the preceding chapters, many of the islands have their own products and handicraft specialities, and these are better purchased where they are produced, unless the visitor is prepared to accept what can be as much as a fifty per cent mark-up. Some of the best bargains can be found in the Dodecanese islands, which still have a limited duty-free status. Thus Rhodes and Kos offer good buys in glassware, textiles, metalwork, furs, wines and spirits and ceramics. Other good decorated pottery comes from Sifnos, Skopelos and Skyros, the latter also specializing in woodcarving and textiles. The best place to buy fruit preserves is Chios; lovers of honey will make their purchases on Thasos or Lemnos; and Lesbos ouzo and Samian wines are of exceptionally good quality. Paros specializes in figures made from its world-famous marble, and where else to buy sponges than on Kalymnos or religious souvenirs than on Tinos? For sizeable purchases most of the popular islands accept the main international credit cards and traveller's cheques; the less visited territories deal strictly in cash.

Hippocratic Hazards

As in all parts of the world, where visitors are exposed to lifestyles, diets, daily routines and general environmental conditions that are different to those experienced at home, the Greek islands pose certain health risks, although these are no greater in the Ionian and Aegean regions than in other parts of the Mediterranean. The two most common complaints, sun-burn and stomach upset, are usually self-inflicted by those who flout precautionary measures, the former being the result of over-exposure and the latter often attributable to over-indulgence. Visitors are strongly advised to take care when relaxing in the summer sun, particularly between 11 a.m. and 3 p.m. in the southern Aegean. It is a common fallacy that when a breeze is blowing the naturally cooled air minimizes the risk of burning. It must be stressed that skin damage results not from the infra-red rays (the heat affect) but from the ultra-violet, which are no respectors of land and sea breezes. Lazing unprotected aboard an island ferry, albeit cooled by the wind, can often lead to serious burning and heatstroke, the latter accompanied by feverishness and diarrhoea.

Stomach upsets can arise from a visitor's exposure to a totally new diet and eating habits, though the chances of contracting something dire from poorly washed salads, re-heated food and certain shellfish are probably no greater in the Greek islands than elsewhere in the Mediterranean. Some travellers tend to be paranoid over the safety of the water. It is treated and drinkable in most areas, and that offered in cafés and restaurants is obviously safe. It is certainly sensible to be cautious, and should doubts persist, there are always the bottled varieties (still and fizzy) and a wide range of flavoured mineral waters. It is in some of the more isolated country districts that piped supplies may be hazardous, and a pitcher of water (usually capped by a fresh lemon) placed near a sink in a privately rented room is a warning that the tap water is to be used for washing purposes only.

In times of distress visitors will find the Greek pharmacies of great help, for they are licensed to dispense pills, medicines and lotions normally available in other European countries only under prescription. Most of the larger island communities have a doctor and a clinic or Red Cross station, and the main towns and cities have hospitals (though, generally speaking, services are not up to Western European standards). Provided UK nationals have completed the EIII form from the DHSS before leaving home, their health cover is the same as that of Greek citizens. Yet for emergencies, which might entail private treatment, it is advisable that the visitor be covered by some form of comprehensive medical insurance. A personal supply of basic cosmetic and pharmaceutical products will also considerably save money (for example, sun oil, TCP, calamine lotion, elastoplast, stomach-settlers, eye drops, pain-relievers etc.) as such items are costly in Greece.

Depending on the season, certain insects can be a source of annoyance in some parts of the Ionian and Aegean. Mosquitos can be kept at bay by repellent lotions and various devices, available locally, that keep them out of bedrooms at night. Flies tend to be more persistent intruders – a case for the sticky paper technique.

Bathing is usually safe at all the recognized tourist beaches, but parts of Greek island waters suffer from pollution (an increasing hazard around the Mediterranean shores) and signs restricting bathing should be strictly adhered to. Most of the polluted stretches occur close to the larger towns and, particularly, near harbours. Certain jellyfish, such as the medusa, can give nasty stings for which medical assistance is needed. Equal precaution is necessary in the countryside, where stout footwear (not sandals) should be worn, for not only is the undergrowth thorny but there is also a chance of encountering snakes (most are harmless) and scorpions.

Whether in the country or in the town, dog bites need immediate attention.

The saga of the Greek WC has already received attention. Here it might be added that the difficulties experienced in hotels are compounded in the public variety, albeit few and far between in the Greek islands. It is indeed necessary and also acceptable to use the facilities of restaurants and hotels, and in the countryside the visitor will soon discover what the alternative is. Few public conveniences are supplied with soap and water but, fortunately, the sea is usually close at hand, the salty Aegean and Ionian waters providing an effective hand-cleansing source. It has to be said that infective hepatitis is a hazard, and it is vital to maintain personal cleanliness at all times.

It is not the intention to end this portrait of the Greek island world on an alarmist note, especially when most of the preceding pages have sung the praises of these unique insular territories. The object of this compendium has been to present some of the attitudes, values and difficulties that the visitor is likely to meet. To be fore-warned is to be fore-armed, for the Greek islands, like all destinations, demand of the visitor an intelligent response to their challenges and a sensible appreciation of their realities.

The Best Island For You

It might be said that the idea and practice of 'island-hopping' was invented in Greece, the precedent being set by such illustrious mythical heroes as Jason, Odysseus and Theseus. Many visitors to the Aegean and Ionian regions, particularly the young and the energetic, currently follow in their footsteps by travelling from island to island, some following carefully researched and organized schedules, others having less rigorous objectives, setting their insular sights as the mood and the opportunity dictates. The time at one's disposal is an obvious governing factor, yet it is feasible to visit a different island for every day spent in the Aegean, and the visitor can land on all the Ionian islands in the space of a week. But not only are such itineraries extremely tiring, the atmospheric gains from 'doing the islands' in as short a time-span as possible is debatable for, at best, only the most superficial of impressions can result. 'If its Tuesday it must be Mykonos' is a syndrome that should be avoided, for the traveller will miss much that is authentic and if the objective is merely to boast x number of visits to island ports, then the answer is an Aegean or Ionian cruise which at least guarantees some measure of relaxation between the succession of destinations. Those who constantly return to the Greek islands will already have realized that their in-depth appreciation is a lengthy, on-going process, and some might argue that their local and regional variety demands a lifetime of pilgrimages. It is far more rewarding to know a few islands well than to visit a host of sea-lapped territories where pressing timetables preclude the traveller from venturing little beyond the waterfront cafés, tavernas and boutiques. Such commercial façades are usually far removed from the more characteristic island realities.

With the time proviso in mind, island-hopping is certainly the best way to enter into the spirit of the Greek islands. However, for the majority of visitors, the two or three week vacation is the norm, which makes the increasingly popular 'package-holiday' the most practicable answer. Each year more islands are added to the organized holiday choice, the competitive brochures promoting their destinations with picturesque views and glowing descriptions of local scenery, special attractions, accommodation and nightlife. This book has attempted to capture the atmosphere of individual islands and it is hoped that intending visitors will be able to gauge something of their appeal as potential holiday venues. To assist in the choice of a destination, the following notes offer further suggestions.

The most accessible islands
For those not intent on an island-hopping itinerary the degree of accessibility naturally plays an important role in the choice of a destination. With the rapid increase in Greek package

holidays and corresponding improvements to airports there are now ten islands (Corfu, Crete, Kos, Mykonos, Rhodes, Samos, Skiathos, Cefalonia, Zakinthos and Lesbos) that receive direct summer flights from Britain. Other islands that offer relatively easy access on from Athens or other Greek airports – by air or sea – are Euboea, Andros, Chios, Karpathos, Thasos, Milos, Cythera and the islands belonging to the Argo-Saronic group (Aegina, Poros, Hydra and Spetses). Islands that demand a lengthier journey from Athens and other Greek airports (e.g. Corfu) include Ios, Syros, Sifnos, Alonnisos, Ithaca, Kalymnos, Patmos, Paxos, Skyros, Skopelos, Lefkas, Samothrace, Serifos and Sifnos. The majority of the remaining Aegean and Ionian destinations can be reached only be irregular and/or long ferry journeys. The visitor should remember that there is a marked correlation between tourist popularity and accessibility, the quieter islands, in terms of commercialization, being those that are more remote from the main ferry lines and airports.

The best for beaches?
The answer to this question depends on what the visitor expects of beaches – unspoilt and uncommercialized sandy coves, or the managed lido-style strands with full facilities and (often) an admittance charge. On many of the islands, even the more tourist conscious, it is still possible to find intimate, empty (and remote) beaches though, increasingly, the large sandy stretches, especially near to island capitals, are being commercialized. Corfu, Crete and Rhodes have many fine sandy beaches as do the islands of Cefalonia, Zakinthos, Mykonos, Paros, Euboea, Skiathos, Ios and Santorini. It should be remembered however, that many of the islands have rocky coasts which, at best, give rise to pebble beaches. Hydra, despite its popularity, is a case in point, and neighbouring Poros has a series of pine-fringed coves where sand is in short supply. If it is exclusively a sedentary beach holiday that the visitor wants, then undoubtedly the most popular beach resort destinations are those of Corfu, Rhodes, Crete and Mykonos.

The best for watersports
The Greek islands are ideally suited to a variety of water sports. Snorkelling and skin-diving have increased in popularity and on most islands snorkelling equipment can be bought inexpensively or rented. There are facilities for learning scuba-diving on Rhodes, Corfu and at Souda Bay, Crete. The Ionian Islands have a number of scuba-diving areas (Corfu, Paxos, Lefkas, Cefalonia and Zakinthos) and the sport is also practised on Mykonos. There are many opportunities for water-skiing, especially on the more popular islands where schools exist on Corfu, Skiathos, Crete (Canea and Elounda), Poros and Spetses. Windsurfing is becoming better organized, but again the hire of equipment is confined to the busy tourist centres. Corfu and Syros have sailing schools and for visitors with the experience, time and necessary finances boats and yachts can be hired. Most islands have facilities to service the growing number of sailing and motor yachts in Greek waters but, with the exception of Rhodes, Crete and Corfu, most of the chartering is done out of Piraeus.

The best islands for children
Few children take to the claustrophobic crowds of Mykonos or the busy commercial atmospheres of Rhodes city, Iraklion or Corfu town. The best family holidays are spent in the less touristy areas, but those that offer a variety of outdoor activities. The islands recommended for visitors with families are Aegina, Kos, Santorini, Spetses, Alonnisos, Andros, Kea, Cefalonia, Patmos, Paxos, Skyros, Thasos and Zakinthos. Teenagers, however, will certainly enjoy the active nightlife of the hotel and beach complexes of the Cretan, Rhodian and Corfiote resorts.

Useful Addresses
National Tourist Organization of Greece – Amerikis 2, Athens; 195–197 Regent Street, London, W1R 8DL. There are NTOG offices in New York, Los Angeles, Chicago, Montreal, Sydney and the majority of European capitals.
Automobile and Touring Club of Greece – Mesoyion 2, Athens. (Branch offices in Salonica, Volos, Patras, Kavala, Corfu, Canea, Iraklion).
British Embassy – Ploutarkhou I, Athens (Also at Corfu, Iraklion, Rhodes, Salonica).
British Airways – Othonos 10, Athens (Also at Corfu, Iraklion, Rhodes, Salonica).
Olympic Airways – Leoforos Syngrou 96, Athens; 141 New Bond Street, London W1; 649 Fifth Avenue, New York.
Greek Water-Skiing Association – Stournara 32, Athens.
Greek Sub-Aqua Diving Club – Ayios Kosmas, Athens-Elliniko.
Greek Sailing Club – Xenofontos 15a, Athens.
Greek Alpine Club – Karageorgis Servias 7, Athens.
Greek Wind-Surfing Club – Filellion 7, Athens.

——— Appendix II ———

The Olympian Gods and the Greek Temple

The ancient Greeks worshipped a large number of deities whose precise origins are lost to legend. Almost every hill, valley and spring was protected by some divinity who jealously guarded his or her domain. Cities and states also had their own protecting gods and goddesses to whom shrines, sanctuaries and temples were erected, their remains forming one of the country's principal historical and archaeological attractions.

Long before classical times the Greeks undertook a systematization of their deities and catalogued them as belonging to one main but extended family – one, however, that proved anything but a unified and accordant household. Rivalry, corruption, intrigue, subversion and deceipt characterized the divine pantheon, for the Greeks also saw their gods as having mortal passions as well as supernatural powers. In various guises they mixed with demi-gods, who never attained Olympian status, and with mortals, spawning offspring whose careers are embroiled with the heroic legends and the country's still powerful body of folklore.

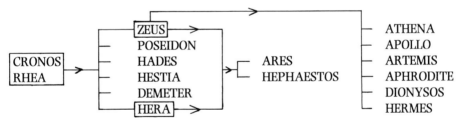

THE OLYMPIAN PANTHEON

Listed below are the members and main offsprings of the Olympian household and the principal attributes and functions that the ancient Greeks (and subsequent civilizations) attached to them.

Zeus, the supreme deity, was god of the heavens and of the weather. The son of Cronos and Rhea (pre-Olympian deities), he overthrew his father and fixed his abode in Mount Olympus. Zeus dispensed good and evil (favours and retribution) to men as he saw fit, though his prime duty was to protect law, order and justice, this authority being manifested with the thunderbolt. A restless leader and, at times, licentious, he fathered many offspring by goddesses, nymphs and mortals.
Poseidon, a brother of Zeus, ruled the seas. He is often represented as a vengeful god carrying a trident with which he could cause earthquakes. Homer constantly refers to him as the

303

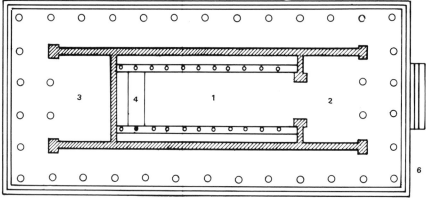

1. CELLA	4. CULT STATUE
2. PRONAOS	5. PERISTASIS
3. OPISTHODOMOS	6. CREPIDOMA

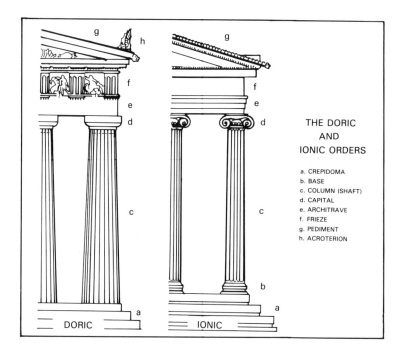

THE DORIC
AND
IONIC ORDERS

a. CREPIDOMA
b. BASE
c. COLUMN (SHAFT)
d. CAPITAL
e. ARCHITRAVE
f. FRIEZE
g. PEDIMENT
h. ACROTERION

DORIC

IONIC

GREEK CAPITALS

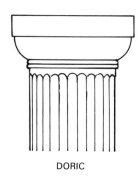

DORIC

IONIC

CORINTHIAN

'earthshaker', and great rivalry existed between him and Zeus.

Hades, the third of the powerful brothers, was lord of the underworld and ruler of the dead. Being less amorous than his brothers, he rarely visited the upperworld, where he delegated the judgement of souls to others. The damned were sent to Tartarus to suffer enternal punishment, but the virtuous entered the Elysian Fields, where Hades had no control.

Hestia was the virgin sister of Zeus, Poseidon and Hades. She was regarded as the kindest of the deities and was the goddess of the hearth, representing the security of the home.

Hera, the queen of Olympus, was both the sister of Zeus and his official wife. Patron of the sexual life of women and of marriage, she was also extremely jealous and persecuted Zeus' illegitimate offspring.

Ares, the son of Zeus and Hera, was the Greek war god and is represented as a fully armed warrior. He was extremely unpopular on Olympus, especially with his parents.

Athena, who sprang fully armed from the head of Zeus, was the goddess of wisdom and patron of intellectual and practical skills. She is represented as a virgin warlike Amazon who became the protectress of Athens (Pallas Athena).

Apollo, or Phoebus Apollo, was the son of Zeus and Leto, and the twin brother of Artemis. He was the much-loved god of light and of the arts but also represented prophecy, archery and healing. His legends are entangled with those of Helios, the sun god, and, subsequently the two deities became one and the same.

Artemis, the chaste goddess of the hunt, was also identified with the moon and with women in childbirth.

Aphrodite, born of Zeus and Dione (though it is also said that she was spawned by the sea's foam), was the goddess of love, beauty and fertility. Beautiful herself, she had the power to grant beauty and charm.

Hermes, messenger of the gods and son of Zeus and Maia, was also patron of merchants, travellers, communications and thieves. He is usually represented with staff, winged shoes and broad hat.

Hephaestos was a legitimate son of Zeus and Hera. The god of fire and patron of smiths and craftsmen, he is depicted as a mighty, bearded and often comic figure. Such was his ugliness that Hera dropped him as a baby from Olympus. He returned as a young man, but this time it was Zeus who disapproved of him, and he was again hurled to the earth, the fall permanently laming him.

Demeter was a sister of Zeus and goddess of the earth. She was the mother, by Zeus, of Persephone, and both mother and daughter were leading figures in the Eleusian Mystery cults which represented the seasonal cycle in terms of death and rebirth. As earth goddess Demeter was patron of corn, harvest and fruitfulness.

Dionysos, son of Zeus and Semele, was the god of wine and fertility whose worship was accompanied by ecstatic rites and rituals. In the country he was patron of vegetation.

With the spread of Greek influence, particularly with the conquests of Alexander, cultural interchange led to the worship of many foreign gods in Greece, especially at such international centres as Delos. The Romans were greatly influenced by Greek civilization, and they blended the Greek deities with their own pantheon, to the extent that Zeus is also known as Jupiter (or Jove), Poseidon as Neptune and Hades as Pluto. The Roman Vesta stands for Hestia, Juno for Hera and Mars for Ares. Aphrodite became the Roman Venus, Athena was Minerva and Hermes was Mercury. Artemis, Hephaestos, Demeter and Dionysos are represented by Diana, Vulcan, Ceres and Bacchus. The popular Apollo retained his Greek name.

Throughout the archaic, classical, Hellenistic and Roman periods, the Greek temple underwent considerable architectural evolution, in terms of both ground plan and decoration. As a religious building it was intended to accommodate only a deity and priests or priestesses, the outside altar being the focus of worshippers at all public ceremonies. Although some Greek shrines were circular buildings, of the type known as *tholos*, the most characteristic temple plan was rectangular and seems to have been derived from the principal room (often the throne room) or *megaron* of the earlier Mycenaean palace-citadels. The temple's main section was the *cella* or *naos*, which was preceded by the *pronaos* (entrance portico). Similar in plan but at the building's other end was a rear chamber (*opisthodomos*). A series of external columns supported the roof and the projecting pediment which was the roof's triangular termination.

From the second half the seventh century BC the typical form was the *peripteral* temple that is, one surrounded by a *peristasis* (colonnade) on all four sides. By the fifth century the temple's classical proportions had been developed with columns at the ends (usually six) and $2x+I$ (i.e., thirteen columns) along the sides. The columns and the entire temple stood on a three-stepped platform known as the *crepidoma*. There was much experimentation in the use of columns, those temples with a double colonnade being known as *dipteral*. Internal columns had both structural and artistic uses.

One of the easiest methods of recognizing the three main orders of temple (and other) architecture – Doric, Ionic and Corinthian – is from the character of the shafts and capitals of their columns or pillars.

The powerful Doric column, tapering towards its top and having sharp-edged fluting, stands directly, without a base, on the uppermost step of the *crepidoma*. Its capital consists of a lower convex moulding (*echinus*) and an upper square slab (*abacus*), above which is the superstructure (*entablature*). The latter is composed of a usually plain horizontal lintel (*architrave*) and a *metope* frieze consisting of sculptured panels separated by sections of mock-columns (*triglyphs*). The pediment is usually ornately sculptured, and its apex (i.e., the roof ridge) is often crowned by a figure or ornament (*acroterion*).

Sometimes known as the 'masculine' order, on account of the austerity of its columns, the Doric differs greatly from the more 'feminine' Ionic whose columns are more slender and untapering and have fluting separated by narrow ridges. The column stands on a base, and the capital is composed of two spiral volutes. The architrave consists of three projecting layers, and the frieze, again usually sculptured (but sometimes plain), is continuous, having no triglyphic subdivisions.

The Corinthian order, often regarded as a hybrid style, has still more slender columns with a finer fluting. Its most characteristic feature is the capital which follows an intricate design of carved foliage (acanthus leaves) with tendrils reaching up to the architrave. Probably the most grandiose of the orders, it flourished in Hellenistic times and was also popular with the Romans, who developed ever more elaborate decorative schemes.

The Greek Islands – Individual Areas and Populations

	Sq. Kilometres	Sq. miles	Population		Sq. Kilometres	Sq. miles	Population
Aegina	83	32	9,550	Leros	53	20	8,500
Alonnisos	64	25	1,425	Lesbos	1,630	629	97,000
Amorgos	121	47	1,800	Milos	151	58	4,500
Anafi	35	14	450	Mykonos	85	33	3,400
Andros	380	147	10,450	Naxos	428	165	14,200
Astypalaea	96	37	1,500	Nisyros	41	16	1,250
Ayios Efstratios	43	17	1,000	Paros	194	75	7,500
Cefalonia	781	3	31,800	Patmos	34	13	2,430
Chios	842	325	52,500	Paxos	3	1	2,200
Corfu	593	229	89,600	Poros	23	9	4,500
Crete	8,259	3,189	465,500	Rhodes	1,398	540	67,000
Cythera	278	107	5,000	Salamis	95	37	23,700
Delos	3·6	1·4	—	Samos	476	184	32,600
Euboea	3,658	1,412	163,000	Samothrace	178	69	3,000
Folegandros	34	13	7,000	Santorini	76	29	6,200
Hydra	50	19	2,550	Serifos	71	44	1,100
Icaria	255	98	7,700	Sifnos	73	28	2,100
Ios	108	42	1,270	Sikinos	41	16	420
Ithaca	94	36	4,150	Skiathos	48	19	3,900
Kalymnos	111	43	13,000	Skopelos	96	37	4,500
Karpathos	301	116	5,400	Skyros	209	81	3,000
Kassos	65	25	1,400	Spetses	22	8	3,500
Kea	134	52	1,660	Simi	58	22	2,480
Kimolos	36	14	1,050	Syros	84	32	18,600
Kos	290	112	16,650	Thasos	379	146	13,500
Kithnos	99	38	1,600	Tilos	60	23	600
Lefkas	299	115	22,900	Tinos	194	75	8,230
Lemnos	476	276	17,400	Zakinthos	402	155	30,200

—— Appendix IV ——

A Chronology of Major Events

There are certain problems in providing an all-embracing chronology of the prehistoric and historic events that governed the cultural development of the Greek islands. Though following the general trends that affected Greece and the Aegean area as a whole, there were times when the islands, individually and collectively, went their own ways, only to be subsequently brought back into the general mainstream of developments. Chapter 2 has attempted to descriptively portray the main episodes in the life of Greece and its islands; the summary reference grids that follow will enable visitors to more easily place archaeological and historical sites in their chronological context. Such period divisions, however, are purely artificial, for what happened in various parts of Greece at particular points in time are but part of a long, continuous and more general process. The detail was enacted in areas that Homer described as a patchwork of 'many glittering seas and many shadowy islands.'

CHRONOLOGICAL TABLE FOR THE CENTURIES BC

	3000BC	2000	1500	1000	800
		BRONZE AGE		IRON AGE (DARK AGE)	ARCHAIC
General	Early Cycladic civilization (central Aegean islands)	Cretan palace civilization	Mycenaean shaft graves / Santorini eruption / Decline of Knossos	Dorian and Phoenician invasions / Introduction of iron / Mycenaean decline	Population increase / Greek colonization of the Mediterranean / International festivals established / Tyrants in control of many cities
Art and Architecture	Cycladic sculpture (female figures in white marble, 2600–2200 BC) Phylakopi, Milos Helladic pottery styles	Great Cretan palaces / Figurine sculpture, fine gold and semi-precious stone work	Santorini frescoes / Beehive tombs	proto-geometric and geometric (orientalizing) pottery	Monumental vases

Timeline of Greek history (rotated table)

	before 600	600	500	400	300	200	AD
Period		ARCHAIC (continued)	CLASSICAL	CLASSICAL	HELLENISTIC	ROMAN EMPIRE	ROMAN EMPIRE
Political developments		Increasing power of city states; Athenian democracy; Rise of Spartan dominance in the Peloponnesus	The Persian invasions; Athens 'Golden Age'; The Delian League; The Peloponnesian War	Athens revival; Rise of Macedon; Alexander's Conquests; Unification of Greece	Rise in power of the Achaean and Aetolian leagues; Alexander's empire of the East	Macedonian Wars; Rome conquers Greece; Greece remains the cultural and intellectual centre of the Mediterranean	
Art and architecture		Archaic black-figure vases. Kouroi and korai sculpture	The great temples at Olympia, Athens, etc; Pheidias, Ictinos (architects), Polygnotos (painter)	Praxiteles (sculptor)	Hellenistic 'baroque' cities and architecture	The marriage between Roman and Greek sculpture and architecture	
philosophy / literature	Phoenician alphabet; Homer, Hesiod, lyric poets	The beginnings of tragedy, comedy and philosophical science: Pindar, Pythagoras, Aeschylus and Sophocles	Herodotos, Euripides, Hippocrates, Plato, Socrates, Aristotle, Epicurus, Thuycdides	Theocritos, Euclid, Archimedes	Foundation of the Library at Alexandria	Horace	Pausanias
Famous dates	776 First Olympic Games; c.950 Foundation of Sparta; c.1450 Destruction of Minoan Civilization; c.1230–1220 The Trojan War	560–543 Solon's social reforms	481 Third Persian campaign; 431–404 Peloponnesian War; 429 Death of Pericles	336 Death of Philip of Macedon; 323 Death of Alexander in Babylon	215 Macedonian Wars	168 Greece becomes a Roman province	AD 50 St Paul's mission to Greece; 67 Nero visits Greece

ROMAN (continued)	AD500 BYZANTINE	AD1200 LATIN
323–37 Constantine transfers Roman capital to Byzantium (Constantinople). Christianity is victorious	527–65 Justinian I emperor. Athens Academy closed. Greek replaces Latin as Byzantine language. Temples destroyed or become churches	1204–6 Fourth Crusade sacks Constantinople
361–363 Emperor Julian favours Greece. Attempt to restore paganism	577 Avars and Slavs raid and settle Greece	1207 The Venetian Marco Sanudo founds Duchy of Naxos
379–395 Edict of Theodosius proscribes paganism. Delphic and Olympian sanctuaries closed, Roman Empire divided into East and West sections	976–1025 Imperial order re-established by Basil II	1261 Michael Palaeologos reconquers Constantinople and imperial rule reinstated. But Latin principalities continue in the islands
393 Last Olympic Games of antiquity	1040–84 Normans of Sicily invade Greece	1308 Dynastic wars throughout Greece and the islands
395 Goths raid Greece	1054 Formal declaration of schism between Greek and Latin churches	1453 Fall of Constantinople to the Turks. Rest of Greece falls to Turks, but Venice keeps the islands
467–477 Vandal raids on Greece	1194 The Italian Orsini seizes the southern Ionian Islands	

CHRONOLOGICAL TABLE FOR THE CENTURIES AD

| TURKISH | KINGDOM OF GREECE | REPUBLIC OF GREECE |
AD1456	AD1832	1974
1456 Turks besiege and conquer Athens	1862–81 Otho abdicates George I becomes 'King of the Hellenes'	1975 New Greek constitution
1579 Duchy of Naxos falls to Turks	1898 Crete granted self-government	1977 Defence agreement with United States
1797 Ionian Islands freed from Venice and after 1815 became Russian, French and British	1908 Crete united with Greece	1979 Treaty of Greece's entry into EEC
1821 25 March Greek independence declared	1912–13 Balkan Wars. Greek territorial gains	1981 Greece joins EEC
1826 Fall of Missolonghi and death of Lord Byron	1919–20 Territorial gains from Treaty of Sèvres	
1827 Battle of Navarino	1920–22 Greco-Turkish War. Asia Minor exchanges of population	
1832 Independence of Greece under Otho of Bavaria	1923 Turkey cedes the Dodecanese to Italy	
	1936–41 Metaxas dictatorship	
	1941–44 Italian, German and Bulgarian occupations of Greece	
	1944–49 Communist rebellion Succession of unstable governments	
	1967–74 Greek Military junta	
	1973 Parliamentary democracy restored. Abolition of the monarchy	

Metric Conversion Tables

Linear measurement

1 metre = 3·28 feet
10 metres = 32·81 feet
50 metres = 164·04 feet
100 metres = 328.08 feet
1 kilometre = 0·621 miles
10 kilometres = 6·21 miles
50 kilometres = 31·05 miles
100 kilometres = 62·1 miles

Square measurement

1 sq. metre = 1·196 sq. yards
10 sq. metres = 11·96 sq. yards
50 sq. metres = 59·8 sq. yards
100 sq. metres = 119·6 sq. yards
1 sq. kilometre = 0·386 sq. miles
10 sq. kilometres = 3·86 sq. miles
50 sq. kilometres = 19·3 sq. miles
100 sq. kilometres = 38.6 sq. miles

Bibliography

I. Mythology and Ancient History

Apollonius of Rhodes (trans. Rieu, E. V.), *The Voyage of the Argo* (Penguin Books, 1979)

Boardman, J., *Pre-Classical – From Crete to Archaic Greece* (Penguin Books, 1967)

Cottrell, L., *The Bull of Minos* (Pan Books, 1955)

Finley, M. I., *The World of Odysseus* (Penguin Books, 1967)

Homer (trans. Rieu, E. V.), *The Illustrated Odyssey* (Rainbird Publishing Group, 1981)

Hutchinson, R. W., *Prehistoric Crete* (Penguin Books, 1962)

Kitto, H. D. F., *The Greeks* (Penguin Books, 1951)

Levi, P., *Atlas of the Greek World* (Phaidon, 1980)

Luce, J. V., *The End of Atlantis* (Paladin, 1970)

Pausanias (trans. Levi, P.), *Guide to Greece* (two vols.) (Penguin Books, 1979)

Payne, R., *The Splendour of Greece* (Robert Hale, 1961)

Thucydides (trans. Warner, R.), *The Peloponnesian War* (Penguin Books, 1954)

Wunderlich, H. G., *The Secret of Crete* (Fontana/Collins, 1976)

II. Byzantine and Latin Greece

Cheetham, N., *Medieval Greece* (Yale Univ. Press, 1981)

Forbes-Boyd, E., *In Crusader Greece* (Centaur Press, 1964)

Obolensky, N., *The Byzantine Commonwealth* (Cardinal, 1974)

Rice, D. Talbot, *Everyday Life in Byzantium* (Batsford, 1967)

Runciman, S., *Mistra: Byzantine Capital of the Peloponnese* (Thames and Hudson, 1980)

Whitting, P. (ed.), *Byzantium: An Introduction* (Blackwell, 1971)

III. Turkish and Modern Greece

Dicks, B., *The Greeks: How They Live and Work* (David and Charles, 1971)

Heurtley, W. A. (et al.), *A Short History of Greece* (Cambridge Univ. Press, 1965)

Howarth, D., *The Greek Adventure* (Collins, 1976)

McNeill, W. H., *The Metamorphosis of Greece since World War II* (Blackwell, 1978)

Pantelouris, E. M., *Greece: An Introduction* (Blueacre Books, 1980)

St Clair, W., *That Greece Might Be Free* (Oxford Univ. Press, 1977)

Tsoucalas, C., *The Greek Tragedy* (Penguin Books, 1969)

Young, K., *The Greek Passion* (Dent, 1969)

Zakythinos, D. A. (trans. Johnstone, K. R.), *The Making of Modern Greece* (Blackwell, 1976)

IV. General Guide Books

Baedeker/AA, *Greece* (Automobile Association, undated)

Bradford, E., *The Companion Guide to the Greek Islands* (Collins, 1970)

Brockway, L. and G., *Greece: A Classical Tour with Extras* (Victor Gollancz, 1967)

De Jongh, B., *The Companion Guide to Southern Greece* (Collins, 1971)

Dicks, B., *Greece: A Traveller's Guide to History and Mythology* (David and Charles, 1980)

Dicks, B., *Portrait of Southern Greece* (Robert Hale, 1982)

Durrell, L., *The Greek Islands* (Faber and Faber, 1978)

Ebdon, J., *Ebdon's Iliad* (Peter Davies, 1983)

Ebdon, J., *Ebdon's Odyssey* (Peter Davies, 1979)

Fodor's, *1986 Guide to Greece* (Hodder and Stoughton, 1986)

Facaros, D., *Greek Island Hopping* (Sphere Books, 1981)

Hellenews, *Tourism in Greece* (1972)

King, F. (ed.), *Introducing Greece* (Methuen, 1956)

Lancaster, O., *Classical Landscape with Figures* (John Murray, 1975)

Marx, G. (ed.), *The Budget Guide to Greece, Israel and Egypt* (St Martin's Press, 1983)

Rossiter, S., *Blue Guide to Greece* (Benn, 1980)

Sheldon, P., *Greece* (Mitchell Beazley, 1983)

Stoneman, R., *A Literary Guide to Travel in Greece* (Penguin Books, 1984)

Webster, T., *Webster's Guide to Greece* (Timsway Publications, 1984)

V. Corfu and the Ionian Islands

Durrell, L., *Prospero's Cell* (Faber and Faber, 1970)

Dicks, B., *Corfu* (David and Charles, 1977)

Forte, J. (ed.), *Corfu: Venus of the Isles* (East Essex Gazette, 1973)

Forte, J., *Wheeler on Corfu: Companion to Venus of the Isles* (East Essex Gazette, undated)

O'Connell, G., *The Ionian Islands and Athens City* (Willowbridge, 1983)

Young, M., *The Traveller's Guide to Corfu and the Ionian Islands* (Jonathan Cape, 1971)

VI. Crete

Bowman, J., *The Traveller's Guide to Crete* (Jonathan Cape, 1972)
Clutton, E., and Kenny, A., *Crete* (David and Charles, 1977)

VII. Kos

Halatsis, C., *Tourist Guide of Kos* (Athens, 1971)

VIII. Northern Islands

Fawcett, J., *The North Aegean Islands* (Roger Lascelles, 1984)

IX. Skiathos

Causton, J. (ed.), *Skiathos: The Shaded Isle* (Cartbridge Press, 1974)

X. Rhodes and the Dodecanese

Currie J., *The Traveller's Guide to Rhodes and the Dodecanese* (Jonathan Cape, 1970)
Dicks, B., *Rhodes* (David and Charles, 1974)
Durrell, L., *Reflections on a Marine Venus* (Faber and Faber, 1969)

XI. Greek Cooking

Paradissis, C., *The Best Book of Greek Cookery* (Efstathiadis, 1971)
Stubbs, J. M., *The Home Book of Greek Cookery* (Faber and Faber, 1963)

XII. Phrase Books and Language Courses

Cortina, *Modern Greek (Cortina Method)* (1962)
Marcopoulos-Gambarotta, E., and Scamp, J., *Breakthrough Greek* (book and tapes) (Pan Books, 1962)
Scott, C., *Collins Greek Phrase Book* (Collins, 1964)
NB For more serious students the Linguaphone and Berlitz language courses in Modern Greek are highly recommended.

XIII. Maps

Most good bookshops now stock useful road/tourist maps of the principal Greek islands, for example, Crete, Rhodes and Corfu. Visitors should purchase these before leaving, as in Greece, should they be available, they are expensive. The Greek equivalents are usually the highly pictorial 'dragons are here' maps, which pay only lip-service to scale, detail, distance and general accuracy.

Picture Credits

The copyright photographs in this book have been supplied by the following. The Author: pp. 28, 36, 40, 48, 51, 55, 59, 61, 62, 64, 77, 79, 83, 99, 100, 103, 104, 113, 114, 116, 124, 126, 130, 131, 139, 158, 172, 182, 184, 186, 187, 191, 197, 200, 203, 205, 212, 215, 216, 219, 223, 226, 228, 232, 237, 239, 241, 244, 249, 250, 255, 257, 259, 262, 273, 274, 277, 283, 286, 287, 294, 296 and all the colour plates. The National Tourist Organization of Greece: 2, 21, 23, 24, 26, 27, 35, 39, 43, 44, 57, 70, 72–3, 80, 82, 89, 91, 93, 94, 110, 119, 123, 133, 137, 142, 147, 150, 153, 155, 157, 166, 168–9, 175, 194, 196, 204, 207, 218, 222, 225, 229, 246, 252, 261, 266, 267, 271, 290, 293, 295. The line drawings are by Lothar Wuttke.

Index